SOUPS, SALADS, SANDWICHES

MATTY MATHESON

Photographs by Quentin Bacon

murdoch books

Sydney | London

*This book is dedicated to my all-time
favorite humans in the world forever and ever.*

*Tricia, you are the greatest.
I love you so much. It's refreshing every day
realizing I get to spend forever with you.*

*This book is also dedicated to our three children:
Macarthur, Rizzo, and Ozzy. Y'all are the
fucking best. I love you. I hope you can always
be yourselves and never hide who you are.*

Y'all my fucking dogs.

CONTENTS

INTRODUCTION 1

PART I: SOUPS 5

Lightest Broth of Garden Herbs with One Chile 8

Court Bouillon with Fresh Garlic and Ginger Oil 13

Rutabaga and Daikon Broth with Tofu 14

Soupe au Pistou 16

Cabbage Soup with Crème Fraîche, Smoked Trout Roe, and Chives 19

Dumplings, Roasted Baby Beets, Pork Belly, and Pork Broth 20

Pumpernickel, Beer, and Cheese Curd Soup 24

Caramelized Maple Parsnip Soup with Sunchoke Chips and Ricotta 27

Broiled and Burnt Roasted Tomato Soup with Grilled Cheese Crostini Thing 29

Broiled Broccoli and Cheddar Soup 30

Cannellini Bean and Kale Soup with Lots of Shallots 33

Corn Maple Parmesan Soup 35

Rhode Island Clam Chowder 39

Cioppino 40

Red Curry Lobster Soup 43

Clam, Sausage, Orecchiette, Kale, and Chicken Brodo 44

Crab Congee 47

Baked Potato Buffet Vichyssoise 48

Cullen Skink 52

Avgolemono 55

Roasted Chicken Leg Pastina Soup 56

Caldo de Pollo 59

Cock-a-Leekie Soup 60

Stuffed Acorn Squash Soup with Emmental and Bread Crumbs 63

Irish Lamb Stew 66

Turkey Drumstick and Barley Soup 69

Crispy Lamb Pho 71

Roasted Bone Marrow in Light Bone Broth with Fresh Peas 72

Bollito Misto 75

Large Crab Cake with Clam Chowder and Aioli 76

Gumbo 81

Creamy Sausage Soup with Rapini and Tortellini 82

Giant Meatball Soup in Beefy Tomato Broth 85

Kimchi Stew 86

Oxtail Barley Yam Soup 89

Cubed Mortadella, Macaroni, and Chicken Broth 91

Smoked Ham Hock with Haddock Soup 94

Beef Noodle Soup 97

PART II: SALADS 107

A Radicchio Salad from Prime Seafood Palace 111

Peaches with Goat Cheese, Mint, Honeycomb, and Olive Oil 112

Celery Salad with Creamy Honey Dressing 115

Broccoli Salad with Bacon Vinaigrette Dressing, Fried Egg, and Gorgonzola 117

Zucchini Salad with Manchego, Salsa Verde, and Pepper and Pine Nut Relish 118

Sichuan Chili Oil Smashed Cucumber Salad and Soy-Cured Egg 121

Rizzo's Wedge Salad 125

Roasted Shallot Salad with Sherry Vinegar and Rye Bread Crumbs 126

Spaghetti with Mint, Ricotta, and Olive Oil–Baked Bread Crumbs 129

Charred Corn Esquites-Style with Fried Oaxacan Cheese Curds 130

Orzo and Goat Cheese Salad 132

Chickpea Casserole 135

Everyone's Mom's Macaroni and Tuna Salad 137

Vasos de Fruta 140

Cranberry Beans with Comté, Tarragon, Mint, and Sherry Vinegar 143

Cannellinis with Roasted Red Peppers, Raisins, Capers, Anchovies, and Parsley 145

Brussels Sprouts with Bacon, Mint, Pistachio, Fish Sauce, Pickled Pepper Caramel, and Lime 146

Butter Beans with Lemon, Confit Garlic, Canned Sardines, and Baby Gem Lettuce 148

Black Beans with Cotija, Cilantro, Red Onion, Crumbled Pork Rinds, Oregano, and Salsa Macha 151

Lupinis with Stracciatella di Bufala, Basil, and Anchovies 152

Roasted Sunchokes, Fresh Ricotta, and Farro 156

Salads continued

Orecchiette with Smoked Mussels and Bottarga 159

Mini Shells with Crab and Basil 160

Cold Ground Pork Larb 163

Bánh Mì Salad with Roasted Pork Belly 164

Chicken Finger Crouton Salad, a Tribute to the Breakfast Beacon 167

Grilled Salami Panzanella Salad 168

Sashimi Salad 172

Frisée aux Lardons Family-Style 175

Warm Potato Salad 176

Leftover Steak Salad 179

Taco Salad 180

PART III: SANDWICHES 189

Taco Submarine 193

Roasted Squash and Mozzarella Grilled Cheese with Honey and Bee Pollen 197

Fried Sprouting Cauliflower 198

Sun-Warmed Tomato 200

Grilled Cheese 203

Croque Madame 204

Matty and Trishy Tuna Melt 207

BLT 210

Stracciatella di Bufala, Caponata, Sun-Dried Tomatoes, Cherry Peppers, and Basil 213

Clubhouse 215

Chicken Parm 216

Beer-Battered Haddock 219

Jerk Shrimp Salad 223

Salmon Katsu Sando 224

Shrimp Burger 226

Bake and Shark 228

Fried Shrimp Po'boy 233

Roasted Chicken Thigh Shawarma with Pickled Turnip and Hot Peppers 235

Jambon Beurre 236

Buffalo Chicken Finger 241

Meatball 242

Pork Katsu Sando 247

Scallion Pancake 248

Italian Combo 253

Beef on Weck with Top Round Roast, Creamed Horseradish, and Beef Au Jus 254

French Dip 261

Not a McRib Sandwich 262

Sabich with Cucumber, Tomato, and Pickled Hot Peppers 264

Canadian Donair with Onion, Tomato, and Donair Sauce 267

Cubano 268

Meatloaf 271

Muffuletta 274

Fried Spam Kimchi Grilled Cheese 277

Philly Cheesesteak 279

Reuben 280

Lasagna Submarine 283

Porchetta 287

Waffle Breakfast Sandwich with Mascarpone, Freezer Strawberry Jam, Fried Egg, and Bacon 288

NYC Bacon, Egg, and Cheese 295

Pain Farce French Toast 296

Fried Egg and Bologna Breakfast Sandwich 299

Banana Bread French Toast with Fried Egg, Peameal Bacon, and Maple Syrup 300

Peanut Butter Cookie with Nutella and Salted Caramel Ice Cream Sandwich 303

Apple Pie Toaster Strudel with Cheddar Cheese 306

Tempura Banana Split Sandwich with All the Fixings 311

Not a Jos Louis 312

Not a Passion Flakie 315

Strawberries and Whipped Cream on Milk Bread 316

Fluffernutter on Wonder Bread with Peanut Butter and Chocolate Chips Microwaved for 10-Second Sandwich 319

Classic Ice Cream Sandwich 321

DRESSINGS AND MORE 333

Creamy Honey Dressing 334

All the Herbs Salsa Verde 334

Scotch Bonnet Salsa 335

Bacon Vinaigrette Dressing 335

Blue Cheese Dressing 336

Coleslaw 336

Vinegar Slaw 337

THANK-YOUS 341

INDEX 344

INTRODUCTION

Soups, Salads, Sandwiches is my most cohesive book, because after writing and making three books, I now know how to make them. So, what is this book? This book is for you! The home cook. Maybe even some chefs will cook from here. I hope they feel some connection and do a twist on a dish or even put it on a menu at their restaurant. I made *Soups, Salads, Sandwiches* with no ego; these are just at-home recipes that are easy and fun.

At first, I had no idea what to do with my third cookbook. It's kinda wild that I'm even doing another one. What the fuck could I make a cookbook about? I really, really tried to figure it out. Like most of my projects, I couldn't force it. I always have to wait for the moment when it all clicks for me. Maybe it's a name or a design or something that triggers a way forward. Something that excites me. Something I can chase. I'm always looking for something like that. I'm a snow leopard in a cage. I need to be free. I need to hunt. I need to soar. I need to live through food. Then the pandemic happened, and I couldn't do a book tour for my little *Home Style Cookery*. That sucked, but I learned something valuable. Being home for as long as I was, I found out how boring and amazing making food at home is and how lucky we are to have restaurants.

There are always things that I love and hate about cooking. I'm sure some of you feel the same. You love doing dishes or grocery shopping or the act of cooking itself, but there's always something that gets you and you're like, *I fucking hate this part*. (On a personal note: I hate doing the dishes. I always have. I love cooking so much and make a mess when I do. I'm a big bad dirty doggy. I just love leaving a hurricane of destruction behind me.)

Sometimes cooking is scary or makes you feel uncomfortable. That's OK. Even I'm uncomfortable when I'm cooking. But the power of cooking always outweighs the anxieties. As long as the love is just a little greater than the fear, we're eating good tonight.

Food has taken me all over the world many times. I'm truly blessed to have had so many years of travel and taste with me. So many stories, so many flavors, so many techniques. Despite this, I keep coming back to the same things that make me happy. The things that make most people happy. The things that you make that are familiar to you. The things that you make that remind you of cooking at home with the people you love.

That's when I thought: soups, salads, and sandwiches. Holy shit, like a book you could open to any chapter and cook from every day. Imagine just being like, *I want a soup and salad*, and boom, just flip the page, and there ya go! Imagine wanting to make a sandwich and being able to make a different sandwich for more than fifty days straight. What the fuck, so sick.

I could eat soup every day, at least twice or even three times. Depending on the soups, that's for sure. Pho for breakfast is my favorite meal. I also love drinking some deep, beautiful beef bone broth, which is just stock, by the way. It's really funny that people made this a thing, but I guess I do love it, too, so I'm part of that problem, like most things.

This book is *that* book. Beautiful, well-thought-out, very delicious recipes that can take those bastard days and elevate them to pure happiness, to holy-shit-we-did-it days. Pick one soup, one salad, and one sandwich, and you literally can cook a different combination for, like, 238,390,283 days straight (not really, but you get the idea). I love that so much. Life is heavy. Life is wild. Why be trapped thinking about what you're gonna make for breakfast, lunch, dinner, or late at night? Just open the book, pick a recipe, cook it, close it, and put it back on the shelf.

Even though there are three huge sections, each has its own path. A choose your own adventure. It's a walk through the woods. It's a riverboat ride, but there's no boat and it's just on an old inner tube. We're going to get wet and wild. We don't need a boat. We thrive in the nothingness. Now, control your destiny.

You know that fun little shelf in your kitchen for the true cookbooks. This is one of those. I'm giving you kitchen-shelf material here. The next time you need me, open it again. Every time that you do, you will be filled with love and light. Embrace the pure joy of freewheeling cooking.

PART I
SOUPS

Every time I think about soup, I still think of my mentor and friend Chef Rang giving me my first taste of pho. That moment—trying something I'd never even heard of, thought of, or known about—changed my life forever. It instantly made me feel so good.

That's the power of soup. That's life. That's friendship. Soup is the friend you've never had but is always there for you. Soup will never turn its back on you.

Why are soups so life-giving? Why does everyone feel better after eating soup? Why do people think broth heals them? I've never heard anyone say, *This cheeseburger saved my life*, in a serious way. But soups are my soul. We drink from the pot of my body. Ladle my body broth into your bowl of life. We give the soup a sip. Food is God, and God is good today, my friend.

I'm always surprised at the number of fond early memories I have of eating soup. We often had canned tomato and cream of broccoli soup at home. They were easy, widely available, and cheap. Soup from a can is an amazing invention. When you open it up, it looks all congealed and like it belongs in *The Matrix*. By simply being heated up, it turns into the most incredible culinary invention in the history of our planet. Having those canned soups made me happy. Tomato soup and grilled cheese is still one of the greatest meals of all time. With all that's happening in the world, why are we making all these elaborate soups? Are we making soups for our egos? Or are we making soups so we can feel good?

There's something about a bowl of ramen, chicken noodle soup, cream of mushroom soup, a seafood chowder, eating a bunch of vegetables and meats and seafood all nestled into a broth or a cream, that somehow makes you feel good. Eating that type of food warms you up. It has so many textures and so many tastes. It makes you feel alive. It's like skydiving for the first time and you know the parachute will work. It's all about trust. I've seen some videos on the internet, and sometimes they don't.

I'm going back to the tough question here: When do you think soups were invented? I'm thinking a long time ago. Who was the first person or creature who made soup? A pterodactyl? A couple of pterodactyls gathered around a lava river simmering some of the first soups? Or was it that only a short fifty million years later, we have people out there chopping down a couple of trees and making a fire? Is that where soup came from? What are we talking about here? Are we opening our eyes? Our minds? Yeah, right, the first canned soup was made in the 1890s! The history of the world doesn't start in the 1890s. Soups have had a long history.

Look how far we've come. From making hippo soup six thousand years ago to (just in America) consuming ten billion soups a year. I'm telling you, people love soup! Listen to me! People are sipping and drinking and spooning and having the greatest times ever. They're pulling up noodles and suckin' on bones.

Soups are the most interactive, most physically demanding acts of culinary dining. And this isn't even counting cereal. Cereal is just cold dessert soup, you know that. We've definitely talked about this. And if we haven't, we don't even need to talk about it. My brothers—as adults—used to not buy any groceries, and for, like, six years, they just ate cereal for three meals a day. They're so fit and skinny and strong. I wasn't doing that, and I'm the only big guy in my family, so I guess I got to eat the cold dessert soup known as cereal.

In this book, I really wanna make some of the tastiest, nicest, and most beautiful soups: the deepest of flavors, the most supple and contagious cravings of soup you've ever looked upon. And I want you to know as you're reading this book: I'm trying to give you the best soups of your life—from my life. We will be making the brothiest of broths, the chowderest of chowders, the creamiest of creams. Once you work on these foundations that I'm laying, you will be able to construct and produce any soup in the world. I am giving you the tools and the knowledge to create and execute your dreams. My dreams and your dreams will become reality. Now, go buy some groceries and make some fucking soup.

LIGHTEST BROTH *of* GARDEN HERBS *with* ONE CHILE

We're starting off the book in a classy way because that's the *only* way. This recipe is so easy and respectable that you're going to be kicking yourself for not putting on your fanciest clothes and making it sooner for the person you love. This broth is a little sipper. Don't be afraid to experiment with different herbs, and don't break your little teapot like I did.

First, make the chicken consommé. In a food processor, pulse the onion, carrot, and celery until finely chopped. Add the ground chicken and eggs and continue to pulse until everything is thoroughly incorporated.

In a stockpot, combine the chicken stock and mixture from your food processor. Vigorously whisk until the chicken mixture is completely dispersed throughout the stock. Heat over medium heat, continuing to stir. You want to go low and slow with this. While the protein in the mixture slowly cooks in the stock, it will pull out any impurities that were previously in it, aka clarifying the stock. As the broth heats, you will notice the mixture float to the top of the stock, forming a gray, scummy mixture. This is what you want. Keep a close eye on it and make sure it never reaches a boil.

After about an hour, the stock should begin to simmer. Turn the heat down to low immediately. If the consommé boils, the mixture will break and the broth will become cloudy. While the broth is gently simmering, the mixture will form into a solid raft floating on top of the broth. If you are feeling brave, you can use a small ladle to gently break a hole in the middle of the raft. This will help the broth simmer up and over the raft to better clarify your broth. Keep an eye on this to make sure the hole doesn't fill back up.

Simmer for another 30 to 40 minutes after the mixture has formed a raft.

Gently ladle the finished broth with the raft through a fine-mesh strainer and into a large vessel. Season with the white shoyu and mirin, as well as a pinch of salt. Use immediately or cool completely, about 30 minutes, and store in the fridge.

If you are using immediately, skip this paragraph. If you are reheating, in a medium pot, heat up your chicken consommé quickly over medium-high heat. Turn the heat down low as soon as you start to see a couple of bubbles float to the surface. If you boil the consommé, you might lose all that fresh chicken flavor.

CONTINUED

SERVES 4

PREP TIME: 2 HOURS

CHICKEN CONSOMMÉ

½ sweet onion, cut into 1-inch chunks

½ carrot, peeled and cut into 1-inch chunks

1 celery rib, cut into 1-inch chunks

1 pound ground chicken

2 eggs

6 cups chicken stock

2 tablespoons white shoyu soy sauce

2 tablespoons mirin

Kosher salt

4 green shiso leaves

4 chive flowers

4 nasturtium leaves and flowers

4 chervil stems

4 lemon thyme sprigs

4 marigold flowers, petals picked

4 spring garlic stems, just the top leaves (or ramp leaves)

2 Thai red chiles, halved lengthwise

LIGHTEST BROTH *of* GARDEN HERBS *with* ONE CHILE CONTINUED

The herbs and flowers used in this recipe are open to interpretation. If you grow herbs yourself or live near a farmers' market, go around and pick anything that seems fresh and interesting. The idea here is to have a nice aromatic, savory tea. Choose your own adventure.

Take all the herbs you have chosen and arrange them into four nice bouquets. Tie each bouquet with butcher's twine. I arranged the leaves on the outside and the stemmed herbs on the inside, with half a Thai chile in each.

In each of four bowls, place one herb bouquet and a couple petals from each flower. Pour 1 cup of hot chicken consommé into each bowl. Serve and consume immediately.

COURT BOUILLON *with* FRESH GARLIC *and* GINGER OIL

This court bouillon is special to me. It's a fundamental stock in French cuisine and has a gentle touch when used in many dishes. It's simple to make but packed with flavor. The ginger, garlic, and joi choi add a touch of brightness and complexity.

In a large pot over medium-high heat, simmer the wine until it has reduced by two-thirds, 30 minutes. Add the water, scallions, shallot, leek, celery, thyme, rosemary, bay leaf, peppercorns, and salt and bring to a boil over high heat, then turn the heat down to low and simmer everything for 30 minutes.

Turn off the heat, add the joi choi and Thai chiles, and allow them to steep in the hot broth for 20 minutes.

Remove the joi choi with tongs and set aside. Strain the remaining contents through a fine-mesh strainer into a large vessel or another pot. Discard any remaining contents. Return the broth to the stove over medium heat.

Once the broth is hot, cut each joi choi quarter into thirds lengthwise. Place four pieces into each of the six bowls with a tablespoon of the fresh garlic and ginger oil and one or two slices of Thai chile (Big Dog likes it hot). Pour 1½ cups broth into each bowl and serve.

SERVES 6
PREP TIME: 1½ HOURS

Half of a 750 ml bottle dry white wine, such as Sauvignon Blanc

10 cups water

1 bunch scallions, thinly sliced

1 shallot, thinly sliced

1 leek, white part only, thinly sliced

2 celery ribs, thinly sliced

8 thyme sprigs

2 rosemary sprigs

1 bay leaf

8 black peppercorns

2 tablespoons kosher salt

2 heads joi choi, cut into quarters (or chicory or mustard greens)

2 Thai chiles, halved lengthwise, plus 2 more for serving

6 tablespoons Fresh Garlic and Ginger Oil (recipe follows)

FRESH GARLIC *and* GINGER OIL

In a small bowl, combine the ginger and garlic. In a small saucepan, heat the grapeseed oil over high heat until it begins to smoke, 2 minutes. Immediately pour the hot oil over the grated ginger and garlic. Once the mixture has cooled, add the sesame oil. Store in an airtight container in the fridge for up to 2 days.

MAKES ABOUT 1 CUP

1 thumb-size knob ginger, grated finely

4 large garlic cloves, grated finely

1 cup grapeseed oil

2 tablespoons toasted sesame oil

RUTABAGA and DAIKON BROTH with TOFU

This is power. This is understanding. This is super soup but still refined and so yummy. The silken tofu makes this mouthfeel that I love. It coats and splashes around like bone marrow, but it's tofu. The pickled shiitakes make it so spicy but well rounded. Daikon is low-key the star. This photo kinda looks like there's just chile oil on top of dirty dishwater after washing old spaghetti sauce–filled Tupperware. Ignore all of that; despite what I said, this soup is fire. Hunt mushrooms, not animals.

A day before you would like to eat this dish, let's make our pickled shiitake mushrooms in chile oil. Using scissors, remove the stems from the shiitakes and reserve the caps in a medium-size bowl. In a small pot over high heat, bring the vinegar, sugar, water, and salt to a boil. Pour the pickling liquid over the mushrooms, making sure that all the mushrooms are covered. If they aren't, cover them with plastic wrap and weight them down with a plate. Let the mushrooms sit in this liquid in the fridge at least overnight but ideally for 24 hours.

Meanwhile, make the chile oil. In a large pot over medium heat, warm the canola oil. When the oil is hot, add the gochugaru and chili powder and whisk vigorously for 30 seconds. Immediately add the cloves, star anise, cinnamon stick, garlic, peppercorns, and sesame oil and continue to whisk vigorously for another 30 seconds, stirring continuously until the oil begins to simmer. Turn the heat down to low and allow everything to steep for 5 minutes. Remove from the heat and allow to cool. Strain the oil through a coffee filter and reserve the oil in an airtight container at room temperature until needed.

Remove the mushrooms from the pickling liquid and dry them with paper towels. Transfer them to a container and cover them with 2 cups of the chile oil. Reserve in the fridge until needed.

The next day, in a large pot over medium heat, bring the dashi up to a gentle simmer. Add the daikon and rutabaga. Turn the heat down to low, cover, and allow the vegetables to poach for 2 hours.

Take the tofu out of its liquid and dry it with paper towels. Press it gently to squeeze out any excess liquid, being careful not to press the tofu too much or it could break apart. Cut it into 1-inch pieces.

After 2 hours, or when the vegetables are almost cooked, add the diced tofu to the broth and continue cooking for no more than 15 minutes. When a fork easily pierces the rutabaga, the vegetables are cooked. Remove the vegetables from the broth. Cut the daikon into 1-inch half-moons and the rutabaga into 1-inch wedges. Add them back to the soup to make sure they are hot for serving.

To serve, ladle a generous amount of the broth, daikon, rutabaga, and tofu into eight bowls. Garnish with a few mushrooms, the scallions, and a pinch of sesame seeds.

SERVES 8

PREP TIME: 1 DAY

PICKLED SHIITAKE MUSHROOMS IN CHILE OIL

1 pound shiitake mushrooms

2 cups malt vinegar

1 cup sugar

2 cups water

1 tablespoon kosher salt

4 cups canola oil

1 cup gochugaru

¼ cup chili powder

4 cloves

2 star anise pods

1 cinnamon stick

8 garlic cloves, chopped

10 black peppercorns

1 tablespoon sesame oil

10 cups dashi

1 daikon, peeled and cut into 4-inch pieces

½ rutabaga, peeled

One 12-ounce package silken tofu

8 scallions, thinly sliced

Toasted white sesame seeds, for garnish

SOUPE AU PISTOU

I'm still a poser, even though I've been to France a handful of times. If you've never been, I won't reveal your secret. This recipe rules, especially if you have a garden that you can pull delicious vegetables from. If you only have green zucchini and not yellow zucchini, I know you already feel like a loser but don't worry. This soup is forgiving. We are just looking to mix and match beautiful vegetables together here. It's one of those awesome soups that has a real choose-your-own-adventure feel to it. Pile that pistou in that soup, add that grated tomato, crunch into that chewy sourdough. Freak what you feel.

In a large heavy-bottomed soup pot or Dutch oven, bring the drained beans and water to a boil. Skim off any foam, then add the bouquet garni. Turn the heat down to low, cover, and simmer for 45 minutes. Add salt to taste after it simmers.

While the soup is simmering, start sautéing the vegetables. Cover the bottom of a large heavy skillet with 1 tablespoon olive oil and heat over medium-high heat. Add the garlic and toast for 1 minute. Then add the green and yellow zucchini, bell pepper, celery, leek, and onion and cook until translucent, about 10 minutes. Stir this mixture into the bean pot and bring the mixture back to a simmer. Add the wine. Cover and simmer over low heat until the beans are fork-tender, 1 hour.

Meanwhile, make the pistou. In a blender, blend the basil, pistachios, olive oil, garlic, and lemon zest together. Keep it chunky; you don't want it pureed. Together, but loose—like me. Taste to see if it needs a little hit of salt. Set it aside.

Prepare the spread. In a small bowl, mix the goat cheese and mascarpone together.

In a large pan over medium-low heat, heat the olive oil. Working in batches, gently fry the sourdough until its lightly browned. Transfer to a paper towel–lined plate to drain and cover with a big spoon of the goat cheese and mascarpone mixture. Hit it with a little salt and black pepper.

In a small bowl, mix your tomatoes and vinegar together. Add a big tablespoon of the mixture to the top of each sourdough cheese piece.

Ladle your soup into four bowls. Do what you like: Add a spoonful of the pistou, some cheese spread, a big ol' piece of the bread, and some grated tomato. Dig in.

SERVES 4

PREP TIME: 2 HOURS

SOUP

1½ cups navy beans, soaked for 6 hours in 6 cups water and drained

8 cups water

A bouquet garni with a few sprigs of tarragon, parsley, and thyme, and a bay leaf

Kosher salt

2 tablespoons extra-virgin olive oil, plus more for serving

4 garlic cloves, smashed

1 cup diced green zucchini

1 cup diced yellow zucchini

1 cup diced red bell pepper

1 cup diced celery

1 cup diced leek (white and green parts)

1 cup diced onion

Half of a 26-ounce bottle dry white wine, such as Sauvignon Blanc

Kosher salt

Freshly cracked black pepper

PISTOU

1 cup basil

1 cup pistachios

1 cup extra-virgin olive oil

3 garlic cloves, halved

Zest of 1 lemon

GOAT CHEESE AND MASCARPONE SPREAD

One 4-ounce log goat cheese

4 ounces mascarpone

2 tablespoons olive oil

1 loaf sourdough, torn into 3-inch pieces

Kosher salt

Freshly cracked black pepper

2 hothouse tomatoes, grated

2 tablespoons sherry vinegar

CABBAGE SOUP *with* CRÈME FRAÎCHE, SMOKED TROUT ROE, *and* CHIVES

This cabbage is soft as butter in the warm broth, then the bounce of the roe hits, then the bacon, then the cream. The dill slaps you in the mouth in the best possible way. It's a dream come true. Imagine a winter day. You're driving down a mountainside. Your car breaks down, and you're stuck for six hours with no heat. Finally, someone shows up on a dogsled with a hot pot of warm bacon cabbage soup. You have a jar of trout roe from your great-aunt in your glove box. Then some other dude pulls up on a snowmobile and has some crème fraîche ('cause you never know when you'll need crème fraîche). Then, you're all eating a hot, brothy cabbage butter soup with the best garnishes in the world. This dish is all time, trust me.

In a large Dutch oven over medium heat, warm the butter, olive oil, and lardon. When the butter begins to melt, add the onion, garlic, and leeks and gently caramelize for 5 to 10 minutes.

Add the pilsner and cook until the liquid is reduced by half. Next, add the cabbage and 6 cups of the water. Make sure the cabbage is covered by at least 1 inch of liquid. Add the bay leaves and kosher salt and pepper to taste. Cover and cook that down for 1 hour, stirring occasionally.

Meanwhile, in a small bowl, whisk the crème fraîche with the remaining 2 tablespoons water. It should be loose enough to drizzle.

In a blender, add the grapeseed oil, dill, and chives. Blend and season to taste with kosher salt. Pass the mixture through a fine-mesh strainer and discard the leftover bits.

When the soup is done, remove the bay leaves and ladle soup into four bowls. Drizzle the grapeseed oil mixture and crème fraîche in circles over your soup. Top each bowl with a tablespoon of smoked trout roe and a generous sprinkle of Maldon salt, pepper, dill, and chives.

SERVES 4

PREP TIME: 1½ HOURS

1 cup unsalted butter

3 tablespoons olive oil

16 slices bacon (about 1 pound), cut into ½-inch lardons (1 cup)

1 large yellow onion, julienned

3 garlic cloves, sliced

1 leek, white and green parts, sliced

One 12-ounce bottle or can pilsner

½ head green cabbage, cored and cut into quarters

6 cups plus 2 tablespoons water

2 bay leaves

Kosher salt and freshly cracked black pepper

1 cup crème fraîche

1 cup grapeseed oil

¼ cup chopped dill, plus extra for serving

¼ cup chopped chives, plus extra for serving

4 tablespoons smoked trout roe

Maldon salt

DUMPLINGS, ROASTED BABY BEETS, PORK BELLY, and PORK BROTH

I always thought eating beets like dumplings with broth would be really cool. Having a full little baby beet burst in my mouth makes me feel so much love toward the noble beet. Then I thought about having baby beets and dumplings together and bonding them together with pork. When the pork belly slaps my tongue like a velvet hammer is true happiness. Slurpin' and sippin' the pork and beet broth is joy, pure joy. Make this and eat it. You'll be warm like I am. We will be warm together.

Make the filling for the dumplings first. We're going to caramelize the shallots. In a small sauté pan over medium heat, warm the olive oil and butter. Add the shallots and cook until they brown evenly, then turn the heat down low and cook for 10 minutes.

In a medium bowl, combine the ricotta, dill, caramelized shallots, and salt and pepper to taste and fold it all together. Set a small bowl of cold water nearby as well. To assemble, lay a wonton wrapper down. Spoon 1 teaspoon of the dumpling filling into the center of the wrapper. Dip your index finger in the water and wet the edges of the wrapper. Fold the wrapper and press the edges together to seal. Repeat with the remaining wrappers and filling until you've used the delicious filling up.

Preheat your oven to 400°F. Rinse and dry the baby beets. Line a baking sheet with parchment paper and cover the parchment with a thin layer of salt. Place the beets pointy side up and roast until fork-tender, about 50 minutes.

Next, take your pork belly out of your fridge and season liberally with salt. Leave out on the counter for it to cure and come up to room temperature.

Remove the beets from the oven and while they are still warm, pinch the skin off with a paper towel. The steam will allow you to pull it off relatively easily. Place the baby beets into a bowl and set aside for later.

In a large pot, add the cold water, chicken stock, and your pork belly. Bring to a boil, then turn the heat down to a low simmer and skim the scum off the top. Add your large purple beet, onion, carrot, bay leaves, thyme, and peppercorns and simmer until the pork belly is soft but not falling apart, 2 hours. You want the skin to be holding it together. Leave a little fat in the water; you just skim the scum while it's simmering.

CONTINUED

SERVES 4

PREP TIME: 3 HOURS

DUMPLINGS

1 teaspoon olive oil

1 teaspoon unsalted butter

2 shallots, finely diced

1½ pounds ricotta

4 ounces (about 2 bunches) fresh dill, chopped

Kosher salt and freshly cracked black pepper

24 wonton wrappers

20 baby beets

Kosher salt and freshly cracked black pepper

2 pounds pork belly, skin on

6 cups cold water

6 cups chicken stock

1 large purple beet, quartered (I prefer Bull's Blood)

1 yellow onion, quartered, with skin on

1 carrot, peeled and halved lengthwise

2 bay leaves

3 thyme sprigs

1 tablespoon black peppercorns

2 ounces (about 1 bunch) dill, finely chopped

DUMPLINGS, ROASTED BABY BEETS, PORK BELLY, *and* PORK BROTH CONTINUED

Remove the pork belly and set it aside. Discard the vegetables and herbs and pass the stock through a fine-mesh strainer into another pot. Place onto the stove and bring up to a rolling simmer over medium heat. Add your dumplings. Add salt until you think it's delicious.

Give your cooled pork a rough chop. Leave the skin, fat, and all the bits and pieces.

To serve, remove the bay leaves and add about 3 tablespoons of pork to each of four bowls along with 5 of your beets in between the pork piles. Ladle your broth on top until it barely covers the beets. Top with a pinch of chopped dill and some freshly cracked black pepper. Eat the beets like dumplings and the dumplings like dumplings!

PUMPERNICKEL, BEER, *and* CHEESE CURD SOUP

This soup is the official soup of Banana Town. The pumpernickel croutons remind me so much of growing up and dipping toasted pumpernickel bread in spinach dip but we are butter roasting it instead. The curds make this so wild. Eating this is just fun. If this isn't fun for you, you're a mutant, so fuck off. This Pumpernickel, Beer, and Cheese Curd is for people who love cheese and beer, maybe people who live in Milwaukee. I love Milwaukee. I've been like five times in the last year. It's an amazing place.

Preheat your oven to 400°F.

Line a bowl with a paper towel. In a large pot over medium heat, cook the bacon until the fat is rendered and the bacon is crisp, 15 minutes. Using a slotted spoon, transfer the bacon to the bowl. Add the onion, jalapeño, garlic, and thyme to the pot. Cook over medium heat, stirring, until softened, 8 minutes. Add half of the beer and cook until reduced by half, about 5 minutes. Add the chicken stock and bring to a gentle simmer for 30 minutes while you make the croutons.

Make the giant pumpernickel croutons. Line a big plate with a paper towel. Toss the pumpernickel cubes with the garlic powder, olive oil, and salt and black pepper to taste. Spread them out on a baking sheet and roast for 20 minutes, tossing every 5 minutes, until they are crunchy-crunchy. Put them all onto the plate.

While the soup continues to simmer, melt the butter in a small skillet over medium-low heat. Whisk in the flour and cook until it's browned, 2 minutes. Pour the roux (you just made a roux) into the soup. Whisk until it's fully combined and bring back to a simmer for 10 minutes. It should be a thick boy now.

Add the cream, sharp cheddar cheese, smoked cheddar cheese, and the remaining beer. Simmer until thick and creamy, 5 minutes. Give it a couple of stirs to help it along. Add in the bacon and season with salt and black pepper.

Ladle the soup into four bowls and top it with the delicious, crunchy pumpernickel croutons. Then hit it with a few cheese curds and a little dash of olive oil, salt, and black pepper.

EAT IT! You're eating fondue at the court of Prince Pumpernickel, but it's soup. It's good for you.

SERVES 4
PREP TIME: 45 MINUTES

8 ounces bacon, diced

1 yellow onion, chopped

1 jalapeño, seeded and chopped

2 garlic cloves, minced

1 tablespoon chopped thyme

One 12-ounce lager

2 cups chicken stock

½ loaf pumpernickel bread, cut into ½-inch cubes

2 tablespoons garlic powder

¼ cup extra-virgin olive oil, plus more for serving

Kosher salt and freshly cracked black pepper

¼ cup unsalted butter

¼ cup all-purpose flour

1 cup heavy cream

8 ounces sharp cheddar cheese, shredded

8 ounces smoked cheddar cheese, shredded

8 ounces cheese curds

CARAMELIZED MAPLE PARSNIP SOUP
with SUNCHOKE CHIPS *and* RICOTTA

Parsnips rule. Make this soup. Sunchoke chips rule. Make these little chips. Ricotta rules. Add this to your soup. Maple syrup is insane. Keep a little bottle up your sleeve like Will Ferrell in *Elf*. This soup will help you figure it all out on a cold winter day; it will make you love your life when it's pitch dark out at 4:30 p.m. and the ol' seasonal depression kicks in.

In a large Dutch oven over medium heat, warm the butter. Add the parsnips and onions and cook until they begin to caramelize, about 10 minutes. Stir occasionally. Add the maple syrup. Guess what? Keep giving it a little stir here and there. We're trying to create a super-sticky, fudgy, super-caramelized mixture here. This should take about 15 minutes. Watch this closely; it will burn if you don't keep moving it.

Next, hit it with the brandy. Flambé. It's a classic. I'm not liable. Let the brandy cook off and then add water to cover, about 6 cups. Simmer for 30 minutes.

While the soup is simmering, let's make the sunchoke chips. Completely submerge them in water and add the vinegar. Let them sit for 20 minutes.

Drain and dry the chips. In a separate large Dutch oven, heat the canola oil over medium-high heat to 360°F. Make sure the chips are very dry. Gently lower them into the oil with a spider. Fry these guys in batches. Never fill the pot up all the way. Gently move them within the fryer. As soon as they get golden brown, 1 to 2 minutes, pull them out and season them with kosher salt.

When the soup has simmered for 30 minutes, throw in the cream. Cook for another 10 minutes, then blend the entire mixture, preferably with a hand blender but a regular blender works too.

In a small bowl, combine the ricotta with the lemon zest and olive oil. Add a healthy pinch of Maldon salt and pepper.

To serve, ladle the soup into four bowls, add a large dollop of the seasoned ricotta, a drizzle with maple syrup, and a few of those delicious sunchoke chips.

SERVES 4
PREP TIME: 1 HOUR

1 cup unsalted butter
2 pounds parsnips, peeled and chopped
1 onion, chopped
1 cup maple syrup, plus more for serving
1 cup brandy
6 sunchokes, thinly sliced or shaved
1 tablespoon white vinegar
6 cups canola oil, for frying
Kosher salt and freshly cracked black pepper
1 cup heavy cream
1 cup ricotta
Zest of 1 lemon
1 tablespoon extra-virgin olive oil
Maldon salt

BROILED *and* BURNT ROASTED TOMATO SOUP *with* GRILLED CHEESE CROSTINI THING

Nothing beats grilled cheese, and nothing beats tomato soup from a can. It just makes you feel like everything will be OK in that moment. If you want to step it up, well now, just look at this fucking thing. Stare at the cheese crostini stacked so high. Stare at the roasted tomato soup. As you slurp up your soup, you can dunk each little cheesy crostini in the delicious tomato liquid. Soak it up one-by-one. You can smell it, which is kinda the best, then taste it, and then you have risen into the heavens. You can look down at all the losers still just eating canned soup (even though it's delicious) like, *Come on! Figure it out.*

Preheat your oven to broil on low. On a baking sheet, toss together the tomatoes, red onion, jalapeños, garlic, olive oil, and salt and black pepper to taste. Broil for 30 minutes, tossing every 10 minutes. Be careful not to burn everything, but you'll want a nice char on the veggies. Leave that broiler on and crank it up to high!

Transfer the charred veggies to a large Dutch oven. Add the tomato puree and vegetable stock. Bring the mixture up to a rolling boil, then cook over low heat for 30 minutes.

While the soup is bubbling away, we're going to make our grilled cheese crostini. Toast your slices of bread, then rub each slice with the garlic clove. Put a nice handful of mozzarella and sharp cheddar on each slice. Put them on a baking sheet and broil for only 2 minutes or so. Watch these; please do not burn them! We need these melty but not browned.

Puree the entire soup mixture and serve with as many grilled cheese crostini as you can stack!

SERVES 6

PREP TIME: 1 HOUR AND 15 MINUTES

SOUP

12 hothouse tomatoes, halved

1 red onion, roughly chopped

3 jalapeños, halved and seeded

4 garlic cloves, smashed

½ cup extra-virgin olive oil

Kosher salt and freshly cracked black pepper

2 cups tomato puree

6 cups vegetable stock, chicken stock, or water

CROSTINI

1 baguette, cut into ¼-inch slices

1 garlic clove, peeled

¼ cup shredded mozzarella cheese

¼ cup shredded sharp cheddar cheese

BROILED BROCCOLI *and* CHEDDAR SOUP

My mother, Joan, always made boiled broccoli with shredded cheese on top and kinda just left it like that. Sometimes, we'd get it with a nice cheese sauce at Christmas or Thanksgiving. I'm still confused as to why cheese and broccoli go together, but they really do. Grilled or broiled broccoli is so good and is so special, but we stan for burnt broc. We're blessed to have access to the best vegetable in all the world, broccoli, so let's make a soup of it. This came from a deep conjuring of trying to elevate this soup that we all know and love.

Preheat your oven to broil on low. On a baking sheet, toss together the broccoli, ¼ cup of the olive oil, and kosher salt and pepper to taste. Broil the fuck out of it so it's nice and charred on one side and beautiful, about 10 minutes. Save 1 cup of the broccoli for our garnish.

When you're almost done broiling that broccoli, in a Dutch oven over medium heat, warm the remaining ¼ cup olive oil and the butter. Add the onion, celery, garlic, and leeks and cook, stirring constantly, until the vegetables are translucent, about 10 minutes. Add the Guinness, broccoli, and water and simmer for 30 minutes.

Add the cream and use a hand blender to blend the soup. Taste and adjust with more cream, butter, Guinness, kosher salt, or pepper. Add the cheese and stir that over medium heat until incorporated. As the cheese is melting away, take your leftover charred broccoli and cover it in the lemon zest, Maldon salt, and pepper.

Once your cheese is melted, ladle the soup into bowls. Garnish with the reserved cheddar and your tasty lemon broccoli.

SERVES 4
PREP TIME: 1 HOUR

4 heads broccoli, cut into florets with stems

½ cup extra-virgin olive oil

Kosher salt and freshly cracked black pepper

½ cup unsalted butter, plus more if needed

1 large yellow onion, diced

3 celery ribs, diced

4 garlic cloves, minced

3 leeks, white parts quartered lengthwise then thinly sliced

¼ cup Guinness, plus more if needed

8 cups water

1 cup heavy cream, plus more if needed

1 pound orange sharp cheddar cheese, shredded, ¼ cup reserved for garnish

Zest of 1 lemon

Maldon salt

CANNELLINI BEAN *and* KALE SOUP *with* LOTS OF SHALLOTS

This is a quick and easy soup that makes you feel good. After you crush this soup, you'll have accomplished making something you probably haven't done before, making a new thing. That's huge. This soup is an easy win. Everyone's life needs more wins and this soup is your big *W* this day! Keep winning, keep soupin'.

In a large Dutch oven over medium heat, add the olive oil, shallots, garlic, fennel, rosemary, and 1 tablespoon of the Calabrian chili peppers. Throw in the tomato paste and cook it down until it starts to caramelize. Add the wine, vegetable stock, and cannellini beans. Turn it down nice and low and cook, covered, for about 1 hour. Skim the scum while the soup cooks down.

Take the lid off and reduce it to a nice hearty soup, about 15 minutes. The beans will have fluffed up. Take the rinds of Pecorino and throw them in. That's nice. Adjust the seasonings to your taste, and when it tastes real good, throw in the kale and cook it down for 10 minutes. Stir that up.

Ladle the soup into bowls. Top each bowl with the grated Pecorino, a drizzle of olive oil, and the lemon juice. Throw in the parsley. It should look like mulch. If you are a spicy boy or girl add some more of that preserved Calabrian chili pepper.

SERVES 4

PREP TIME: 1 HOUR 15 MINUTES

1 cup extra-virgin olive oil, plus more for serving

6 shallots, sliced

6 garlic cloves, smashed

1 fennel bulb, diced

2 rosemary sprigs

2 tablespoons preserved Calabrian chili peppers, chopped

1 heaping tablespoon tomato paste

1 cup Italian white wine

6 cups vegetable stock

2 cups dried cannellini beans, soaked for 6 hours and drained

Two 2-inch pieces Pecorino rind

Kosher salt and freshly cracked black pepper

1 large bunch Tuscan black kale, chopped into 1-inch-wide pieces

½ cup grated Pecorino cheese

Juice of 1 lemon

1 bunch curly parsley, chopped

CORN MAPLE PARMESAN SOUP

I love frozen corn. It's a deep fondness that tugs at my heartstrings. I think it's because frozen corn has this bad reputation. I have always thought people (like scientists) think it's bad for you. I'm not a food scientist. I do come from a long line of alcohol and drug addiction, so I pray that corn isn't that bad for you. Making this soup is very yummy (much like alcohol), but like anything that's fun and high in carbs: too much and it could kill you.

In a large Dutch oven over medium heat, warm the butter and olive oil. Add the onion, poblano, and garlic and cook until the onion and garlic are translucent, 5 minutes. Add the wine and cook until the liquid is reduced by half. Next, add the corn and water. Bring that up to a boil and give it a stir. The frozen corn is going to release a lot of liquid. Simmer for about 20 minutes, and then add the cream. It's going to look like vomit until you blend it.

While the soup is simmering, make the charry crema. Get a cast-iron skillet smoking hot. Throw in the corn with nothing else. Let it get nice and charred. Swish it around to get it hot, hot, hot, until it's burned on one side, 3 minutes. Put it on a paper towel. Throw it in a large bowl with the sour cream, mayonnaise, Parmesan, lime zest and juice, and salt and black pepper to taste and mix it all together. Set it aside.

Add the maple syrup to the soup and simmer until it is reduced by a third, 10 minutes more. Then, add the Parmesan and bourbon. Cook for 5 more minutes, until the booze smell reduces a little bit. Throw everything into a blender, working in batches if needed, and blend.

Add salt and black pepper to taste and stir in a splash of water or cream if the soup is too thick. Bring it back up to temperature. Everyone wants a hot soup.

For serving, ladle the soup into four bowls. Keep the chili powder, paprika, cayenne, and charry crema on the side for guests to dress their soup themselves.

SERVES 4

PREP TIME: 1 HOUR

SOUP

¼ cup unsalted butter

¼ cup olive oil

1 yellow onion, diced

1 poblano pepper, seeded and diced

3 garlic cloves, minced

2 cups dry white wine, such as Sauvignon Blanc

3 cups frozen corn

2 cups water, plus more if needed

2 cups heavy cream, plus more if needed

1 cup maple syrup

1 cup Parmesan cheese

1 ounce bourbon

Kosher salt and freshly cracked black pepper

2 tablespoons chili powder, for serving

2 tablespoons smoked paprika, for serving

1 tablespoon cayenne, for serving

CHARRY CREMA

1 cup frozen corn

½ cup sour cream

½ cup mayonnaise

1 cup grated Parmesan cheese

Zest of 2 limes

Juice of ½ lime

Kosher salt and freshly cracked black pepper

RHODE ISLAND CLAM CHOWDER

Rhode Island is a special place. They make chowder different from everyone else, and it's pretty fire. It reminds me of the way my family makes chowder, without the milk and cream. I hate roux-based chowders. They get this glossy look that tastes like nothing. I like brothy, milky, cloudy chowders. They are more warming, and eating thick soup is kinda gross. Rhode Island knows what's good and *Family Guy* rules, so eat this soup.

In a large soup pot or Dutch oven, heat the olive oil over medium heat. Add the bacon and cook until it becomes crispy, 5 to 7 minutes. Drain off any excess fat, but leave the bacon in the pot. Add the onion, garlic, and leeks and cook until the onion and leeks become translucent, 3 minutes. Stir in the potatoes, bay leaf, thyme, clam juice, and water.

Bring the mixture to a boil, then reduce the heat to a simmer. Let it simmer until the potatoes are tender, about 30 minutes. Add the clams and celery to the pot and continue to simmer until the vegetables are tender, an additional 10 minutes. Remove the bay leaf and season with salt and pepper to taste.

Garnish with the chopped parsley and serve with a handful of saltine crackers on the side.

SERVES 4
PREP TIME: 1 HOUR

2 tablespoons olive oil

1 cup diced bacon or salt pork

1 yellow onion, finely chopped

2 garlic cloves, minced

1 cup diced leeks, white part only

2 cups 1-inch cubes Yukon gold potatoes

1 bay leaf

3 sprigs thyme

4 cups clam juice

1 cup water

24 medium-size quahog clams, rinsed and roughly chopped

2 large ribs celery, diced

Kosher salt and freshly cracked black pepper

Chopped fresh parsley, for garnish

Saltine crackers, for serving

CIOPPINO

Befriend your fishmonger and bring the ocean to you. Truthfully, you should have already done this when you moved to whatever neighborhood you now call home. Having a good fishmonger close to you is an amazing privilege, and you should support small fish shops. They are few and far between. Even though I live close to a lake, I don't have access to a lot of fish. Living land locked kinda sucks. Them bringing in fish from all over is an amazing luxury.

This soup is a love story to your local fish shop.

Heat a large Dutch oven over medium heat. Add enough olive oil to coat the bottom, then add your fennel, onion, sweet peppers, and garlic. Cook and stir until the vegetables are lightly caramelized, about 10 minutes. Next, we're going to add the ground fennel, Old Bay, paprika, cayenne, and dried chile flakes to build that flavor. Toast for about 3 minutes, being careful not to burn the spices.

Next, we're going to add our wine and Pernod. We want to burn off all the alcohol. If you want to flambé, go ahead, but do not end up on the internet for being stupid. After about 10 minutes, once the alcohol has burned off, add your tomato puree and fish stock. Season with salt and pepper. Cover and cook for 30 minutes, stirring occasionally.

Add the cod and clams to the stew and cook for 5 to 8 minutes, until the clams open. Add in the scallops after the clams begin to open up. Lightly stir to combine. Cook for 2 more minutes. Now we're going to add the mussels and shrimp to the pot and cook for 1 minute. The mussels should open up quickly. Once this beauty has finished coming together, top with the lemon juice, black pepper, olive oil, parsley, and fennel tops. Serve with a slice or two of your favorite crusty bread.

SERVES 4

PREP TIME: 1 HOUR AND 15 MINUTES

Olive oil

2 cups diced fennel (save your tops for garnish)

1 cup yellow onion, diced

5 small sweet peppers, diced

3 garlic cloves, smashed

1 tablespoon ground fennel

1 tablespoon Old Bay Seasoning

1 tablespoon paprika

1 teaspoon cayenne

½ teaspoon dried chile flakes

Half of a 26-ounce bottle white wine, such as Sauvignon Blanc

1 cup Pernod

1 cup tomato puree

4 cups fish stock

Kosher salt and freshly cracked black pepper

1 pound cod, cut into 2-inch segments

1 dozen littleneck clams, cleaned

1 pound scallops, cleaned

1 pound mussels, cleaned

1 pound shrimp, peeled and deveined

Juice of 2 lemons

¼ bunch parsley, stemmed and chopped

1 loaf your favorite crusty bread, sliced, for serving

RED CURRY LOBSTER SOUP

Lobster bisque is good, but Red Curry Lobster Soup is a new level. It's spicy, it's tangy, it's creamy, and it's really strong. And the shiitakes just make the mouthfeel that much better. I like pairing mushrooms with seafood because they have the same kind of chew and bounce in the mouth. Don't tell anybody, but these were just frozen lobster tails because lobster is so expensive. Just be sure to thaw them for at least an hour before getting started.

First, let's make the curry paste. In a blender, combine the lemongrass, shallot, chiles, garlic, lime leaves, cilantro leaves, gochugaru, mace, cumin, coriander, white pepper, tomato paste, and fish sauce and blend until smooth. Transfer to an airtight container and store in the fridge until needed, up to 1 week.

Now let's make the soup: In a large pot, warm your neutral oil over medium-high heat. When the oil is hot, add the lobster tails cut-side down and sear. You want to go as hot and fast as possible. Once the cut side is caramelized, remove the tails right away and allow them to cool.

In a blender, blend your cilantro stems, scallions, ginger, and garlic as finely as possible.

In the same pot you used to cook the lobster, over medium heat, add your vegetable paste and sweat it for 5 minutes. Stir constantly to prevent the vegetables from burning. Once most of the water from the vegetable paste has cooked off and the vegetables are translucent, add your red curry paste. Sear for another minute, stirring constantly. You can add as much or as little of this paste as you like, 3 tablespoons will make it spicy but not insanely spicy. Add your chicken stock and bring to a simmer. Add your carrots, red onion, shiitakes, and 1 tablespoon of kosher salt and simmer for 30 minutes.

While this is happening, remove most of your lobster meat from the shells. Save a few tails with meat still in them for a cool Instagram photo. You can add the shells immediately to your simmering soup to help impart some flavor—just be sure to remove them before serving. Dice the lobster into big chunks (about 1 inch).

After your soup has simmered and the carrots are tender, add your coconut milk and lobster meat and simmer for another 5 minutes.

Add salt and black pepper to your liking. Roughly chop your cilantro leaves and add them to your soup just before serving. Give your limes a nice squeeze over top and enjoy.

SERVES 4
PREP TIME: 2 HOURS

RED CURRY PASTE

1 lemongrass stalk

1 shallot, peeled

2 red finger chiles, seeded

6 garlic cloves

5 makrut lime leaves

Cilantro leaves

2 tablespoons gochugaru

½ teaspoon ground mace

¼ teaspoon ground cumin

¼ teaspoon ground coriander

¼ teaspoon ground white pepper

1 cup tomato paste

½ cup fish sauce

SOUP

½ cup neutral oil

4 frozen lobster tails, thawed and split in half

1 bunch cilantro, stems and leaves separated

1 bunch scallions, trimmed

1 knob ginger, peeled

6 garlic cloves, peeled

1 cup Red Curry Paste (see above)

6 cups chicken stock

1 large carrot, peeled and diced

1 red onion, diced

6 shiitake mushrooms, stemmed and diced

Kosher salt

One 13.5-ounce can coconut milk

Freshly cracked black pepper

3 limes, quartered

CLAM, SAUSAGE, ORECCHIETTE, KALE, *and* CHICKEN BRODO

When I was a young bad boy, I used to hang out at the mall where Trish worked. She killed it at a clothing store and became the boss. There was this restaurant inside of the mall that served a sausage rapini and orecchiette pasta that was pretty basic but always hit. It was delicious but I was young and we couldn't afford to eat there every day. We could have been that cute couple who brought packed lunches to each other and ate them in the courtyard outside the mall or in the food court like full freaks. I guess what I'm saying is: make this for someone you love, bring it to work, and eat it on your lap because it'll be super easy with all the clam shells. See, I am an idiot. We could have thrown those clam shells into the wishing fountain at the mall. That restaurant in the mall is now closed, and so is her old workplace. So also, I'm saying this is more long-lasting than two whole businesses. This is forever, just like my love for Tricia.

Bring a large pot of water to a boil. Season with salt until it tastes like the sea and boil your orecchiette pasta al dente (removing 2 to 3 minutes before it's done according to the package instructions). Drain and toss with a few tablespoons of olive oil to prevent it from sticking to each other. Keep covered until ready to use.

In a large pot over medium-high heat, warm up the ¼ cup olive oil and brown your sausage meat, breaking it up into bite-size pieces. Add your onion, garlic, and anchovy and cook until the vegetables are translucent, about 5 minutes.

Next, add your wine. Lower the heat to medium and simmer until it has reduced to a few tablespoons of liquid, 10 minutes. Then, add your chicken stock, rosemary, thyme, chile flakes, smoked paprika, and 1 tablespoon of salt. Turn the heat down to low and simmer for 1 hour.

While the soup is simmering, take a pot brush and really scrub the shells of your clams. Get in every nook and crack. You don't want any sand. Hold these in cold water in the fridge until you are ready to use them.

Once the soup has simmered, add your clams and cook until they open, about 10 minutes, then immediately remove them with tongs. If some don't open, get rid of them. Never force a clam shell open.

Add your kale and simmer for 10 more minutes. Adjust your salt as you see fit. When the soup is done, add your cooked clams and orecchiette back in. Ladle a generous amount into four bowls, drizzle with olive oil, and sprinkle with black pepper. If you want, you can also top with Parmigiano-Reggiano.

SERVES 4
PREP TIME: 2 HOURS

2½ cups dried orecchiette pasta

Sea salt

¼ cup olive oil, plus a few tablespoons for the pasta and for serving

5 hot Italian sausages, removed from their casings

1 white onion, diced

4 garlic cloves, roughly chopped

1 anchovy

1 cup dry white wine, such as Sauvignon Blanc

10 cups good-quality chicken stock

1 rosemary sprig, leaves picked and finely chopped

6 thyme sprigs, leaves picked and finely chopped

1 teaspoon red pepper flakes

1 teaspoon smoked paprika

2 pounds littleneck clams

1 bunch Tuscan black kale, roughly chopped

Freshly cracked black pepper

Parmigiano-Reggiano (optional)

CRAB CONGEE

The first time I ever had congee with all these kinds of toppings on top was at Boon Café in Australia. It was chock-full of all these accoutrements. I never had congee like that before. It usually comes out with nothing on it. My kids love congee so much, but I just think they like salty porridge. Trish makes what she calls magic soup, which is just chicken soup with a lot of veggies. So, when I made congee for the first time and Mac asked what I was making, I told him I was making magic congee and he loved the sound of that. What kid wouldn't love savory and salty chicken stock rice porridge?

Make the congee. Wash the rice in a fine-mesh strainer under cold running water. Add the rice to a large pot along with 8 cups of the chicken stock, the ginger, and garlic. Bring it to a boil, then turn it down to a simmer and cook, stirring every 15 minutes. until the rice is very overcooked. This will take 1½ to 2 hours. Use the remaining chicken stock if needed to get the desired texture. The grains will have burst open and the mixture should be thick.

Toward the end, stir it with a whisk like you're making whipped cream—really work it. I like mine very smooth and thick, like a warm smoothie consistency. It should not be runny or thin. Season with salt. You can pick out the ginger and garlic, but I like chewing on it like sugarcane.

In a small pot, simmer the shiitakes in the soy sauce, water, and sesame oil until soft, about 10 minutes. Reserve till assembly.

Make the congee sauce. In a small bowl, combine the chile oil, sesame oil, soy sauce, lime zest and juice, garlic, and cilantro. This is a great condiment for really anything, like grilled fish or pork, but it's best for congee.

Now let's make our omelet. In a small bowl, whisk your eggs. In a medium cast-iron pan over medium-high heat, add your oil and butter. Just before the butter starts to brown, add your eggs. Let them begin to cook while pulling the forming egg curds into the middle with a spatula and allow the liquid to keep filling the empty spots. Once it looks formed, take your spatula and fold it into thirds. I like an omelet, but you can do poached, fried, soft-boiled, whatever you feel like to accompany the dish!

Now let's assemble. Ladle the congee into bowls, 1 cup should do per bowl. I like to place everything on top, then mix everything together:

At the 12 o'clock position, place a spoonful of crab. At the 3 o'clock position, place some congee sauce. At the 6 o'clock position, place the cilantro and sprinkle on the white pepper. At the 9 o'clock position, place the shiitakes with a slotted spoon (discard the liquid).

But assemble as you like—it's a blank canvas, run wild, not everything has to look like the pictures!

SERVES 8
PREP TIME: 2½ HOURS

CONGEE
1 cup basmati rice
8 to 10 cups chicken stock
1 thumb-size knob ginger, quartered
2 garlic cloves, smashed
3 tablespoons kosher salt

MUSHROOMS
10 shiitake mushrooms, stemmed and sliced
½ cup soy sauce
1 cup water
2 tablespoons sesame oil

CONGEE SAUCE
2 tablespoons chile oil (page 172)
2 tablespoons sesame oil
2 tablespoons soy sauce
Zest and juice of 1 lime
1 garlic clove, grated
Small handful of cilantro stems, thinly sliced

OMELET
3 eggs
2 ounces grapeseed oil
2 tablespoons unsalted butter

TOPPINGS
One 6-ounce can good lump crabmeat
Handful of chopped cilantro
Ground white pepper

BAKED POTATO BUFFET VICHYSSOISE

This recipe is one of those that comes to you in a fever dream, and the subject of that dream is the beautiful potato. There's nothing better than potatoes (shout-out to Prince Edward Island) and all the toppings you can fit on it. It's a baked potato bar that you can set up and eat with everyone you love in your life. Is it time for the baked potato bar to make a comeback? This is my effort to get everyone eating potatoes with delicious toppings on them. We set this up for my kids for the photoshoot for the book and it was pure chaos.

In a large Dutch oven over medium-high heat, warm the butter. Add the leeks, onion, and potatoes. Cover with just enough water (about 8 cups) and simmer until the potatoes are fork-tender, about 10 minutes.

Add the cream and milk and puree with a hand blender. Pass the mixture through a fine-mesh strainer into another pot set over medium-low heat. Season to taste with salt and put a lid on it to keep it warm. Be sure to give it a stir with a spatula every 5 minutes.

Set up your baked potato topping bar. Ladle your soup into four bowls. Share the toppings. Don't share the toppings. Be loved. Be hated. Become the soup.

SERVES 4

PREP TIME: 35 MINUTES

SOUP

1 cup unsalted butter

4 leeks, trimmed and white parts quartered lengthwise then thinly sliced

1 large white onion, thinly sliced

6 Yukon gold potatoes, peeled and cubed

1 cup heavy cream

1 cup whole milk

Kosher salt

BAKED POTATO TOPPING BAR

2 cups sour cream

2 cups shredded sharp cheddar cheese

6 slices thick-cut bacon, cooked and crumbled

1 knob horseradish, peeled and grated

½ bunch chives, thinly sliced

Hickory Sticks

CULLEN SKINK

I'm Scottish, as you can tell by my last name, Matheson. I've only been to Scotland once, and it was very, very beautiful. I remember when I was in second grade, me and my brothers snuck downstairs at, like, 5:00 a.m. to watch *Highlander* on VHS. We all wanted to see it so badly, but my parents were good parents who wouldn't let us watch R-rated movies, especially because this one has dudes just cutting off each other's heads and there's some bad sex stuff, that's for sure. This soup should make you feel good, like you're the one last remaining Highlander. You've cut everyone's head off, and you can finally just live your life. Scotland forever, baby! Freedom.

In a medium pot over medium heat, combine the milk, haddock, and bay leaf. Bring to a gentle simmer and simmer for 5 minutes. Remove from the heat and let steep for another 15 minutes. Gently remove the haddock and peel and discard the skin. Flake the fish and reserve until needed. Reserve the milk as well and discard the bay leaf.

In a separate medium pot over medium heat, slowly cook your bacon until it is lightly browned, about 10 minutes. Add your onion and leeks and cook everything until the vegetables are translucent, trying to prevent as much browning as you can. Add your potatoes and cook for 1 minute. Add the chicken stock and gently simmer until your potatoes are tender, 30 minutes.

Use a slotted spoon to transfer approximately one-quarter of the potatoes to a bowl. Blend the removed potatoes in a food processor or blender with a bit of potato liquid until smooth. Then add the blended potatoes and the reserved milk back into the pot, gently mixing with a spatula. Continue to simmer until the soup thickens, about 10 minutes.

If the soup still has some fat floating to the top, you may need to strain a bit more of your potatoes and mash them into your soup. The starch will help emulsify and incorporate everything.

Once the soup is the consistency of a chowder, add the flaked fish and salt. Adjust the salt to your liking. Serve with a nice crusty piece of bread.

SERVES 6
PREP TIME: 1½ HOURS

4 cups whole milk

1 pound smoked haddock

1 bay leaf

8 ounces double-smoked bacon, cut into meaty ½-inch chunks

1 yellow onion, diced

3 small leeks, white parts only, finely diced

4 Yukon gold potatoes, peeled and cubed

6 cups chicken stock

3 tablespoons kosher salt

1 small loaf sourdough, for serving

AVGOLEMONO

This was a request from my collaborator, Garrett. I had no idea what this recipe was and had yet to learn about the wonders of avgolemono soup. We made it and it's pretty fire, but holy shit, what a name. I have no idea how to pronounce this, but I love chicken, I love lemon, and I love soup, so I fucking love this.

In a large pot over medium heat, heat the olive oil. Add the onion, carrots, celery, 1 teaspoon of salt, ½ teaspoon of pepper, and the bay leaf and cook until the onions are translucent, 5 minutes.

Add the whole chicken breasts and chicken stock to the pot. Bring the mixture to a boil, then lower the heat to medium-low, skimming off any scum. Cover and simmer until the chicken is cooked through, about 20 minutes. Remove the chicken breasts from the pot and set them aside until cool enough to handle.

While the chicken is cooking, bring a separate small pot of salted water to a boil. Cook the orzo until al dente according to the package instructions. Drain and toss in olive oil to prevent sticking. Set aside.

In a medium bowl, whisk together the eggs and lemon juice until well combined. While whisking continuously, gradually add ½ cup of the warm chicken soup to the egg and lemon mixture. This step is essential to prevent the eggs from curdling when they're added to the hot soup. Continue to whisk until the avgolemono sauce is smooth. Set aside.

Shred the chicken into big chunks using two forks. Return the shredded chicken and the cooked orzo to the soup. Slowly pour the avgolemono sauce into the soup, stirring continuously.

Heat the soup gently for a few more minutes to allow the flavors to meld together and the soup to thicken slightly. Keep the heat low to prevent curdling.

Taste and adjust the seasoning with salt and pepper as needed. Stir in the dill. Ladle the soup into bowls and garnish with additional dill.

SERVES 4
PREP TIME: 1 HOUR

¼ cup olive oil, plus more to coat the orzo

1 small yellow onion, finely chopped

2 carrots, finely diced

2 celery ribs, finely diced

Kosher salt and freshly cracked black pepper

1 bay leaf

2 boneless, skinless chicken breasts

4 cups chicken stock

1 cup orzo pasta

2 eggs

Juice of 2 lemons

¼ cup dill, chopped, plus more for garnish

ROASTED CHICKEN LEG PASTINA SOUP

It really was amazing making this book, but I love this photo so much. I laugh at it all the time. This soup just looks like fucking risotto, doesn't it? It's like, *Is this it, with just a chicken leg on it?* But hey, it *is* a soup and this is my book. Fight me. Make this soup, and you'll be like, *Holy shit, this is the best soup I've ever made.* Your cool butcher will have chicken carcasses, just ask for them!

First, we're going to make the chicken stock. Preheat your oven to 400°F. Add your chicken carcasses, wings, and feet (if using) to a roasting pan and lightly cover with just enough olive oil to coat evenly. Roast until the chicken is golden brown and most of the fat has rendered, 1 hour. Strain the chicken fat through a fine-mesh strainer and reserve for your schmaltz. Add the roasted chicken pieces to a stockpot.

In the same roasting pan, add your onion, carrot, celery, garlic, and tomato paste. Mix everything together until the tomato paste coats everything evenly. Roast until golden brown, 45 minutes. Add to the stockpot with the chicken pieces.

Add the water to the stockpot along with your parsley, thyme, and bay leaf. Bring this up to a gentle simmer over medium-low heat and cook for 4 hours. Strain the stock through a fine-mesh strainer and allow it to cool. Set aside 6 cups for this recipe and store the rest in an airtight container in the fridge until ready to use, up to 3 days.

While the stock is going, let's make the roasted garlic schmaltz. In a small pot over low heat, combine the chicken fat, garlic, shallot, and thyme. Simmer until the garlic and shallot are golden brown and tender, about 30 minutes. Remove the shallot and thyme and discard them both. Using the back of a fork, gently mash the garlic to incorporate it into the fat. Once the mixture is cool, transfer to an airtight container and keep in the fridge until needed, up to 3 days.

We're going to preheat our oven to 400°F again. In a heavy-bottomed pot over medium heat, warm your olive oil. Add your onion and carrot and cook until the vegetables are translucent and any liquid has been cooked off, 15 minutes. Add your garlic and cook for another 5 minutes. Add your tomato paste and cook for an additional 2 minutes, stirring constantly to prevent the tomato paste from browning. Add the 6 cups of chicken stock, the crushed tomatoes, salt, sugar, thyme, bay leaf, and oregano. Simmer on low for 30 minutes.

Meanwhile, prep your chicken. Rub your chicken legs with olive oil and season with salt. Place on a rack on a baking sheet and roast until the legs reach an internal temperature of 165°F, 30 minutes. Remove the chicken from the oven and let it rest for about 10 minutes. (This should line up around the time your soup finishes.) Add the pastina to the soup and cook until the pasta is tender, about 8 minutes. Serve a ladle of the pastini soup in a shallow bowl, top with a roasted chicken leg, a drizzle of roasted garlic chicken schmaltz, and a few cracks of pepper.

SERVES 4

PREP TIME: 1 DAY

CHICKEN STOCK

4 chicken carcasses

1 pound chicken wings

1 pound chicken feet (optional)

Olive oil

1 large yellow onion, diced

1 large carrot, peeled and diced

4 celery ribs, diced

4 garlic cloves, peeled

One 6-ounce can tomato paste

14 cups water

½ bunch parsley

½ bunch thyme

1 bay leaf

ROASTED GARLIC SCHMALTZ

1 cup roasted chicken fat (reserved from above)

1 head garlic, peeled and lightly crushed

1 shallot, halved

¼ bunch thyme

¼ cup olive oil, plus more to prep the chicken

1 small sweet onion, diced into ¼-inch pieces

1 small carrot, peeled and grated

4 garlic cloves, minced

1 tablespoon tomato paste

4 cups crushed tomato

Kosher salt and freshly cracked black pepper

1 tablespoon sugar

4 thyme sprigs, leaves picked and chopped

1 bay leaf

1 tablespoon dried oregano

4 chicken legs

1 pound dried pastina pasta

CALDO DE POLLO

This soup is pure and simple, but it can change your life. Caldo de Pollo is a chicken soup with a vegetables, that's it! Unadorned food is the hardest to make, and this is a recipe that can go terribly wrong because of its simplicity. Don't worry, I have your back and we will work through this recipe and maybe solve your childhood trauma. No guarantees. That is why everyone always makes fun of something that has restraint. But here we are. Do we crack under the pressure? Or do we show up for ourselves and control this soup situation? We show up and control. That's who we are! Maybe don't make this for your in-laws the first time they come over to the new apartment, huh? Or make it. And challenge yourself. Your in-laws will love it, and they'll buy you that TV from Costco.

Preheat your oven to 400°F.

Place your chicken legs on a baking sheet and coat them liberally with salt. Roast until the chicken is golden brown, about 35 minutes. Set the chicken aside and scrape the rendered chicken fat that has collected on the baking sheet into a stockpot.

Set the stockpot over medium-high heat and add the onion, carrot, celery, and garlic. Cook until the vegetables are translucent, stirring frequently to prevent browning, about 10 minutes. Add your roasted chicken, the water, jalapeño, and cilantro stems. Turn the heat down to medium-low and simmer for 2 hours.

Gently remove your chicken and reserve until needed. Strain the stock through a fine-mesh strainer into a large vessel.

In a stockpot, add your corn, potatoes, zucchini, and cabbage. Pour your stock over top, add 2 tablespoons of salt, and simmer over medium heat until the potatoes are tender, 30 minutes.

Add your cooked chicken, cilantro leaves, and oregano. Simmer for another 10 minutes to heat the chicken through. Adjust your seasoning with as much salt and pepper as you like.

Ladle the soup into six bowls and serve with a communal bowl of chips, sour cream, and limes for people to add to their liking.

SERVES 6

PREP TIME: 3 HOURS

6 chicken legs, split in half

Kosher salt and freshly cracked black pepper

1 large yellow onion, quartered

1 carrot, peeled and roughly chopped

1 celery rib, roughly chopped

4 garlic cloves, roughly chopped

10 cups water

1 jalapeño, halved and seeded

1 bunch cilantro, stems separated and leaves roughly chopped

2 ears corn, husked and cut into 2-inch rounds

2 Yukon gold potatoes, skin on, cut into quarters

1 zucchini, diced

¼ head green cabbage, diced

1 tablespoon dried oregano

One 12-ounce bag tortilla chips

2 cups sour cream

2 limes, quartered

COCK-A-LEEKIE SOUP

Please tell me the last time you opened up a cookbook and there was a recipe for cock-a-leekie soup. It's a Scottish icon that's a chicken and leek soup with barley and prunes. Nobody out here is like, *Damn, the world needs more cock-a-leekie soup,* but fuck that, we need cock-a-leekie soup more now than ever. The time is now. This book is for you, so we have to bring out the big tasty treats. I also like making soups with bone-in chicken because sucking on chicken bones is the best. We love it, even if you are nasty, because I know you all are nasty. Stay nasty and stay making cock-a-leekie.

Cut the legs, breasts, and wings off your chicken. Remove the drumstick from the thigh, chop each breast in half, and remove the drumette from the flat of the wing. Set these pieces aside.

Chop up the remaining carcass of the chicken into 1-inch pieces. Place these pieces in a large pot with any remaining vegetable scraps from the ingredient prep. Add the water and simmer gently until you are left with 8 cups of chicken broth, about 2 hours. Strain the stock into a large vessel and set aside while you prepare your soup.

In a large Dutch oven over medium-high heat, add your canola oil and allow that to get hot. Season your reserved chicken with salt and pepper and fry it until it is golden brown on both sides, 10 minutes. Transfer to a plate. Discard the remaining oil.

In the same pot, melt your butter over medium heat. Add your garlic, celery, onion, three-quarters of your sliced leeks, and your carrot and cook until they are translucent, about 10 minutes. Add your browned chicken with all its resting juices and cover with your chicken stock. Simmer over low heat for 1 hour.

Add the barley and prunes. Continue simmering on low heat until the barley is completely cooked, about 30 minutes. Add salt and pepper to taste.

Line a baking sheet with paper towels. For the garnish, in a medium bowl, mix together your cornstarch, onion powder, and garlic powder. Toss together the cornstarch mixture and your reserved leeks. Really work the leeks into the mixture to make sure they are all separated and coated. Dust them off and fry them in a cast-iron pan with a thin layer of canola oil over medium-high heat until they're lightly golden brown, remove them with a slotted spoon, and place them onto the baking sheet to drain. Season with salt.

To serve, place a nice large ladle of soup in a bowl and garnish with crispy leeks.

SERVES 6
PREP TIME: 4 HOURS

1 whole chicken (5 to 6 pounds)

12 cups water

½ cup canola oil plus more for the leeks

Kosher salt and freshly cracked black pepper

2 tablespoons unsalted butter

4 garlic cloves, thinly sliced

3 celery ribs, thinly sliced

1 yellow onion, thinly sliced

5 large leeks, green and white parts, thinly sliced

1 carrot, peeled and diced

1 cup pearl barley

½ cup pitted prunes, chopped

1 cup cornstarch

½ teaspoon garlic powder

½ teaspoon onion powder

STUFFED ACORN SQUASH SOUP *with* EMMENTAL *and* BREAD CRUMBS

This soup reminds me of winter. I associate it with the smell of firewood burning and the feel of being hugged when coming in from the cold. Being hugged as a cold person is so beautiful. If you make this, that's what this is like. It's like coming in from shoveling a milelong driveway after a snowstorm. The person inside the home has made this powerful soup. Your exterior snowperson, your Jack Nicholson at the end of *The Shining*, melts away. It's just you in your little down jacket with your little snow boots, and you're not a threat to Danny or anybody.

Preheat your oven to 400°F.

Let's prep the acorn squash. Cut the tops off. Then, using a metal spoon, scoop out all the guts and seeds and scrape the squash until there's a ¼-inch border all around. Discard the guts and seeds but save the tops. Drizzle the inside with olive oil and season with salt and pepper to taste. Put the tops back on.

Take some aluminum foil, bunch it up, and set the foil bunches on baking sheets. Press your acorn squash bases into the foil bunches so that they're upright. We do the foil bunches to keep them stable instead of cutting the bottoms off, because otherwise, we might have a soup leak—and we are not fans of soup leaks. Protect ourselves at all costs. Roast the acorn squashes for 30 minutes, then take them out. Leave the oven on and turn it up to 450°F.

While the acorn squashes are roasting, let's get your butternut squash cookin'. In a large pot, boil the squash with enough water to cover. Season with about 1 tablespoon of kosher salt. Bring to a boil, then simmer until fork-tender, 30 minutes or so.

Using a spider strainer, take out your squash and throw it into your blender. Reserve that water. Blend the squash until it is a puree. Add ½ cup of water from the pot you boiled your squash in and blend again until fully incorporated. Throw in the cream and butter. Blend again. Add the maple syrup and brandy, then blend one more time. We want this to be smooth. Once it is all fully incorporated, taste and add salt, pepper, and maple syrup to taste. Blend one last time if needed.

In a medium bowl, toss your torn bread in 1 tablespoon of olive oil, the garlic powder, nutmeg, and salt and pepper to taste. Spread out on a baking sheet and roast at 450°F until crunchy. Remove, let them cool, then blitz in a food processor with the nutmeg. We love a garlicky, crispy bread crumb in our soups, don't we? Stir in the parsley once you are happy with the size and texture of the crumb after blitzing.

CONTINUED

SERVES 4

PREP TIME: 1 HOUR AND 15 MINUTES

4 acorn squash (each the size of a softball)

Olive oil

Kosher salt and freshly cracked black pepper

8 cups diced butternut squash

½ cup whipping cream (35% fat)

½ cup unsalted butter

3 tablespoons maple syrup, plus more as needed

2 ounces brandy

2 big handfuls day-old sourdough or hearty bread, torn or cubed

1 tablespoon garlic powder

1 teaspoon ground nutmeg

½ bunch flat-leaf parsley, finely chopped

4 cups shredded Emmental cheese

STUFFED ACORN SQUASH SOUP *with* EMMENTAL *and* BREAD CRUMBS CONTINUED

Set your oven to high broil. Make sure the acorn squashes are still upright. Set your tops aside for serving. Pour the hot soup into each acorn squash, leaving about ½ inch of space at the top because we're gonna jam a big handful of cheese in there. Divide the Emmental evenly among the squash and broil until the cheese is oozing and overflowing!

Once the cheese is bubbly and golden brown—it should look like a French onion soup except it's an acorn squash, obviously—take the baking sheet out of the oven. Using your hands, gently transfer each squash into a beautiful bowl. Be very careful; it's hot. Do not use tongs because you will squash your acorn squashes.

Spoon a nice big tablespoon of bread crumbs on top of your golden, bubbling cheese. Garnish with the acorn squash top, serve, and enjoy. Doesn't that smell nice? Holy shit, Martha, watch out—Big Dog is coming.

IRISH LAMB STEW

My love for soups started with pot roast and gravy, which is pretty much stew. My love for lamb comes from my father. Lamb stew reminds me of him and my grandfather. People who don't love lamb are kinda whack. Lamb isn't gamy; it's lamby, and lamby is tight! Some rendered lamb fat with shallots and lemon juice spooned over boiled potatoes is incredible, or even over some bitter chicories. Holy cow, lamb rules. This stew is for you and the people who love you.

Heat a large Dutch oven over medium heat. Add the bacon and cook until crispy. Remove the bacon with a slotted spoon and set it aside, leaving the bacon fat in the Dutch oven. Rub the lamb chunks with the tomato paste. Working in batches to not crowd the pan, add them to the Dutch oven and brown on all sides, about 10 minutes. Remove the browned lamb and set it aside with the bacon.

Preheat your oven to 325°F.

Add the onion to the pot and cook until it becomes translucent, about 5 minutes. Stir in the garlic and cook for an additional minute. Sprinkle the flour over the onions and garlic, stirring well to coat. Cook for 1 to 2 minutes to remove the raw flour taste. Pour in the Guinness and wine, scraping the bottom of the pot to loosen any browned bits. Allow the liquid to come to a simmer and cook until the liquid reduces by half, about 20 minutes.

Return the lamb and bacon to the pot, along with the carrots, potatoes, turnips, 3 cups of the beef stock, the bay leaves, and thyme. Season with 1 tablespoon each of salt and pepper. Bring the stew to a boil, cover the pot, and transfer to the oven. Roast for 2 to 2½ hours, until you can cut the lamb with the side of a fork. Stir occasionally and add more beef stock if needed to maintain a slightly thick, soupy consistency.

Remove the stew from the oven and let it cool slightly. Remove the thyme sprigs and bay leaves. Adjust the seasoning with more salt and pepper. Serve hot in a bowl with lots and lots of salt-buttered bread.

SERVES 8

PREP TIME: 4 HOURS

6 ounces bacon (double smoked if you can get it), diced

2 pounds lamb shoulder, cut into 2-inch chunks

2 tablespoons tomato paste

1 large yellow onion, chopped

4 garlic cloves, minced

2 tablespoons all-purpose flour

One 14.9-ounce can Guinness

Half of a 750 ml bottle full-bodied red wine

4 large carrots, peeled and sliced

1 pound new or baby potatoes

2 turnips, peeled and diced

3 to 4 cups beef stock

2 bay leaves

5 thyme sprigs

Kosher salt and freshly cracked black pepper

1 stick salted butter, for serving

Bread, for serving

TURKEY DRUMSTICK *and* BARLEY SOUP

I guess I love barley because, fuck it, barley rules. It's very good for you. I'm breaking my own rule here. We are cooking the barley in this soup. I usually like cooking my pasta or grain separately. Only make enough for one night. Because if you don't, then guess what? After sitting in the fridge all night, the barley will soak up all the liquid and you'll have a literal cube of food. Like a giant bouillon cube of flavor, which is cool but not really.

Heat a large pot over medium-high heat and add the olive oil. Add the drumsticks and brown them on all sides, about 5 minutes. Remove and set aside.

In the same pot over medium-high heat, add a little more olive oil if your turkey sucked up all of the oil in the pot. Add the onion, carrots, celery, and garlic. Sauté the vegetables until they start to soften, about 5 minutes. Stir in the pearl barley, thyme, rosemary, and bay leaf and cook for another 2 to 3 minutes, allowing the barley to toast slightly.

Return the browned turkey drums to the pot and pour in the chicken stock. Once the soup comes to a boil, turn the heat down to low, cover the pot, and let it simmer, stirring occasionally, until the turkey is tender and the barley is fully cooked, 1½ to 2 hours.

Remove from the heat and remove your herbs. Taste and add more salt and pepper, if you like. Garnish the soup with chopped parsley.

SERVES 4

PREP TIME: 2½ HOURS

2 tablespoons olive oil, plus more if needed

2 turkey drumsticks

1 yellow onion, finely diced

2 carrots, diced

2 celery ribs, diced

3 garlic cloves, minced

1 cup pearl barley

4 thyme sprigs

1 teaspoon fresh rosemary, minced

1 bay leaf

6 cups chicken stock

Kosher salt and freshly cracked black pepper

Chopped parsley, for garnish

CRISPY LAMB PHO

This recipe is for an old friend and was inspired by a memory of one of the best things I've ever eaten. Danny Bowien used to have a burrito spot called Mission Cantina on the Lower East Side, and some days they would serve pho. 'Cause why not? The lamb pho really hit me hard because it was two things that I love but had never really had together. The deep lamb pho broth and the crispy lamb ribs blew my mind. I hope you enjoy my version inspired by Danny's genius.

Let's make pho. First, let's char our onions and ginger in a cast-iron pan over medium-high heat. You want them to get carmelized to give our broth a deep flavor. Set aside.

In a large pot, place the marrowbones, lamb shoulder, and lamb ribs and cover the goods with cold water. Bring to a boil for 5 minutes to blanch and then drain and quickly wash off all the bones, shoulder, and ribs.

Place everything back into the pot and add your 15 cups water, fish sauce, rock sugar, salt, monosodium glutamate, and garlic cloves. Bring to a boil and then immediately reduce it to a simmer. Skim the scum and add your charred onions, charred ginger, cinnamon, coriander, star anise, and cloves.

Keep simmering the pho broth, removing the scum from the surface of the water until the liquid is clear and no more scum rises to the surface. There will be a lot of it—the lamb ribs are very fatty. After about 2½ hours (when you can almost pinch through the ribs), take them and the lamb shoulder out. Let them cool on a wire rack and move to the fridge.

Let the broth continue to simmer for another 4 hours. Keep adding water if too much is cooking off. In the end we should have about 6 to 8 quarts of delicious broth. Strain after 4 hours.

Preheat your oven to broil on high. When you are ready to serve, slice your lamb shoulder meat and ribs into 1-inch-thick pieces, then cover all your lamb in the mala spice and season with salt. Broil until they are nice and crispy, 5 to 10 minutes.

To serve, boil the noodles according to the package instructions. Divide among four bowls. Put the lamb shoulder and ribs on top. Bring the broth to a rolling boil and ladle it over all that deliciousness in your bowls.

Set up your garnishes on a large plate and serve. I don't fuck with bean sprouts, but go ahead if you do.

SERVES 4

PREP TIME: 1 DAY

SOUP

2 large yellow onions, cut in half

One 8-inch piece ginger, cut in half

3 pounds marrow bones

1 bone-in lamb shoulder (take out of the fridge 2½ hours before starting recipe)

2 racks bone-in lamb ribs (take out of the fridge 2½ hours before starting recipe)

15 cups water

½ cup fish sauce

2 tablespoons rock sugar

1 tablespoon kosher salt, plus more as needed

½ teaspoon monosodium glutamate

4 garlic cloves, halved

1 cinnamon stick, broken in half

1 tablespoon coriander seeds

2 star anise pods

3 or 4 cloves

½ cup mala spice (I like Fly By Jing)

1 pound dried pho noodles

GARNISHES

Shiso leaves

Culantro (Vietnamese cilantro)

White onion, sliced

Scallions, sliced

2 limes, quartered

Handful of bean sprouts

Bird's eye chiles

Thai basil

ROASTED BONE MARROW *in* LIGHT BONE BROTH *with* FRESH PEAS

Peas are one of the first things to come out of the garden in spring. I love it. After you bask in the early morning sun of spring, you are going to have to go to the market. Bone marrow is relatively easy to get now. Ask your favorite butcher for some. This soup is truly a two-ingredient beauty. Peas and marrow: they just work so well with each other. I made this soup the very first time I cooked in NYC for a *Keep It Canada* TV party at Kinfolk in Brooklyn. It's pretty crazy thinking back to almost ten years ago, and this soup still makes me feel good.

The day before you want to have this delicious broth, completely submerge 5 marrowbone pieces in cold water in the fridge for 24 hours to remove impurities.

Fast-forward to the morning you make the soup. In a large pot over medium-high heat, add the remaining 5 marrowbone pieces and cover them with cold water. Bring it up to a boil for 5 minutes, then drain and rinse the bones to remove impurities. Return the bones to the pot, cover with cold water again, and bring back up to a simmer. Then, add a large pinch of salt, your onion, peppercorns, and bay leaves. Skim the scum. Put a lid on it and simmer gently for 12 hours. Read a self-help book and continue skimming the scum every 30 to 45 minutes while it simmers, topping off the water when needed. During the first hour or two, skim it multiple times, it's going to release a lot of scum.

Strain the liquid and discard the bones and vegetables. Set the broth aside. The bones and vegetables will be very overcooked and look disgusting. If you want to, take a bite, but I don't recommend it.

Preheat your oven to 400°F. Take the refrigerator bones out of the water and place them into a roasting pan. Roast until golden brown and molten in the middle, about 20 minutes.

You need the fresh peas, never the canned! You want them to have that crunch. Heat the peas up gently in the bone broth.

Add a delicious roasted marrowbone piece to each of four bowls. Then remove the marrow from the last remaining piece. Top up each bone with the marrow you just removed. Ladle your delicious broth into the bowls and fill your boots if you didn't chomp on that gross meat.

SERVES 4 COLLAGEN-POSITIVE PEOPLE
PREP TIME: 2 DAYS

Ten 4-inch pieces beef marrowbones
Kosher salt
1 large yellow onion, skin on
2 tablespoons black peppercorns
2 bay leaves
4 cups peas, shucked

BOLLITO MISTO

This is super special for me and really speaks to people. Maybe you'll do it like twice a year and eat it for a week. Boiled meats. Everyone, that's the new shit. Everything doesn't have to be caramelized or smoked and roasted dark. Boiled meat is real adult shit, OK? We mature as fuck over here. We boil our meats.

In a Dutch oven or large pot, add the marrowbone, tongue, and brisket and cover with 3 inches of water. Add the onion whole with the skin on, so we can get the purest beef broth possible. Bring the mixture up to a boil and skim the scum. Turn it down to a low simmer and cook it for about 6 hours. Remove from the heat and allow to cool completely at room temperature overnight.

While the broth is going, make the salsa verde. Make sure everything is washed, dried, and cut. In a blender, add the parsley, basil, mint, cilantro, capers, anchovies, mustard, garlic, chiles, olive oil, and lemon zest and juice. Blend until emulsified. Season to taste with salt and black pepper as desired and put in an airtight container in the fridge for the next day.

The next day, remove the cold meat from the broth. Scrape the tendon off the bone and chop it up. Take the brisket and slice it across from the thinner side, making sure that you go across the grain. With a paring knife, peel the skin off the ox tongue, then slice it into rounds from the tip to the base so it's the same thickness as the brisket. Place the tendon, brisket, and ox tongue onto a baking sheet. Cover with a towel and put in the fridge for later.

Bring your broth back up to a simmer over medium heat. When the mixture reaches a simmer, place your whole chicken and sausage in the broth. Add the serrano, bay leaves, garlic, fennel, carrots, and celery. Make a cheesecloth bouquet of the peppercorns, coriander seeds, star anise, and cloves. Tie it up with twine and throw it in the broth. Throw the potatoes in whole. Gently simmer for 1 hour.

Turn the heat off and allow the mixture to steep for 30 minutes. Get your salsa verde out of the fridge and set this aside. Remove the sausage and chicken and place on a baking sheet to cool. Once they're almost room temperature, slice off the chicken breasts, legs, thighs, and wings. Slice the cotechino sausage in rounds the same thickness as the brisket and ox tongue. Remove the vegetables and place them onto a separate baking sheet to cool.

In a casserole dish, place the bone marrow tendons, sliced ox tongue, and brisket. Then pour 1 cup of broth over the top and wrap the dish with plastic wrap to help the meats come back up to room temperature. Now we are ready to plate our meal. Set out the casserole dish or trays of separated meat and vegetables beside the pot of broth. Everyone can build their bowl to their liking. Sip the broth alongside a plate of meats or make a bowl of it and eat it with a spoon. Add potatoes or not! Dress with salsa verde and choose your own adventure.

SERVES 8
PREP TIME: 2 DAYS

SOUP

Five 2-inch pieces marrowbone

1 ox tongue

2 pounds fatty brisket

1 Spanish onion

1 whole chicken

2 cotechino sausages (mild Italian is OK if you can't get your hands on these)

1 red serrano pepper

4 bay leaves

3 garlic cloves, smashed

1 fennel bulb

5 carrots, peeled

6 celery ribs

1 tablespoon black peppercorns

1 tablespoon coriander seeds

1 star anise pod

2 cloves

3 Yukon gold potatoes, peeled

SALSA VERDE

1 cup tightly packed flat-leaf parsley

1 cup tightly packed basil

1 cup tightly packed mint

1 cup tightly packed cilantro

¼ cup capers, drained and rinsed

2 anchovy fillets

1 tablespoon Dijon mustard

2 garlic cloves, minced

1 teaspoon crushed red pepper flakes

1½ cups extra-virgin olive oil

Zest and juice of 1 lemon

Kosher salt and freshly cracked black pepper

LARGE CRAB CAKE *with* CLAM CHOWDER *and* AIOLI

I always had an idea to make a crab cake soup, but, like, how do you actually go about making that? Is it as easy as just making a crab cake and pouring chowder all over it? Yes, the answer is yes. Most things with chowder poured over them are perfect. Here you go—you now have the keys to Perfection Town and you're the mayor. You're welcome. Also, I just thought to crust the crab with the Goldfish crackers 'cause that just makes sense, no? Yeah, I'm a genius.

Rinse your clams really well under cold water. Use a pot brush to help loosen and wash away any stubborn sand. Soak them in a large bowl full of cold water mixed with 3 tablespoons of salt for at least 1 hour to get out all the sand. Drain them off and set aside.

In a large stockpot, heat up the neutral oil over medium-high heat. When the oil is very hot, add the shallots and garlic and, working quickly, stir them until they are fragrant, 10 seconds. Add your clams and wine. Place a lid on the pot and allow the clams to boil in the wine until the clams have opened up, 5 to 10 minutes. Turn off the heat and discard any clams that have not opened.

Use tongs to remove the clams from the pot and set them aside to cool. Set a fine-mesh strainer lined with a coffee filter over a large bowl and strain the remaining liquid through it. Discard anything left in the coffee filter. Once the clams have cooled, pry the meat out and discard the shells. Reserve until needed.

Let's make the chowder. In the same stockpot you used earlier or a large pot or Dutch oven over medium heat, melt the butter. Add the onion, leek, celery, and garlic and cook, stirring occasionally, until the vegetables are wilted and translucent, 10 minutes. Add the flour and cook, stirring constantly to ensure there are no lumps, an additional 2 minutes. Add the milk in two batches, stirring frequently to prevent sticking or lumps and allowing the mixture to come to a simmer before adding the second batch. Add the half-and-half in two batches, following the same method as the milk. Finally, add the reserved clam liquor and potatoes and simmer for an additional 30 minutes. Stir occasionally until the chowder has thickened slightly. If it thickens too much, you can add more milk.

Five minutes before serving, add the clam meat and salt to finish the chowder. Adjust the seasoning as you see fit.

To serve, place a crab cake in the center of a bowl, ladle a generous amount of chowder over the top of the crab cake, and finish with a dollop of aioli.

CONTINUED

SERVES 8
PREP TIME: 1 DAY

4 pounds littleneck clams

Kosher salt

½ cup neutral oil

2 shallots, thinly sliced

3 garlic cloves, thinly sliced

Half of 750 ml bottle dry white wine, such as Sauvignon Blanc

1 cup unsalted butter

1 sweet onion, diced small

1 leek, white part only, diced small

3 celery ribs, diced small

4 garlic cloves, minced

¼ cup all-purpose flour

4 cups whole milk, plus more as needed

2 cups half-and-half

2 large Yukon gold potatoes, parboiled, peeled, and diced into ½-inch pieces

2 teaspoons kosher salt

8 Crab Cakes (recipe follows)

Garlic Aioli (recipe follows), for serving

LARGE CRAB CAKE *with* CLAM CHOWDER *and* AIOLI CONTINUED

CRAB CAKES

Make your Goldfish cracker crumbs. In a food processor, pulse the Goldfish until they form coarse crumbs.

Make the garlic aioli. In a small bowl, whisk together the egg yolk, garlic, mustard, and vinegar until well combined. Slowly drizzle in the olive oil while continuously and vigorously whisking. It's important to add the oil gradually to create a stable emulsion. The mixture should start to thicken and become creamy. If the aioli becomes too thick, you can add a small amount of water, a teaspoon at a time, to thin it out.

Taste the aioli and season with salt according to your preference. Separate out ¼ cup of the aioli. Transfer the remaining aioli to a container with a tight-fitting lid. It can be stored in the fridge for up to 1 week.

In a medium bowl, combine the ¼ cup of aioli, the mustard, garlic, Old Bay, Worcestershire sauce, lemon zest, butter, 1 cup of the Goldfish cracker crumbs, and 1 of the eggs. Mix to combine thoroughly. Gently squeeze the crabmeat to remove any excess water. Lightly fold the meat into your mixture. Cover and refrigerate overnight to allow the mixture to set.

The following day, weigh the crab cakes into 3-ounce balls and shape them into little pucks. You can use a metal ½-cup measuring cup to help form the pucks if you choose. (Line the cup with plastic wrap, press the mixture into the cup, and pop it out.)

It's time to bread the crab cakes. Set up your breading station. Place the flour in a shallow bowl. In another, beat the remaining 6 eggs, and in a third, place the remaining Goldfish crumbs. Dust the crab cakes in the flour, dip them into the eggs, and coat them with the Goldfish crumbs.

Line a plate with paper towels. In a cast-iron skillet over medium heat, heat the neutral oil to 350°F. Gently place the crab cakes in the oil, working in batches. Fry on each side until they are golden brown, 5 minutes, then transfer them to the paper towel–lined plate to drain.

MAKES 8 CRAB CAKES

CRAB CAKES

3 (6.6-ounce) bags Goldfish cracker crumbs

1 tablespoon Dijon mustard

2 garlic cloves, grated

1 tablespoon Old Bay Seasoning

1 teaspoon Worcestershire sauce

Zest of 1 lemon

1 tablespoon unsalted butter, melted

7 eggs

1 pound crabmeat

2 cups all-purpose flour

2 cups neutral oil, for frying

GARLIC AIOLI

1 egg yolk

2 garlic cloves, minced

½ tablespoon Dijon mustard

¼ cup white wine vinegar

1 cup olive oil

Kosher salt

GUMBO

My parents love making gumbo. When I was younger, I didn't like it. I was a typical kid, and there are a lot of things going on in a gumbo. To this day I hate canned diced tomatoes, and I especially hate them in soups. I'm also still on the fence about okra, but I seem to be coming around. This spicy gumbo is my ideal version of a gumbo. It's also kinda difficult to find some of these ingredients. I get it. I live in Canada. Finding real andouille is very hard. We try our best. Please try your best. The soup deserves it.

In a large Dutch oven, heat the vegetable oil over medium-high heat. Add the flour and stir constantly to make a smooth paste. Lower the heat to medium-low and continue to cook, stirring constantly, until the roux turns a deep brown color. If it burns, start over. This entire process can take 30 minutes to 1 hour. Once the roux is ready and looks like milk chocolate, remove it from the heat and set it aside. Don't be alarmed, the residual heat will make the roux even darker.

In a large Dutch oven, cook the sausage over medium-high heat until it's browned, about 5 minutes. Transfer the sausage to a plate and set it aside. In the same pot, quickly sear the shrimp on both sides and transfer to the same plate with the sausage. If the Dutch oven is looking dry, add 1 tablespoon of vegetable oil. Then, add the chicken pieces and cook until they are no longer pink, about 10 minutes. Transfer the chicken to the plate with the sausage and shrimp and set it aside. Turn the heat down to medium, add the onion, bell pepper, and celery, and cook until the vegetables become tender, 5 to 7 minutes. Add the garlic, bay leaves, thyme, oregano, paprika, and cayenne and cook until the spices become fragrant, another 2 to 3 minutes. Stir in the tomatoes and chicken stock and bring to a gentle simmer.

Return the Dutch oven to medium heat. Slowly ladle the hot soup into the roux, stirring vigorously until there are no lumps. Bring the soup back to a simmer before adding more liquid. Once all the soup has been added to the roux, return the sausage and chicken to the pot. Bring the mixture to a boil, then turn the heat down to low. Let it simmer, uncovered, for 30 minutes to 1 hour, stirring occasionally. About 20 minutes before serving, add the okra and continue to simmer. Then add the shrimp and cook for 8 to 10 minutes. Taste and adjust salt and black pepper, if needed. Remove the bay leaves and serve over steamed white rice.

SERVES 6
PREP TIME: 3 HOURS

¾ cup vegetable oil, plus more for preparing the gumbo

¾ cup all-purpose flour

12 ounces chorizo or andouille sausage, sliced ½ inch thick

1 pound tiger shrimp, tails on, shelled

2 pounds boneless, skinless chicken thighs, cut into bite-size pieces

1 large yellow onion, diced

1 green bell pepper, diced

3 celery ribs, diced

4 garlic cloves, minced

2 bay leaves

1 teaspoon dried thyme

1½ teaspoons dried oregano

1½ teaspoons paprika

¾ teaspoon cayenne

One 28-ounce can diced tomatoes

6 cups chicken stock

3 cups frozen okra, roughly chopped

Kosher salt and freshly cracked black pepper

Medium-grain rice, cooked, for serving

CREAMY SAUSAGE SOUP *with* RAPINI *and* TORTELLINI

This is an all-time banger dish. Creamy sausage with cheesy tortellini and rapini, just enough to satisfy all of those creamy food dreams. Now that I'm thinking of it, you can make this even creamier. The next day you could just pour or scoop this into a casserole dish and cover it with mozzarella and bake it. That would be insane. Maybe one day, I'll do a whole book of leftovers. When I see some of these photos, I think instantly of what I could turn these into after the first meal. What's day 4 of leftovers truly look like? Pain? Truth? Happiness? Fear? You tell me!

Bring a large pot of salted water to a boil. Cook the tortellini until al dente according to the package instructions. Drain and set aside. Cover them with olive oil to prevent sticking.

Heat a large Dutch oven over medium-high heat. Add the guanciale and cook until it's crispy and the fat has rendered. Crumble the sausage into the pot and cook, breaking it into smaller pieces with a spoon, until it's browned and cooked through, about 5 minutes.

In the same pot, add the onion, garlic, and thyme. Sauté until the onion becomes translucent, 2 to 3 minutes. Pour in the wine to deglaze the pot, scraping up any brown bits, and simmer until it is reduced by half. Add the cream and simmer until it is reduced by half again. Pour in the chicken stock and bring it back to a simmer. Add the cooked sausage and Parmesan and simmer uncovered for 30 minutes.

Five minutes before the soup is finished, add the rapini to become tender and the tortellini to heat through. Season the soup with salt and lots of pepper. Garnish with additional Parmesan and pepper.

SERVES 2
PREP TIME: 1 HOUR

8 ounces fresh ricotta tortellini or flavor of your choice

Extra-virgin olive oil

4 ounces guanciale, diced

2 mild Italian sausages, removed from their casings

1 yellow onion, finely chopped

2 garlic cloves, minced

4 sprigs fresh thyme

1 cup dry white wine

1 cup heavy cream

2 cups chicken stock

½ cup grated Parmesan cheese, plus more for garnish

1 small bunch rapini, cut into 1-inch pieces

Kosher salt and freshly cracked black pepper

GIANT MEATBALL SOUP IN BEEFY TOMATO BROTH

Who doesn't love a meatball? Only a fucking psycho doesn't love meatballs, or maybe vegetarians. BUT I LOVE VEGETARIANS, so that's fine. Meatballs are cool, but meatball soup? Come on, this shit slaps. You know that. Everyone loves it when you tell them you're making meatball soup for dinner. Well, everyone except for you-know-who. This soup is not only for giants but people who just love simply braised meatballs. Which I'm guessing is you!

In a large bowl, place all the ground meat with the eggs, Parmesan, bread crumbs, 3 teaspoons of the garlic, the parsley, ½ teaspoon of salt, and lots of black pepper. Mix with your hands until fully incorporated.

Line a baking sheet with parchment paper. Put a little olive oil on your hands and roll the mixture into 4 softball-size meatballs. Place on the prepared baking sheet, then set aside until ready to roast.

Preheat your oven to 500°F.

In a large pot over medium-high heat, heat enough olive oil to cover the bottom. Add the onion, bell peppers, jalapeño, and remaining 4 teaspoons garlic and cook until translucent, about 5 minutes. Add the tomato paste and cook for 2 minutes more. Pour in the diced tomatoes, beef stock, and bay leaves. Simmer for 15 minutes.

When the soup starts to simmer, roast your meatballs until brown, hopefully less than 10 minutes. After they begin browning, give them a shake so they can get golden brown evenly all over.

Remove the meatballs from the oven and drop them into the soup. Continue simmering for 1 hour. At the 1-hour mark, pour in the pasta and cook until it is al dente according to package instructions.

Remove the bay leaves. Get a big ol' ladle of everything into a bowl with a meatball in the middle. If you want to get fancy, cut the meatball into segments like an orange in the bowl. Garnish with olive oil, black pepper, Parmesan, and parsley.

SERVES 4

PREP TIME: 2 HOURS

1 pound ground beef

8 ounces ground veal

8 ounces ground pork

2 eggs

1 cup grated Parmesan cheese, plus more for serving

1 cup dry bread crumbs

7 garlic cloves, minced (about 7 teaspoons)

¼ bunch parsley, chopped, plus more for serving

Kosher salt and freshly cracked black pepper

Canola oil

1 large yellow onion, diced

2 red bell peppers, diced

1 jalapeño, diced

1 tablespoon tomato paste

One 28-ounce can diced tomatoes, not drained

Two 32-ounce boxes beef stock

2 bay leaves

2 cups dried ditalini pasta

Extra-virgin olive oil

KIMCHI STEW

Nothing beats a kimchi stew. There's a spot in Toronto that's open twenty-four hours, and the number of times I've gone in there at 3:00 a.m. for some is remarkable. It's kinda saved me for years, to be honest. If you drank a lot the night before, it's OK for you to make this and eat it. It will make you feel so good, then you can fall back asleep or watch all the director's cuts of *The Lord of the Rings*, and everything will be fine. Life is a struggle most of the time. Lighten up and make this soup, then get drunk or don't. This soup will be there for you one way or the other.

In a large Dutch oven over medium-high heat, add a drizzle of vegetable oil and your onion, ginger, and garlic. Cook for 5 minutes, then add your pork belly and quickly toss it in the wilted vegetables. Add your soy sauce, mirin, sugar, gochugaru, sesame oil, gochujang, dashi, kimchi, and kimchi liquid. Cook this on a high simmer until the pork belly is tender but NOT falling apart, 1 hour. This is not a low-and-slow soup; you want to cook it as quickly as you can without completely boiling it. Hot and fast.

Ten minutes before serving, stir in your scallions and place your tofu on top. Try not to stir once the tofu is added to avoid breaking it into small pieces. You just want to heat it through. Add salt and sugar as you see fit.

Sprinkle sesame seeds on top and eat as is or serve it over the steamed white rice.

SERVES 4
PREP TIME: 2 HOURS

Vegetable oil

1 yellow onion, thinly sliced

1 knob ginger, roughly chopped

4 garlic cloves, roughly chopped

1 pound pork belly, skin removed, cut into 1-inch pieces

¼ cup soy sauce

¼ cup mirin

1 tablespoon sugar, plus more as needed

1 teaspoon gochugaru

1 tablespoon sesame oil

2 tablespoons gochujang

6 cups dashi (made from instant dashi powder)

1 pound kimchi, cut into small pieces

¼ cup kimchi liquid

7 scallions, cut into 1-inch pieces

Half of a 16-ounce package silken tofu, rinsed, drained, and cut into 1-inch cubes

Kosher salt

Sugar

Toasted sesame seeds, for serving

2 cups short-grain rice, cooked, optional, for serving

OXTAIL BARLEY YAM SOUP

This soup is just plain and simple power soup. Oxtail is the dankest and most succulent of the beefs. You need to make this and suck on those oxtails. Then the yams hit like little starbursts. Then that barley is like, *I'm here for the tendon-sucking party.* Then the Scotch bonnet salsa is like, *I'm waiting on all y'all, what the fuck? Let's all just chill and be on top of each other, OK?* This soup is best for your frisky friends who aren't afraid of eating food with bones. Those people suck.

Liberally season your oxtail with salt and pepper on both sides.

In a large pot over medium-high heat, add enough oil to cover the bottom of the pan and sear the oxtail, about 5 minutes per side. You want a nice deep sear on these guys. Pour in your beef stock. Turn the heat down to low, cover with a lid, and simmer until your oxtail is tender and can be pulled apart with a fork, 2 to 3 hours. Pull your oxtail out of its braising liquid and reserve in a bowl until needed. Strain your braising liquid through a fine-mesh strainer into a large vessel and hold until needed.

In the same pot used to braise the oxtail, warm 2 tablespoons of oil over medium heat. Add your onion and garlic and cook until they are translucent, 5 to 10 minutes. Pour your reserved braising liquid into your pot and add your carrots, celery, bay leaves, thyme, and rosemary. Turn the heat down to medium-low and simmer for 45 to 60 minutes. Your carrots should be 90 percent cooked. Test them with a knife; if you can poke them and still feel some resistance, you are just about there. At this point, add your pearl barley and yam. Simmer until your vegetables are tender, another 30 minutes.

Add your reserved oxtail and simmer for 5 more minutes to heat it through. If you don't like big bones in your soup, you can pick the meat off before adding it to your soup. Add salt and pepper to your liking. Serve with a generous spoonful of scotch bonnet salsa.

SERVES 4
PREP TIME: 4 HOURS

4 pounds oxtail, cut into 1-inch segments

Kosher salt and freshly cracked black pepper

Grapeseed oil

12 cups beef stock

1 large yellow onion, cut into 1-inch pieces

4 garlic cloves, smashed

1 large carrot, peeled and cut into 3 pieces

2 celery ribs, cut into 1-inch pieces

2 bay leaves

4 thyme sprigs

½ rosemary sprig

2 cups pearl barley

1 large yam, peeled and cut into large chunks

Scotch Bonnet Salsa (page 335)

CUBED MORTADELLA, MACARONI, *and* CHICKEN BROTH

OK, bear with me. I hope this will be something like the bologna bowl if it catches on because, holy shit, this works. It is definitely not just hot dog soup or hot dog–flavored water, to quote the great Limp Bizkit. Look at it. Like, really take a moment to look at this. It's so beautiful. The melting mortadella and the macaroni and olive work so well together. It's literally just pimento loaf soup. I'm so happy with this, like after Dr. Frankenstein made the creature. But please don't make this for your Italian grandparents. Nonna and Nonno will be upset.

In a large pot, bring the broth to a boil. Add the onion, celery, carrot, bay leaf, and parsley and simmer for 20 minutes. Discard the bay leaf. Take the broth off the heat and set aside.

In a separate pot, cook the pasta until al dente by going 2 to 3 minutes shorter than the package instructions. Drain the pasta and set aside.

We want to keep the mortadella soft. When the broth is ready, add the mortadella, olives, and pasta. Ladle this beautiful liquid into bowls. Finish with Parmesan, pepper, and olive oil.

SERVES 4
PREP TIME: 45 MINUTES

- 8 cups chicken broth
- 1 yellow onion, diced
- 2 celery ribs, diced
- 2 carrots, peeled and diced
- 1 bay leaf
- 4 parsley sprigs
- 3 cups dried ditalini pasta
- 2 cups cubed mortadella
- 1 cup green olives, sliced
- Finely grated or powdered Parmesan cheese, for serving
- Freshly cracked black pepper, for serving
- Extra-virgin olive oil, for serving

SMOKED HAM HOCK *with* HADDOCK SOUP

I made this soup for some branded video thing I did years ago. It never saw the light of day, so here ya go, something from the vault. It's a perfect soup for a chilly spring or fall day. Eat it with a sweater on. Then maybe take it off 'cause you are too hot now. That is the best and the worst. How many times have I taken off my shirt halfway through a meal? I wish I could do it at restaurants.

In a heavy-bottomed Dutch oven over medium heat, add your olive oil and ham hock. Lightly brown the ham hock, about 10 minutes. Add your carrot, onion, leek, celery, and garlic and cook until the onion is translucent, another 10 minutes. Stir frequently to prevent unnecessary coloring. Add your chicken stock and 1 tablespoon of salt and simmer for 30 minutes.

Add the beans to your soup along with the thyme and rosemary and continue to simmer for an additional 15 minutes. At this point, the broth should have thickened and concentrated slightly.

Dry your haddock fillet with paper towels. Dice it into ½-inch cubes and add it to your soup. Continue to simmer the soup for 5 minutes before removing it from the heat. Adjust your seasoning with salt and pepper.

When the soup is almost done, make the salad. Place your parsley, tarragon, and celery leaves in a bowl. Rinse the shallots in cold water, dry them with paper towels, and add them to the bowl with your herbs.

When the soup is finished, dress your salad. Add your anchovies, olive oil, lemon zest and juice, salt, and pepper to the bowl and toss to combine.

To serve, ladle a generous portion of soup into six bowls, top it with a good amount of the herb salad, an additional drizzle of olive oil, and a few cracks of black pepper.

SERVES 6 PEOPLE
PREP TIME: 1½ HOURS

SOUP

¼ cup olive oil, plus more for serving

1 pound smoked ham hock, skin removed, cut into ½-inch cubes

1 large carrot, diced

1 white onion, diced

1 leek, white parts only, diced

4 celery ribs, diced

4 garlic cloves, thinly sliced

8 cups chicken stock

Kosher salt and freshly cracked black pepper

One 15.5-ounce can cannellini beans, drained and rinsed

One 15.5-ounce can bean medley, drained and rinsed

10 thyme sprigs, leaves picked and finely chopped

1 rosemary sprig, leaves picked and finely chopped

1 frozen haddock fillet

SALAD

½ bunch flat-leaf parsley, picked and roughly chopped

½ bunch tarragon, picked and roughly chopped

1 head's worth of celery leaves (½ cup), roughly chopped

1 shallot, thinly sliced

3 anchovies, roughly chopped

¼ cup olive oil

Zest and juice of 1 lemon

Kosher salt and freshly cracked black pepper

BEEF NOODLE SOUP

I eat beef noodle soup at least once a month. I'm a big wonton, BBQ duck, and noodle soup person, but every once in a while, you need that pure beef noodle soup. Beef shin is challenging to find; you'll have to go to a real butcher shop. So it's not actually that difficult. You'll enjoy making this. Like most good things, this will take some time to make the shin and the broth so it's perfectly balanced with taste and texture. You want the shin to melt in your mouth up to a point because all the connective tissues and tendons do have the slightest bite to them. Don't cheat on the time, because if you do, you'll cheat yourself with flavor. Good luck.

Bring a large pot of water to a boil. Add the beef and blanch it for 4 minutes. Drain and rinse the beef under cold water to remove any impurities. Set the beef aside.

In a large, clean pot over medium heat with your neutral oil heated up, add the onion, garlic, and ginger and cook until golden brown, about 4 minutes. Add the doubanjiang and continue to stir until it is lightly caramelized, about 1 minute. Next, add the cinnamon stick, star anise, and bay leaves and cook until aromatic. Add the rice wine and cook until reduced by half (this will also cook off the alcohol). Stir in the soy sauce, rock sugar, and water, bring the mixture to a boil, then reduce the heat to low. Return the beef to the pot. Cover and simmer until the beef is tender enough to pierce with a knife but doesn't fall apart, about 2 hours. Skim off any impurities that rise to the surface.

While the broth is simmering, cook the noodles until they are tender and chewy. Drain and set aside.

When the stock is ready, set the beef aside and strain the stock through a fine-mesh strainer into a large vessel. Discard the solid ingredients. You should be left with a dark flavorful broth. Return the strained broth to the pot with the beef and bring it to a gentle simmer. Taste and adjust the seasoning with salt as needed.

Remove the beef from the pot and turn off the heat. Let's arrange all the sides on the table. Put the noodles, bok choy, scallions, cilantro, and chili crisp in different plates and bowls. Slice your beef into ½-inch slices and arrange on a plate. Then take your pot of broth and put on a trivet on the table. Now your guests can make their own delicious beef noodle soup with the toppings piled high.

SERVES 4
PREP TIME: 2½ HOURS

2 pounds beef shank
2 tablespoons neutral oil
1 yellow onion, quartered
3 garlic cloves, smashed
One 2-inch piece ginger, sliced
2 tablespoons doubanjiang
1 cinnamon stick
3 star anise pods
2 bay leaves
¼ cup rice wine
¼ cup soy sauce
1 tablespoon rock sugar
10 cups water
1 pound dried white wheat noodles, medium-thick
Kosher salt
3 baby bok choy, halved
6 scallions, thinly sliced
½ cup cilantro, stemmed
Chili crisp, for garnish

PART II
SALADS

My dad used to make fun of salads. Every time we were at a restaurant, if anyone asked if he wanted soup or salad, he would say, "Do I look like a rabbit to you?" It was embarrassing, but dad jokes be dad jokes and good ol' Steve Savage can get away with it.

I was never a big salad guy, but then I started dating Tricia, and whenever I ate with her family, there was a salad on the side. My mother-in-law, Carol, was always whipping up a salad with dinner. I guess it's an Italian thing. My reaction was "What is that?" I just didn't grow up eating salads. As you get further into this section, you'll see that my family's definition of a salad was taco salad. No greens, no lettuces. It was just ground beef with Fritos on top. Come on! People are out here making salads with just vegetables, oil, vinegar, salt, and pepper?

Actually, why do people think salads are just vegetables? That's the biggest problem. Salads are anything that's mixed up. Just mix it up, it's a salad! When was the last time you mixed something up and ate it? You eat five things at once and, boom, there's a mouth salad. Just think, you've got pasta salads, seafood salads, lettuce salads, citrus salads, grain salads, bean salads—there are so many salads! You can make anything a salad. I want this book to represent freedom, especially this section. I want to be at the top of the mountain screaming, "I LOVE SALADS! I LOVE GRILLED SALAMI!!!" Grilled salami should be a salad. If you keep reading, you'll see I did just that.

Here's a little love letter to shitty salads. I am a huge fan of an iceberg lettuce chopped salad, whether it's at an old diner or a shitty steakhouse chain. I love the shitty house chef—chopped salad—whatever the fuck they choose to call it. You know, the one where you get to pick if you want ranch, blue cheese, French, Thousand Island, or Italian. I love that we live in a world where (for the most part) there's only one salad and five dressings that exist. For some reason, I'm attracted to that. Every time I go to any restaurant that has it, I've posted it, and I'm more excited about the shitty salad. A perfect single slice of green pepper, canned black olives, a splash of ranch, and six-day-old dried croutons. That salad better be served in a little wooden bowl. You know the ones I'm talking about.

That is the lowest form of salad. The bare minimum salad. And yet I love it. I truly do. It's one of my favorite things of all time. That salad tastes just as good to me as a beautiful, fresh ripened persimmon plucked off a tree. Yeah, that's cool. You're on a boat in the middle of the ocean, and you're eating a freshly shucked scallop? Yeah, that's nice; that'll change your life. But so can a piece-of-shit salad in the middle of Palm Springs.

We are going to make salads in this book that are beautiful, that are mundane, that are hard to make, that are easy to make. Salads that are good and fresh and salads that are even better three days later. Salads that I hope you'll make for the rest of your life. Salads that are healthy and salads that are probably not that good for you. Salads that you can bring to your friends' houses to brighten up their day. Salads that you can make in a bowl and by the time you've completed it, you've already eaten half of it because it's that good and you're not going to share with anybody because you ate it like a big ol' hog.

I love how I can take anything I want and make it into a salad. If you took a bunch of stuff and put it all in a pot, it would be gross. Just think, if you took all these salads and boiled and blended them, how gross would that be? But somehow, in the salad bowl of life, they are beautiful, they are tasty. Isn't that weird? Doesn't that make you think?

Dressing a salad properly is one of the most difficult things to do. People either drown their salads with dressing or they don't put enough in and it tastes like nothing. Understanding how to dress a salad is essential. Whatever kind of salad it is, it needs to be dressed and seasoned properly. A lot of people don't even use salt and pepper when making just a simple green salad. What the heck is that? It only makes sense if you just put some oil and vinegar and salt and pepper on it. Why are people doing things that don't make sense? I want salads to make sense. I want salads to be delicious. Now there are so many salads when we go out to eat. Power bowls, super bowls, all this shit, and you go and order it and it all tastes the same. Nothing is seasoned properly! But now, you can take these salads and make them at home and season them and have them actually taste good. ALWAYS SEASON YOUR SALADS PROPERLY! You want to taste everything! You want to layer seasoning; you want to develop full flavor across the board! PLEASE! Treat your romaine lettuce the same as your A5 Wagyu YouTube fuckin' steak! Come on!

Let's make some salads. Cook from the heart. And for fuck's sake, make sure you season properly.

A RADICCHIO SALAD *from* PRIME SEAFOOD PALACE

This salad is based on the idea of a present that we serve at my restaurant in Toronto, Prime Seafood Palace. There is this beautiful tower of radicchio, and inside is a warm vinaigrette of rendered pork fat, honey, beet, and lardon that soaks into all the leaves. All the lardon pools into these little leaf baths of flavor. Oh, and the Thunder Oak Gouda is profound and really brings this all together. The bitterness of the radicchio, the fatty pork vinaigrette, and honey and beet juice are just nutso. Then, as you start cutting into it, the whole salad turns into a beautiful mess, you'll see.

In a small skillet, add the bacon and cook until the fat is rendered and the bacon is completely cooked. Then, add the shallots and cook until they are translucent, about 5 minutes. Add the beet juice to deglaze the pan and bring the mixture to a boil for 4 minutes. Add the honey and water and continue boiling for another 10 minutes. Turn the heat down to low and add the vinegar and pork fat. Stir everything together. Season with salt and pepper. Keep the dressing warm.

On a grill or grill pan, set over medium heat, grill the radicchio core until it is tender, about 6 minutes. Set it aside.

Lay two stacks of 6 radicchio cups on a tray with the cups facing up. Fill each cup with 1 tablespoon of the dressing. Divide the cheese evenly among the cups, then stack the cups into a perfect stack. Season with olive oil and Maldon salt.

SERVES 2

PREP TIME: 30 MINUTES

DRESSING

½ cup double-smoked bacon, cut into ¼-inch lardons

1 large shallot, minced

¼ cup beet juice

¼ cup honey

¼ cup water

¼ cup sherry vinegar

¼ cup pork fat

Kosher salt and freshly cracked black pepper

1 head radicchio, pulled apart (keep leaves in a cup shape and save the core)

½ cup shaved Gouda cheese (we use Thunder Oak)

Extra-virgin olive oil

Maldon salt

SALADS

PEACHES *with* GOAT CHEESE, MINT, HONEYCOMB, *and* OLIVE OIL

Everyone is giving me complete shit about this dish, and that's fine. This looks like a stupid appetizer your great-auntie pulled from a glossy magazine and served to you as part of Sunday lunch. You are correct. But I have the vision. I start talking about recipes and ideas for dishes all the time. I can see them. I wish I was just some old auntie pulling recipes from magazines and cooking them for all their loved ones. This dish is a tribute to my love of the mundane and to living life to the fullest at least once a year. Also, it's coming to my attention that I love honeycomb.

First, let's make the maple walnuts. Line a baking sheet with parchment paper. In a small pot, combine the maple syrup and sugar. Set it over medium-high heat, melt the mixture, and allow it to bubble. When the bubbles grow to be about 1 inch high and the mixture appears to be thick and caramelized, add your walnuts and stir vigorously with a spatula. The mixture will soon go from gooey to powdery (this is what you want). Transfer to the baking sheet and allow it to cool completely. Chop them after they cool. Store your extra in your cabinet for a few days and use them on other salads.

Get a grill as hot as you can! Sear all your peaches and the lemon halves as quickly as you can, about 30 seconds per side. If you start to cook the fruit, it will fall apart on you. Allow these to cool. Once your fruits have come to room temperature, cut your lemon into quarters.

Now, assemble the salad on a platter. Dollop the salsa verde in six spots and place each peach cut-side up on the salsa verde. For each peach, add one chunk of goat cheese, ½ teaspoon of the chopped maple walnuts, a piece of honeycomb, some mint leaves, some parsley leaves, Maldon salt, and pepper. Give them a little hit of fancy olive oil. Add your grilled lemon to the platter as well to use as you like.

SERVES 4 TO 6

PREP TIME: 30 MINUTES

MAPLE WALNUTS

½ cup maple syrup

1 cup sugar

2 cups walnut halves

3 nice and ripe peaches, halved

1 lemon, halved lengthwise

½ cup All the Herbs Salsa Verde (page 334)

¼ cup goat cheese

3 tablespoons honeycomb

10 mint leaves, torn

10 parsley leaves, torn

Fancy olive oil

Maldon salt and freshly cracked black pepper

CELERY SALAD *with* CREAMY HONEY DRESSING

Celery deserves to be a star in salads, and this is a star dish. It's kinda like a Waldorf, but not. Let the celery shine, let the honeycomb sing, let the walnuts dance, let the cheese soar, let the dates scream from the rooftops. This salad seems freaky deaky, but it's the truth. The mouthfeel of this is just wild, but you'll enjoy all the textures and tastes for your life-loving mouth.

You'll want to add your celery to a salted ice bath. This little salt bath is going to make our celery very crunchy. For every 4 cups of water, add 2 tablespoons of salt. Make sure the salt is completely dissolved. Add a handful of ice and keep the celery in the mixture for 10 minutes, then drain and set aside.

In a large bowl, combine your celery, walnuts, and dates. Season with Maldon salt, pepper, and the dressing. When ready to serve, give the salad a little mix. Top with a little mound of cheese and a beautiful piece of honeycomb that your friends can break up and add to the top of their portions.

SERVES 4

PREP TIME: 15 MINUTES

1 head celery, hearts and leaves chopped thin with white parts removed

½ cup toasted walnuts

½ cup roughly chopped dates

Maldon salt and freshly cracked black pepper

1 cup Creamy Honey Dressing (page 334)

½ cup shredded Limburger cheese

3½ ounces fresh honeycomb

BROCCOLI SALAD *with* BACON VINAIGRETTE DRESSING, FRIED EGG, *and* GORGONZOLA

A broccoli salad makes sense. Broccoli loves you, and you love it, so everything is going to be fine. Well, once we make one. Gorgonzola rules, don't be scared, and eggs rule, so don't worry. Bacon vinaigrette is always nice and warm. We will get through this and make this right. This salad low-key could be made in any season, warm or cold. Also it's a fire dinner or breakfast. Dang, just eat this every day, all day. You'll become so strong.

Preheat your broiler on high. Line a large baking sheet with aluminum foil.

Chop the broccoli so it's all different shapes and sizes. Lay out the broccoli and shallots on the prepared baking sheet and season with a good amount of olive oil, salt, and pepper.

Broil your vegetables until they're burned, 10 minutes. It's not just the time. Watch!

While the vegetables are broiling, fry the eggs in the butter in a cast-iron pan over medium heat. Do you want that over easy or fried? The choice is yours.

Lace your broccoli and shallots with the bacon vinaigrette. Place your individual fried eggs on the salad and add chunks of the gorgonzola on top. Give your guests some bowls and dig in.

SERVES 4

PREP TIME: 30 MINUTES

3 heads broccoli, including stems

1 shallot, sliced as thinly as possible

Olive oil

Kosher salt and freshly cracked black pepper

4 eggs

2 tablespoons unsalted butter

Bacon Vinaigrette Dressing (page 335)

4 ounces gorgonzola, cut into 8 chunks

SALADS

ZUCCHINI SALAD *with* MANCHEGO, SALSA VERDE, *and* PEPPER *and* PINE NUT RELISH

It's really tough making zucchini taste good. It's so full of water, it's like a weird gourd. You can shave it raw, but it doesn't really have flavor. It's pretty funny actually. Like, why we even trying to grow these things? Roasting it seems to be best, or shredding it and making fritters. But this is the section on salads, so we did a hard sear in the cast iron to char it and develop some kind of taste. Still, they are more texture than taste, so that's why we make the relish. That shit is banging. This is a pretty dish and is great for parties, especially ones that you know aren't going to be that fun. You show up with this and it'll definitely be a talking-point salad. Big points for you, and you'll make the host look like a dum-dum.

First, let's make the pepper and pine nut relish. Preheat your broiler on high. On a baking sheet, lay out your poblanos, bell pepper, jalapeños, and Anaheim pepper. Broil them until they are blistered and charred, about 8 minutes total. Make sure to flip them over and get all sides.

Transfer the peppers to a bowl and cover them with plastic wrap for 20 minutes. The skin should come off pretty easily when you begin to peel. Remove the stems and seeds from the peppers. You can leave the charred skin on. Dice each type of pepper individually into about ¼-inch pieces.

In a small pot, bring your pickled jalapeño liquid, vinegar, and sugar to a simmer. In a small bowl, stir together your cornstarch and water and slowly pour it into the pot, whisking constantly until the mixture thickens. Add your chopped peppers, pine nuts, pickled jalapeños and cherry peppers, and a pinch of salt, and stir to combine thoroughly. If you are using it right away, set aside. If you are making it for later, let it cool, and transfer to an airtight container and refrigerate.

Lightly season the cut sides of your zucchinis with salt and a touch of olive oil. Let this cure for at least 10 minutes.

Heat up a small cast-iron pan over medium-high heat. Add the zucchini in batches and quickly sear both cut sides of each piece, about 45 seconds a side. Try not to cook the zucchini too much. Transfer to a plate and let cool, then cut them into ½-inch pieces.

To build your salad, lay your sliced zucchini cut side up. Spoon your salsa verde and spread it in a smooth layer. Then top with your pepper and pine nut relish. Garnish with the whole mint leaves.

Finish by zesting and juicing the lemon over top of everything. Add a nice healthy drizzle of olive oil, a sprinkle of Maldon salt, and a few cracks of black pepper. Finally, using a vegetable peeler, shave nice big curls of Manchego onto your salad. Cover the whole thing or let your guests add it as they like.

SERVES 4

PREP TIME: 2 HOURS

PEPPER AND PINE NUT RELISH

2 poblano peppers

1 red bell pepper

2 jalapeños

1 Anaheim pepper

¼ cup pickled jalapeño liquid

¼ cup white vinegar

½ cup sugar

1 tablespoon cornstarch

2 tablespoons cold water

1 cup pine nuts, toasted

1 cup pickled jalapeños, sliced

4 pickled cherry peppers

Kosher salt

4 zucchinis, cut into quarters lengthwise

Kosher salt

Fancy olive oil

All the Herbs Salsa Verde (page 334)

½ bunch mint, picked

1 lemon

Maldon salt and freshly cracked black pepper

1 block Manchego cheese (at least 12 ounces)

SICHUAN CHILI OIL SMASHED CUCUMBER SALAD *and* SOY-CURED EGG

This is just one of the best things ever. The textures and tastes set you up for a perfect meal. Normally, smashed cucumbers are often served simply as a side to just nibble on while you're waiting for noodles or dumplings to come out. I think this treatment takes the cucumbers to more of a comprehensive dish. This is so refreshing. The soy eggs are just Banana Town. Since we're making a cookbook, we could make something beautiful like this a main event. I'm so hyped on this salad, and I know this will be a staple for you and your family or friends, or maybe your lover.

First, we're going to make the soy sauce eggs. Bring a large pot of water to a boil. Lower each egg into the pot and set your timer for 6 minutes. Transfer the eggs to an ice bath until they get cold, then peel them.

To marinate the eggs, place a Ziploc bag in a small bowl. Fill it with the water, soy sauce, and mirin. Add the eggs and squeeze the air out of the bag to ensure the eggs are covered in the soy sauce mixture. Seal the bag closed and store in the refrigerator. Ideally wait 24 hours, but they can be used after 6 hours.

When you are ready to make your salad, get ready to smash your cucumbers. Lay them on a cutting board and smash them with the bottom of a pot. Transfer them to a strainer set over a bowl, generously salt them, and place them in the fridge for 30 minutes. Salting them draws out a lot of the moisture in the cucumbers. Press them with paper towels to remove all the moisture you can.

In a large bowl, mix the red onion, cilantro, and scallions.

Make the black vinegar chili crisp dressing. In a small bowl, mix up the chili crisp, black vinegar, soy sauce, sesame seeds, lime zest and juice, garlic, ginger, and grapeseed oil.

Carefully remove your beautiful little soy eggs from their salty bath. Break them gently with your hands. Do it artfully, we are trying to make art here.

When you're ready to serve, get a large platter out. First put down your smashed cucumber. Toss with the dressing. Top it with the broken-up soy eggs. Add the onion, cilantro, and scallions and top with the sesame seeds.

SERVES 4 TO 6
PREP TIME: 1 DAY

SOY SAUCE EGGS

6 eggs

½ cup water

1 cup soy sauce

¾ cup mirin

CUCUMBER SALAD

2 English cucumbers, cut into 2-inch strips

Kosher salt

½ red onion, sliced as thinly as possible

½ bunch cilantro, chopped

½ bunch scallions, chopped

2 tablespoons toasted sesame seeds

BLACK VINEGAR CHILI CRISP DRESSING

¼ cup chili crisp

2 tablespoons black vinegar

2 tablespoons soy sauce

3 tablespoons toasted sesame seeds

Zest and juice of 1 lime

2 garlic cloves, grated

1 small knob ginger, grated

2 tablespoons grapeseed oil

RIZZO'S WEDGE SALAD

This salad is my idea of an Italian wedge steakhouse salad. The green bell pepper is very, very important. I used to hate green bell peppers, but why? My daughter Rizzo loves them, and I think I've grown because now I love green peppers too. But there's a lot more to this salad than the pepper—the pancetta is so great, and the blue cheese dressing is perfect for real. I obviously love Rizzo way more than this salad, but this salad is 10/10.

Preheat your oven to 400°F. Line a baking sheet with aluminum foil.

We're going to make the dressing first. In a blender, add the mayonnaise, gorgonzola, buttermilk, vinegar, sugar, and salt and pepper to taste. Blend until smooth.

Place the pancetta on the prepared baking sheet and press with another baking sheet. Bake for 10 minutes. Remove from the oven and put the pancetta on paper towels to dry.

We're going to put it all together on a beautiful platter. First put down your iceberg lettuce. Then top with tomato, onion, bell pepper, pancetta, and blue cheese. Dress with the dressing, oregano, good olive oil, and salt and pepper to taste.

SERVES 4
PREP TIME: 30 MINUTES

BLUE CHEESE DRESSING

¾ cup mayonnaise

½ cup crumbled gorgonzola

½ cup buttermilk

2 tablespoons white vinegar

1 teaspoon sugar

Kosher salt and freshly cracked black pepper

½ cup sliced or diced pancetta

½ head iceberg lettuce, cut into 6 pieces

1 Roma tomato, diced

1 small red onion, thinly sliced

½ green bell pepper, diced

1 large (6-ounce) wedge blue cheese

½ teaspoon dried oregano

Extra-virgin olive oil

Kosher salt and freshly cracked black pepper

ROASTED SHALLOT SALAD *with* SHERRY VINEGAR *and* RYE BREAD CRUMBS

You should make this salad for a first-date night because if you do, you'll have a second date. That's for three reasons: (1) They will love shallots. (2) Anyone who loves shallots is good in my book. (3) A raw shallot salad kiss could be the most incredible kiss of all time and could bring about world peace. But probably not.

Make your bread crumbs. Preheat your oven to 350°F. Butter both sides of the bread. Place on a baking sheet and bake for 20 minutes, flipping the slices halfway through. Allow the bread to cool completely on your counter; it should be completely dried out. Break it into chunks and pulse in a food processor until fine. You should have about ¼ cup of bread crumbs. Leave the oven on.

Reserve one of your shallots. Slice it into thin disks and discard the core. Let the slices soak in ice water for 10 minutes, carefully separating out its individual rings while it's soaking in the ice bath. This is going to make them a little less wild. Drain and dry the rings on a paper towel.

Take your remaining shallots and cut them in half lengthwise. In a medium cast-iron pan over medium-high heat, melt the butter. Sear the shallots in batches, cut-side down, until they are nice and caramelized and your butter is brown and frothy. Add more butter for each batch if needed. When they are all seared, add the vinegar to deglaze your pan and season with a big pinch of salt. Scrape up those browned bits. Remove from the heat and add your walnuts, dates, and thyme.

Place your pan into the oven and roast until the shallots are slightly tender but still hold their shape, 10 minutes. Remove your pan from the oven and let it cool down slightly.

While the shallots are still warm, cut them in half again widthwise and separate the individual petals. Add the roasted shallots and everything remaining in the pan to a medium bowl. Toss with the lemon juice and adjust the seasoning with salt and pepper.

In a small bowl, mix together the reserved sliced shallot rings and the parsley. Dress this with the olive oil and a pinch of salt.

To serve, lay out your cooked shallot salad on a nice serving platter. Top this with your herb and shallot salad and bread crumbs. To finish it off, garnish with the large piece of Gouda on top.

SERVES 4
PREP TIME: 1 HOUR

2 slices dark rye bread

¼ cup unsalted butter, plus more for searing the shallots and buttering the bread

16 large shallots, peeled, root on

¼ cup sherry vinegar

Kosher salt

½ cup toasted walnuts, roughly chopped

½ cup dates, halved

6 thyme sprigs

Freshly cracked black pepper

Juice of ½ lemon

½ cup parsley leaves

1 tablespoon extra-virgin olive oil

1 big chunk (8 ounces) aged Gouda cheese

SPAGHETTI *with* MINT, RICOTTA, *and* OLIVE OIL–BAKED BREAD CRUMBS

Look at this photo. Shouldn't it be hanging in the Louvre? Maybe this should be served at a very fancy, high-end restaurant. Pasta salad is so good, but it's also weird sometimes. And I think spaghetti salad is the weirdest of them all. It's a beautiful little thing. We plated this and wrote instructions to make it this way, but we all know you could just make a bowl of this and pour the garnishes on it and it'll be fine. But if you want that big gold star, you gotta try your best. It's so annoying, but beauty can kill.

Make your croutons. Preheat your oven to 400°F. On a large baking sheet, combine your bread with the olive oil, garlic powder, and salt and black pepper to taste. Roast until crunchy, 15 to 20 minutes. Let cool, then pulse the croutons in a food processor. Put that into a medium bowl and set aside.

In a separate medium bowl, whisk together three-quarters of the ricotta (reserve the rest for serving), the lemon zest and juice, and buttermilk. It should be loose enough to coat the back of a spoon. Set aside.

Bring a large pot of salted water to a boil. Cook your pasta al dente, about 8 minutes. Drain and transfer to a baking sheet. Cover in olive oil to prevent it from sticking until we need it.

While the pasta is cooking, let's make the garnish mix. In a bowl, combine the bread crumbs, chile flakes, chives, and black pepper to taste.

To plate your dish, take four plates and dollop some of the reserved ricotta in the center of each one. Grab a large bowl and mix together the whisked ricotta with your noodles. If you are fancy, take your plating tweezers, pull up one portion, and, keeping the noodles straight, begin to twirl. You can also do this with two forks. Then, take your garnish bowl and keep twirling the noodles on the crumbs; it should coat the outside. Plate each twirled portion on your ricotta dollops. Once you have the noodles built, top with your lemon supremes and mint.

SERVES 4
PREP TIME: 45 MINUTES

¼ loaf Italian bread, cut into croutons

¼ cup extra-virgin olive oil, plus more for coating the pasta

1 tablespoon garlic powder

Kosher salt and freshly cracked black pepper

One 15-ounce container ricotta cheese

Zest and juice of 1 lemon

¾ cup buttermilk

8 ounces spaghetti

1 tablespoon chile flakes

½ bunch chives, finely diced

Maldon salt

1 lemon, cut into segments

1 lemon, supremed (see page 152)

½ bunch mint, roughly chopped

CHARRED CORN ESQUITES-STYLE *with* FRIED OAXACAN CHEESE CURDS

Mexico is one of the most flavorful places in the world, period. We all know it. Combining crema with charred corn is the best. Esquites are such a great snack and easy eating while walking around or chilling. But I wanted some cheese. We need some cheese, so why not fry some Oaxacan cheese curds and blast the fuck off? Why can't we make the crispiest, cheesiest little fried daddies and put them on top of this corn salad? Why can't we? Guess what? We can.

To char the corn, get a grill on high heat or preheat your oven to high broil. Brush the corn with the vegetable oil and season it with salt and pepper to taste. Grill the corn, turning it occasionally, until it's charred and cooked through, 10 to 12 minutes. Remove from the grill or oven and let it cool slightly. Cut the kernels off the cobs and place them in a large bowl.

In a separate large bowl, whisk together the flour, beer, Mexican chile powder, morita powder, 1 teaspoon of salt, and 1 teaspoon of black pepper until you have a smooth batter. The batter should be thick enough to coat the back of a spoon.

Line a plate with paper towels. Heat 2 inches of vegetable oil in a large Dutch oven over medium heat until it reaches 350°F. Lightly dust the Oaxacan cheese cubes in flour and dip them into the beer batter, allowing any excess batter to drip off. Carefully place them in the hot oil and fry until they turn golden brown and crispy, 2 to 3 minutes. Remove with a slotted spoon and place them on the plate to drain. Season with a sprinkling of salt.

In a small bowl, whisk together the mayonnaise, sour cream, lime juice, garlic, and the cilantro to make your crema. Adjust the seasoning with salt and pepper to taste. Pour the dressing over the corn and toss to coat.

Now layer your salad in a few parfait cups if you got 'em. If you don't, this also works on a plate or in a bowl. Start your base with charred corn kernels, then crema, pickled and fresh jalapeños, more corn, crema, cotija cheese, and crema, then top with your fried Oaxacan cheese. Sprinkle with the Tajín and serve with lime wedges to be squeezed over top.

SERVES 4
PREP TIME: 1 HOUR

6 ears corn

2 tablespoons vegetable oil, plus more for frying

Kosher salt and freshly cracked black pepper

1 cup all-purpose flour

1 cup Mexican lager like a Corona

1 teaspoon Mexican chile powder

½ teaspoon morita chile powder

8 ounces Oaxacan cheese, torn into bite-size pieces

½ cup mayonnaise

½ cup sour cream

Juice of 2 limes, plus more lime wedges for serving

2 garlic cloves, minced

½ cup chopped fresh cilantro leaves

½ cup sliced jalapeños

½ cup sliced pickled jalapeños

½ cup crumbled cotija cheese (or feta cheese)

2 tablespoons Tajín

ORZO *and* GOAT CHEESE SALAD

This is a tasty Mediterranean shovel-fest salad. Have this with some grilled chicken or lamb chops. Holy cow shit. Orzo is white hot. You'll see; you are ahead of the curve. You will be the most fantastic kids at the function. Whoever pulls up with the orzo and goat cheese salad is going to be bringing something. Orzo's gone full circle. Does anyone even care about orzo? HELLO, does anyone care about orzo salads?

Bring a small pot of salted water to a boil. Cook the orzo until it's al dente, about 8 minutes. Drain and rinse under cold water to stop the cooking process. Let it cool completely.

Heat a large cast-iron pan over medium-high heat. Toss the zucchini with 2 tablespoons of the olive oil and season with salt and pepper. Cook the zucchini on the cut side until lightly charred and tender. Remove from the heat and let cool slightly.

In a small bowl, whisk together 2 tablespoons of the olive oil, the lemon juice, mustard, garlic, and salt and pepper to taste. Taste and adjust the seasoning as needed.

In a large bowl, combine the cooled orzo, charred zucchini, and cherry tomatoes. Gently fold in the crumbled goat cheese, reserving a small amount for garnish. Drizzle the vinaigrette over the salad and toss everything together to coat the ingredients evenly.

Add the basil, tarragon, and parsley, and reserved goat cheese. Finish with the remaining 2 tablespoons olive oil, salt, and pepper.

SERVES 2
PREP TIME: 45 MINUTES

1 cup dried orzo pasta

1 medium zucchini, cut into ¼-inch halved coins

6 tablespoons extra-virgin olive oil

Kosher salt and freshly cracked black pepper

1 tablespoon fresh lemon juice

1 teaspoon Dijon mustard

1 small garlic clove, minced

1 cup cherry tomatoes, halved

3 ounces goat cheese, crumbled

2 tablespoons basil leaves, chopped

2 tablespoons tarragon, chopped

2 tablespoons parsley

CHICKPEA CASSEROLE

This is a cold casserole served as a salad. Don't be scared. I think this would be best for a summer BBQ or outdoor cookout. It would be unreal with some BBQ lamb or smoked fish. The combination comes from my love of mutter paneer and mango chutney. Toronto is so rich with Indian roti shops. Living in Parkdale and eating at Mother India saved my life at least thirty-six times. I would always get a mutter paneer and add lamb. I feel like this dish would be fire if you pair it with a bunch of roti. Show up with that bounty (and maybe some samosas with tamarind sauce) to the cookout and it would be much loved and respected.

Preheat your oven to 400°F.

Toss a ½ cup of chickpeas with your olive oil and spread them out on a baking sheet. Bake these until they're crispy and crunchy, 12 minutes, then toss them with the yellow curry powder and salt.

Halve your pickled onions and separate the layers.

In a large bowl, toss together the remaining chickpeas, parsley, mint, yellow curry dressing, lime zest, and lime juice. Adjust the seasoning with salt and pepper. Layer the mango marmalade on top of the chickpea salad, and top with the toasted chickpeas, pickled onions, and almonds.

CONTINUED

MAKES 1 BIG PLATTER (SERVING 6)

PREP TIME: 2 DAYS

Two 15.5-ounce cans chickpeas, drained and rinsed

2 tablespoons olive oil

2 tablespoons yellow curry powder

Kosher salt

6 Pickled Red Pearl Onions (recipe follows)

½ cup chopped parsley

½ cup chopped mint

2 tablespoons Yellow Curry Dressing (recipe follows)

Zest and juice of 1 lime

Freshly cracked black pepper

2 tablespoons Mango Marmalade (recipe follows)

½ cup toasted almonds, roughly chopped

CHICKPEAS *with* YELLOW CURRY DRESSING, MANGO MARMALADE, ALMONDS, *and* PICKLED RED PEARL ONIONS CONTINUED

PICKLED RED PEARL ONIONS

Place the onions in a resealable jar. In a medium saucepan over high heat, combine the water, sugar, vinegar, bay leaf, and peppercorns and stir until the sugar has completely dissolved. This will take about a minute or two. Allow the pickling liquid to come to a boil and immediately pour the liquid over top of the onions, covering with a lid. Allow the pickled onions to cool at room temperature for about 30 minutes, then refrigerate the jar for at least 24 hours to allow the flavors to develop and the onions to pickle. Use within 1 week.

1 pound red pearl onions, peeled
1 cup water
1 cup sugar
½ cup white vinegar
1 bay leaf
6 black peppercorns

YELLOW CURRY DRESSING

In a medium bowl, thoroughly mix together all the ingredients. Transfer to an airtight container and refrigerate. This is best made the night before you plan to use it.

1 cup mayonnaise
1 cup full-fat Greek yogurt
1 tablespoon yellow curry powder
1 teaspoon kosher salt
Zest and juice of 1 lime

MANGO MARMALADE

Place your dried mangoes in a bowl. Boil 1 cup of the water and pour it over the mangoes, allowing them to steep for 15 minutes. Drain and chop the rehydrated mangoes until they reach the consistency of a paste.

In a small saucepan, combine another 1 cup of the water with the sugar and vinegar. Bring to a boil over medium-high heat and add your fresh mango and mango paste. Turn the heat down to low and simmer for 15 minutes. The sauce will thicken a little bit.

Remove the pan from the heat and add your chiles and a pinch of salt. Allow this mixture to cook for 30 minutes before using. Transfer any leftovers to an airtight container and store in the fridge for up to 1 week.

1 cup dried mangoes
2 cups water
1 cup sugar
½ cup white vinegar
3 Ataulfo mangoes, diced
2 green chiles, thinly sliced
Kosher salt

EVERYONE'S MOM'S MACARONI *and* TUNA SALAD

This is another hitter! I love coming home and seeing this giant, old, classic, pink Tupperware bowl with a white lid in the fridge. It takes up a whole shelf. And it's just for Trish, lol. I really have no idea why she always makes so much, but I don't ever ask. I think it's one of her aunt's recipes, and it's for Canada Day picnics or something insane like that. It's so fucking good, I swear, but it's just so much. We have ourselves a Tupperware bowl filled with a month's worth of tuna salad. This should feed a full family of sixteen or a football team or a dance recital.

The most important thing about making pasta salad is to overcook your pasta in salted water. However long the box of pasta says to cook it for, add 3 minutes. You want it to be soft when it comes out. After your pasta is cooked, drain it.

Add the still-warm pasta to a large bowl with the tuna, celery, carrot, bell pepper, onion, parsley, and mayonnaise and mix it vigorously until everything comes together into a nice homogeneous mixture. Add salt and pepper to taste. Place this into a large casserole dish and cover it tightly with plastic wrap. Keep in the fridge until ready to serve. This should last forever in the refrigerator but after a few days it's pushing it.

Beat the shit outta that. Rip it. Add salt and pepper. Once that's in a beautiful state, serve it at parties.

SERVES 8

PREP TIME: 35 MINUTES

One 16-ounce box elbow pasta (little ones)

Four 5-ounce cans tuna in water, drained

1 cup diced celery

1 cup diced carrot

1 cup diced red bell pepper

½ cup diced red onion

½ cup chopped parsley

3 cups mayonnaise

Kosher salt and freshly cracked black pepper

VASOS DE FRUTA

One of the first times I went to LA, I went to a fruit stand and it brought me so much joy. This is back when I was still drinking and having FUN. When you are living like that, being hungover is inevitable, and luckily these fruit stands are all over the place. Eating these spicy, salty fruit cups is the best cure for anything. They just make you feel good. It was definitely the first time I had salty, savory fruit, and it flipped my brain. I loved it. By cutting everything the same size, you can eat it all in the same bite. When you make this salad, you'll fill your mouth with one of the biggest, best flavor grenades ever. And usually they include jicama, but I couldn't get any the day of the photo shoot, so whatever, we're here now.

In a large bowl, combine the pineapple, mango, watermelon, and dragon fruit.

In a separate bowl, combine the serranos, Thai basil, honey, lime zest and juice, chamoy, and Tajín. Adjust with salt to your liking.

Pour the dressing over the fruit mixture. Gently toss everything together to ensure an even coating. Cover the fruit salad with plastic wrap or a lid and refrigerate for at least 30 minutes before serving to allow the flavors to meld. Give the salad another gentle toss before serving. Add an additional sprinkle of Tajín over top for extra kick and give a few cranks of freshly cracked black pepper.

SERVES 6

PREP TIME: 40 MINUTES

Half of a pineapple, cut into 1-inch pieces

2 mangoes, cut into 1-inch pieces

One-quarter of a large watermelon, cut into 1-inch pieces

1 dragon fruit, cut into 1-inch pieces

2 serrano peppers, thinly sliced

½ cup Thai basil leaves, chopped

2 tablespoons honey

Zest and juice of 2 limes

2 tablespoons chamoy

2 teaspoons Tajín, plus more for serving

Kosher salt and freshly cracked black pepper

CRANBERRY BEANS *with* COMTÉ, TARRAGON, MINT, *and* SHERRY VINEGAR

In *Indiana Jones and the Last Crusade*, Harrison Ford must overcome three challenges. He has to kneel, spell *God*, and take a leap of faith across an abyss. That's what we are doing here, but with cranberries. We're making a cranberry vinaigrette. Then, we're going to pair that with cranberry beans and dried cranberries. If you pass the challenges of the cranberries you are rewarded with treviso, Comte, and everlasting life.

First, let's mix up this cranberry vinaigrette. Put the vinegar, cranberry juice, olive oil, lemon zest and juice, mustard, and honey in a mason jar and just shake the piss out of it. Really let it go—it should look like creamy cranberry juice. Do not drink it!

Next, let's arrange this bad boy. In a large bowl, toss the cranberry beans, dried cranberries, hazelnuts, tarragon, and mint with the dressing. Lay the treviso out on a platter and pour your salad over it. To finish, either cover the entire thing with Comté cheese or leave it on the side for guests to help themselves. Welcome to the cranberry flavor zone.

SERVES 4
PREP TIME: 30 MINUTES

CRANBERRY VINAIGRETTE

2 tablespoons sherry vinegar

1 tablespoon cranberry juice

¼ cup olive oil

Zest and juice of 1 lemon

1 teaspoon Dijon mustard

1 teaspoon honey

2 cups cooked and drained cranberry beans

1 cup dried cranberries

1 cup hazelnuts

1 bunch tarragon, diced

1 bunch mint, diced

2 treviso, cut into four wedges

2 cups shaved Comté cheese

CANNELLINIS *with* ROASTED RED PEPPERS, RAISINS, CAPERS, ANCHOVIES, *and* PARSLEY

All bodies look beautiful when they are glistening in the sun with a little bit of oil. Hot body summer for all. Let your freak flag fly. This salad is for us and all the real freaky deakies. Whole roasted pep-peps is the move. They slurp up so nice with those slippery, salt salamander–looking anchovies. This is a heater dish. This book has no duds, just like my friend circles.

Start by roasting the peppers. On a gas stove, roast each pepper on high and, using tongs, turn them occasionally until the skin is blistered and black, 3 minutes. Transfer to a bowl and cover tightly with plastic wrap. Let stand until the skin starts to loosen and the peppers are cool, about 10 minutes.

While you wait for the peppers to sweat, in a large bowl, add your cannellini beans, raisins, capers, and parsley. Toss with the olive oil, lemon juice, and salt and black pepper to taste. Set aside.

Carefully rub off and discard the blistered skin of the peppers. Remove the seeds but leave the peppers as whole as you can. Line them all up on a platter and cover them in the bean mixture. Then lay the anchovies on top and garnish with the lemon zest, a drizzle of olive oil, and more black pepper.

SERVES 4

PREP TIME: 30 MINUTES

4 shepherd peppers

2 cups canned cannellini beans, drained

½ cup Italian raisins (or just the best raisins you can get your hands on)

½ cup capers, drained

½ bunch Italian parsley, roughly chopped

½ cup extra-virgin olive oil, plus more for drizzling

Zest and juice of 1 lemon

Kosher salt and freshly cracked black pepper

7 anchovies

BRUSSELS SPROUTS *with* BACON, MINT, PISTACHIO, FISH SAUCE, PICKLED PEPPER CARAMEL, *and* LIME

Twelve years ago, you couldn't walk into a restaurant and not get fried Brussels sprouts with a spicy sauce or something. It was like wildfire. This is the 2020s redux version of something we all used to love that got beaten down so hard from triple-trickle-down restaurant folks. But these fried Brussels deserve to live again because this is something special. The deep caramelization from frying combined with that super-bouncy crunch of the raw is world class. This salad is so fucking good. Wow. Let's honor the 2010s.

Preheat your oven to 450°F.

Take the stems off the peppers. In a blender, puree the red bell pepper, jalapeño, scotch bonnet, Thai chiles, serranos, fish sauce, and vinegar.

While the peppers are blending, start your caramel. In a small pot over medium-low heat, combine the sugar and water and reduce until thickened and dark amber in color. This will take time and you need to keep stirring it pretty consistently. Then add the blended peppers mixture into your caramel and stir to combine. Turn the heat off and remove the pan and let it chill out for a second. Don't want it to be fudge.

On a baking sheet, toss your halved Brussels sprouts and bacon in olive oil and season with salt and black pepper to taste. Roast until golden brown, 25 to 30 minutes. Let them cool for 10 minutes. Then cut your bacon into small pieces, about a quarter of an inch.

In a large bowl, combine the roasted Brussels sprouts and bacon with the pistachios. Don't add all the caramel in at once. Add it gradually and toss everything together.

Plate the salad on a nice platter. Cover with the shaved Brussels sprouts, mint, and lime zest and juice. Toss and serve to your best friends only, no borderline people, only ride-or-dies.

SERVES 4 TO 6
PREP TIME: 1 HOUR

1 red bell pepper

1 jalapeño

1 scotch bonnet

2 Thai chiles

2 red serrano peppers

½ cup fish sauce

1 cup white vinegar

1 cup sugar

1 cup water

4 pounds Brussels sprouts, half halved and half shaved

Extra-virgin olive oil

Kosher salt and freshly cracked black pepper

4 ounces bacon

1 cup pistachios, toasted and chopped

½ bunch mint, finely chopped

Zest and juice of 1 lime

BUTTER BEANS *with* LEMON, CONFIT GARLIC, CANNED SARDINES, *and* BABY GEM LETTUCE

When I look at this salad, I think about how it would be nice to eat it outside with the bees and birds and while looking at trees moving. Maybe in France or my rural Ontario. Or Northern California, who knows? This salad is so fresh and all about the simplicity. The lemon slices, the creamy beans, the confit garlic, the beautiful tinned fish. Now I'm not trying to tell all of you that tinned fish is some new hot trend that I'm jumping on. I grew up working class, and eating canned fish and smoked mussels or oysters was not some lavish lifestyle choice. It was humiliating. Imagine going to school as a kid with a can of smoked mussels and some saltines. Now people are paying seventy-five clams for some anchovies, bruh. That shit is crazy, but this salad is pure. Don't make fun of these sardines. This ain't a fad. It's shame from early childhood trauma. Catch me as I trust-fall into your arms.

Set the stage by gently cooking the onions over medium-low heat in a skillet in the butter and olive oil. Let them become these fatty, buttery things. They should be a little bit translucent after 10 minutes. Take the pan off the heat and hit it with the lemon zest and juice. Let the onions sit there and steam uncovered. Season with salt and pepper to taste and let cool.

In a large bowl, mix your butter beans with the cooled lemon onion rings, olive oil, and salt.

Make the confit garlic. Put the cloves into a small saucepan, cover them with the olive oil, and cook over medium heat until they are fully caramelized on the outside, about 15 minutes. Take them off the heat and set aside.

Lay your lettuce onto a beautiful platter, then top with your butter bean and onion mix. Garnish with lemon triangles, confit garlic, sardines, reserved sardine oil, and fresh cracked black pepper.

SERVES 4

PREP TIME: 25 MINUTES

LEMON ONION RINGS

3 onions, cut into thin rings

1 tablespoon unsalted butter

2 tablespoons extra-virgin olive oil

Zest and juice of 1 lemon

Kosher salt and freshly cracked black pepper

1 cup canned butter beans, dried and rinsed

CONFIT GARLIC

1 cup garlic cloves

2 cups olive oil

SALAD

4 heads baby gem lettuce, chopped

½ lemon, sliced super thin into triangles

One beautiful (4-ounce) tin sardines, drained and oil reserved

Freshly cracked black pepper

BLACK BEANS *with* COTIJA, CILANTRO, RED ONION, CRUMBLED PORK RINDS, OREGANO, *and* SALSA MACHA

This one's a heater and could set it off for a whole night because of how powerful it is. The flavor and the mouthfeel are bonkers. It's going to light y'all up. Don't be scared, jump in. It's like jumping off a small bridge in the dark into a creek. You gotta just trust me, OK? This is also one of those salads that you could easily wrap into tortillas and bake with some enchilada sauce or scoop atop cheese quesadillas. This is just a fire condiment that I'm calling a salad. Don't tell anybody—it's our secret. Make the salsa macha the day before, it will come together in a snap after that.

First, let's make the salsa macha. In a skillet over medium heat toast the garlic in oil, until golden brown, about 1 minute. Add the ancho and guajillo chile powders and simmer for 1 minute, stirring constantly. Add the peanuts and sesame seeds and simmer on very low heat until the the seeds turn golden brown, 4 more minutes. Remove from the heat and allow to cool for 10 minutes. Stir in the vinegar, salt, and oregano. Pour the mixture into a blender or food processor and pulse several times until the salsa is nicely combined. Don't overprocess it; you want to have nice crispy bits, not a puree. Store in an airtight container, refrigerated, for up to several months.

The next day, in a large bowl, combine the black beans, cilantro, red onion, bell pepper, dried oregano, and jalapeño. Toss with the olive oil, lime juice, and salt and pepper to taste.

Put the mixture on a platter, then drizzle 3 tablespoons of your salsa macha over everything and top with your pork rinds, Manchego, and cotija.

SERVES 4

PREP TIME: 8 HOURS

SALSA MACHA

4 garlic cloves, chopped

2 cups vegetable oil

2 tablespoons ancho chile powder

2 tablespoons guajillo chile powder

½ cup peanuts, toasted

¼ cup toasted sesame seeds

1 teaspoon apple cider vinegar

½ teaspoon kosher salt

½ teaspoon dried Mexican oregano

Two 15.5-ounce cans black beans, drained and rinsed

1 bunch cilantro, chopped

1 red onion, thinly sliced

1 red bell pepper, diced

2 tablespoons dried Mexican oregano

1 jalapeño, chopped (seeds in or out, it's up to you)

¼ cup extra-virgin olive oil

Juice of 6 limes

Kosher salt and freshly cracked black pepper

2 cups pork rinds, crushed

8 ounces Manchego cheese, shredded

12 ounces cotija cheese, crumbled

LUPINIS *with* STRACCIATELLA DI BUFALA, BASIL, *and* ANCHOVIES

Lupini is a bean, but it was also the name of our canary. Rest in paradise, Lupini. This recipe is my version of a love song to my wife, who loves lupinis, the bean, and obviously loved our bird. Sadly our last canary, Garbanzo, passed away this spring. We named it Garbanzo to keep with the bean theme, but Lupini will always be our first love. Please make this salad and feel the love from me, Trish, and our beloved fallen birds, Lupini and Garbanzo. P.S. We would like to welcome our third canary Waffles to the world.

Use your thumb and forefinger to pinch and squeeze the bean from its skin. Soak these in water overnight to help reduce their salinity.

The next day, soak the basil leaves in cold water for 10 minutes and pat them dry. Soak the shallots in ice water for 10 minutes to help take some of their spiciness away.

Cut the top and bottom off the orange. Place the orange on one of its sliced ends. Carefully work your way around the orange with your knife to remove the remaining peel and proceed to cut between each rib like a wedge to get your segments. Squeeze out the leftover pith to get your orange juice for the dressing.

Make the dressing. In a large bowl, whisk together your garlic, chile flakes, lemon zest and juice, reserved orange juice, and olive oil. Rip up your basil and toss that, the shallots, beans, and orange segments in.

To serve, lay everything out on a nice big plate. Try to make sure you have all your basil, shallots, and orange segments spread out over top with some lupini beans sticking through. To garnish, place a very generous dollop of the stracciatella in the center of your salad, lay out your anchovies, and sprinkle on the nice big, chunky olives. Drizzle with a healthy dose of olive oil, a bunch of big cracks of pepper, and some flaky salt.

SERVES 4 TO 6
PREP TIME: 12 HOURS

4 cups jarred lupini beans, rinsed and dried

1 cup basil leaves

1 shallot, thinly sliced

1 orange

1 pound stracciatella di bufala

4 anchovies

8 chunky green olives, pitted

DRESSING

2 garlic cloves, grated

2 teaspoons dried red pepper flakes

Zest and juice of 1 lemon

Juice of ¼ orange (reserved from above)

Extra-virgin olive oil

Freshly cracked black pepper

Maldon salt

ROASTED SUNCHOKES, FRESH RICOTTA, *and* FARRO

Wow, wow, wow, wow, wow. Sunchokes are so special. I feel like no one really fucks with them, but holy cow, they rule. After you roast them, they turn into custard/crème brulee dessert-like food. With the ricotta, it's so fire. Farro is cool, too, but holy piss sunchokes, come on! It's impossible not to think of over-easy fried eggs looking at these bad boys. This is my version of molecular gastronomy.

Preheat your oven to 400°F. Line a baking sheet with parchment paper.

In a small pot, bring 2 cups of water to a boil. Add your farro, carrot, celery, red onion, bay leaves, thyme, and salt. Simmer for 20 minutes because we don't wanna cook it to shit. Spoon it all out onto a baking sheet and discard everything but the farro. Add a few glugs of olive oil to make sure it doesn't become sticky or clumpy and season with salt. Let it cool.

Scrub any dirt off the sunchokes and rinse them under cool water. Make sure you dry them off. Add the sunchokes to the prepared baking sheet and season them with olive oil, salt, and pepper. Roast until the sunchokes are fork-tender, about 20 minutes. Remove from the oven and allow to cool for about 15 minutes. Cut the sunchokes into chunks, a little larger than bite-sized.

While the sunchokes are cooling, let's make our ricotta mixture. In a bowl, mix together the ricotta, milk, 2 tablespoons olive oil, a healthy pinch of salt, and pepper.

In a large bowl, add the farro, sunchokes, mint, and basil. Spoon that over a few times to incorporate. Toss together to make it a loose falling salad. We are back to the moment where we start layering it up.

In four small bowls, spoon some of your sunchokes and farro. Make a dimple in the center with the back of your spoon and fill it with the ricotta mixture. Make another dimple in your ricotta and add a dollop of the marmalade.

SERVES 4
PREP TIME: 1 HOUR

1 cup farro

¼ carrot, peeled and halved

¼ celery rib

½ red onion, peeled and halved

2 bay leaves

4 thyme sprigs

1 tablespoon kosher salt, plus more for roasting and seasoning

Olive oil

Freshly cracked black pepper

1 pound sunchokes

3 shallots

1 cup fresh ricotta

3 tablespoons milk

½ bunch mint, torn

½ bunch basil, chopped

½ cup orange marmalade (preferably Bonne Maman)

ORECCHIETTE *with* SMOKED MUSSELS *and* BOTTARGA

Shapes and sizes matter when making salads. Can you fit everything onto a forkful or spoonful? This recipe is a perfect example of salad eating with a spoon at its finest. Everything is the same size and is a journey of texture. We have nice little cups of pasta filled with shallots and smoked mussels. This is an umami bomber with the bottarga, but if you don't love it, leave it out. Although if you don't like bottarga, then you probably don't like smoked canned mussels, so why are you even eating this and shoveling it in your mouth with a spoon so fast? If you do love bottarga and smoked mussels, you'll love this. The freshly grated tomato vinaigrette-sauce is so good. I'm trying to give you pasta salads like you've never seen before.

Bring a large pot of salted water to a boil. Cook the orecchiette until al dente, then drain and set aside.

In a large bowl, grate the tomatoes. Lace it with ½ cup of the olive oil and Maldon salt and pepper to taste. Add one-quarter of the parsley, one-half of the shallots, the garlic, lemon zest and juice, and orecchiette. Mix it all together.

Then in another small bowl, add your mussels with the remaining 2 tablespoons olive oil and the remaining shallots and parsley. Season with Maldon salt and black pepper.

Time to plate. Split the orecchiette salad into four portions. Then divide the mussels mixture equally, shave the bottarga, and dust with smoked paprika.

SERVES 4

PREP TIME: 20 MINUTES

1 pound dried orecchiette pasta

6 large hothouse tomatoes

½ cup extra-virgin olive oil, plus 2 tablespoons for the mussel mixture

Maldon salt and freshly cracked black pepper

½ bunch parsley, chopped

2 shallots, thinly sliced

3 garlic cloves, grated

Zest and juice of 1 lemon

Two 4.2-ounce cans smoked mussels, drained

4 ounces bottarga, grated

Smoked paprika, for garnish

MINI SHELLS *with* CRAB *and* BASIL

Crab salad, tuna salad, and other canned seafood salads seem to be something that everyone enjoys. I always think they are going to be sweet like marshmallows, but they aren't, because they are seafood. This is a very elegant take on a crab salad. The amount of basil and tarragon will pay out tenfold in your mouth. Basil and seafood go really well together. It's a very intense herb, but crab also has a distinctive taste, so why not put two superstars in the ring together? Cold casserole salads forever.

Bring a large pot of salted water to a boil. Throw in the pasta and cook to al dente. Drain, then put the pasta on a baking sheet. Gently squirt a little bit of olive oil on it and move it around so it doesn't get sticky. Let them cool down—we don't want to put hot pasta shells with our crab and mayo; it could make someone barf.

In a huge bowl, throw in your carrots, fennel, red onion, and celery. We need to make a giant dressing. Add the mayo and sour cream and incorporate with a spatula to coat everything. That's gonna be our base dressing. Sprinkle salt and pepper to taste on top. Then add the lemon zest and juice. Throw in the pasta a handful at a time and fold it in; repeat until all the pasta is in.

Gently fold the crab in, trying your best not to mash it up too much. Mix in the tarragon and finish with a drizzle of olive oil and pepper. Garnish with the basil. I think what you're gonna have is a nice little crab shell pasta salad. Make it, get on the Peloton, then eat a bowl of it.

ONE BIG-FUCKING TUPPERWARE CONTAINER, TRISHY SIZE

PREP TIME: 35 MINUTES

One 16-ounce box mini shell pasta

Extra-virgin olive oil

1 cup finely diced carrots

1 cup finely diced fennel

1 cup finely diced red onion

1 cup finely diced celery

2 cups mayonnaise

2 cups sour cream

Kosher salt and freshly cracked black pepper

Zest and juice from 1 lemon

1 cup lump crabmeat, drained (if you can't get crab, this is fire with tuna too)

½ bunch tarragon, chopped

½ bunch basil, sliced into thin strips

COLD GROUND PORK LARB

This is just a larb, but a good larb. You can call it a salad because, like we've said many times, anything can be a salad. Pork fish sauce salad. Very tasty, very good for you. I love the toasted crushed rice. It's so good and crunchy. Raw cabbage is the perfect vessel for this. This is my version of a hot dog sandwich but for salads.

Make the larb sauce. In a small bowl, mix together the fish sauce, lime zest and juice, Thai chiles, serrano, garlic, ginger, and cilantro. Set aside.

In a dry pan over medium-low heat, toast the rice until golden and fragrant, about 15 minutes. Transfer the toasted rice to a mortar and pestle and grind until fine. Set aside.

Set a large pot over medium heat. Add the canola oil and pork and cook until gray, about 5 minutes. Stir in the larb sauce, mint, Thai basil, cilantro, shallot, and toasted rice. Continue to cook until the mixture begins to toast, another 3 minutes. Remove from the heat and set aside.

Cut the cabbage into quarters and peel off layers to form little cups. Spoon the meat into the cups. Garnish each one with a little bit of chicharrón and serve limes on the side for your guests to squeeze on top.

SERVES: 4

PREP TIME: 30 MINUTES

LARB SAUCE

½ cup fish sauce

Zest of 1 lime

Juice of 6 limes

2 Thai red chiles, thinly sliced

1 serrano pepper, thinly sliced

1 garlic clove, minced

One 2-inch piece ginger, peeled and minced

½ cup cilantro, finely chopped

PORK

¼ cup uncooked sticky rice

2 tablespoons canola oil

1½ pounds ground pork

¼ cup chopped mint

¼ cup chopped Thai basil

¼ cup chopped cilantro

½ shallot, thinly sliced

1 head white cabbage

½ cup chicharrón, crushed into small pieces

2 limes, sliced into wedges for serving

BÁNH MÌ SALAD *with* ROASTED PORK BELLY

The bánh mì is one of my favorite sandwiches. It's special and all about the ingredients coming together. That's why I thought, *Let's turn it into a salad*. It's such a powerful combination of flavors. Rang and I had them in Hanoi. It was a special experience that we're going to re-create here. It's one of my favorite memories eating good. Thank you, Vietnam, for the greatest food things in the world.

Prep your pork belly. Cover the skin of your pork belly with at least ¼ cup salt. Place it on a baking sheet and refrigerate, uncovered, for 2 days to allow the skin to dry.

Rub the salt off the pork belly skin with a dry paper towel. Score the bottom flesh all over with a knife or a box cutter. Cut it shallow like a kitty cat would. Season with the five-spice powder and salt.

Preheat your oven to 350°F. Set a rack in a baking sheet. Place the pork belly onto the rack and add 1 cup of water to the pan to prevent the flesh from burning. Roast for 3 to 3½ hours. The thickest part of the meat needs to hit at 145°F. Then turn the heat up to 500°F and roast until all the skin has puffed and becomes crunchy-crackling, about 10 minutes. You want to check on it frequently at this stage to make sure it doesn't burn. Remove from the oven and allow it to cool for 30 minutes.

While the pork belly is roasting, let's make the pickled carrots and daikon. In a medium bowl, combine the carrots, daikon, sugar, and salt. Using your little fingers, get in there and massage the salt and sugar until they disappear. Add the water and rice wine vinegar. Pack it into a mason jar. Seal whatever you don't use and store in the fridge for up to 1 week.

We can also make our nuoc mam gung. In an small bowl, whisk the fish sauce, water, and sugar until the sugar is completely dissolved. Next, add the garlic, lime juice, and Thai chiles and stir to combine.

In a large bowl, toss together the napa cabbage, pickled carrots and daikon, bean sprouts, jalapeño, Thai basil, culantro, and cilantro with the nuoc mam gung. Cut your pork belly into 1-inch cubes and place it on top. Top this with your chopped peanuts.

Serve with the fresh lime wedges and Thai chiles on the side for people to add as much as they like.

SERVES 4
PREP TIME: 2 DAYS

2 pounds pork belly, skin on

Kosher salt

1 tablespoon five-spice powder

PICKLED CARROTS AND DAIKON

1 carrot, peeled and julienned (about 1½ cups)

1 cup peeled and julienned daikon

¼ cup sugar

1 tablespoon kosher salt

1 cup water

½ cup rice wine vinegar

NUOC MAM GUNG

¼ cup fish sauce

¼ cup water

2 tablespoons sugar

5 garlic cloves, minced

Juice of 1 lime

2 Thai chiles, seeded and minced, plus more for serving

1 small napa cabbage, shredded

1 large handful bean sprouts

1 jalapeño, sliced into thin rounds

½ bunch Thai basil, picked

½ cup culantro, roughly chopped

½ bunch cilantro, picked

1 cup roasted peanuts, chopped

3 limes, cut into quarters, for serving

CHICKEN FINGER CROUTON SALAD, A TRIBUTE TO THE BREAKFAST BEACON

Let me set the stage for this one. One day, Lisa, Keenan, Coulson, and I all went to Breakfast Beacon, an iconic breakfast and lunch spot in Crystal Beach that absolutely crushes. I got the club sandwich with added pickles and onion. Keenan got the same because he's a copycat. And Coulson, I think, got a cheeseburger, but Lisa got the Beacon Salad. We didn't really blink an eye, but it came out so fast, and let me tell you, all four of our jaws dropped. I've been going to the Beacon for a very long time, since Mac was a newborn. No one had ever ordered a salad at the Beacon. In all its glory, this salad looked like a bowl of cheese topped with cut-up deep-fried chicken fingers. The rest of us asked at the same time if we could try it. We all did and were like, *This is chicken finger croutons.* Underneath the cheese and the cut-up chicken fingers were iceberg lettuce, diced green peppers, diced white onion, and diced tomato. It was served with ranch dressing. It was insane perfection. It was the greatest salad we'd ever seen. We all ate the salad within minutes, Lisa didn't even get a bite. We had to order a new one for her. Anyway, this is how you make the world's most excellent salad ever.

First, we're going to marinate the chicken. In a big Ziploc bag, add the chicken breasts, 1 cup of the buttermilk, the salt, and cayenne. Seal the bag and carefully move the bag around to make sure the chicken is evenly coated. Place in the fridge for at least 4 hours, or up to overnight.

When you're ready to fry, in a large bowl, mix together the flour, baking powder, garlic powder, and paprika. Add salt. Next, add the remaining ¼ cup buttermilk and stir it with a fork. It'll be clumpy. Line a baking sheet with parchment paper or aluminum foil. Remove a few pieces of chicken at a time from the bag and toss it into the flour mixture. Press the chicken firmly to coat it on all sides—this will get messy. Set up the chicken tenders on the baking sheet.

Next, we're frying the chicken. Line a plate with paper towels. In a large Dutch oven over high heat, heat the canola oil. This guy should get up to at least 360°F. Using tongs, cook a few pieces of chicken at a time until golden brown, about 5 minutes. Then flip and fry a few minutes more. Set the cooked chicken on the plate. When they're all fried, chop into bite-size bits and set aside.

Let's assemble this beauty. In a large bowl, place the iceberg lettuce. We're going to make little piles of beautiful toppings all around. Make this beautiful with the buttermilk chicken, onion, red and green bell peppers, tomato, cheddar cheese, and bacon bits. Add as much or as little ranch as you like. You're welcome and I love you, Breakfast Beacon.

SERVES 4 TO 6

PREP TIME: 6 HOURS

BUTTERMILK CHICKEN FINGERS

2 pounds chicken breasts, thinly sliced

1¼ cups buttermilk

2 teaspoons kosher salt, plus more for breading

1 teaspoon cayenne

2 cups all-purpose flour

2 teaspoons baking powder

2 teaspoons garlic powder

1 teaspoon paprika

4 cups canola oil

SALAD

2 heads iceberg lettuce, cored and chopped

½ white onion, diced

1 red bell pepper, diced

1 green bell pepper, diced

1 hothouse tomato, diced

2 cups shredded cheddar cheese

1 cup bacon bits

Ranch dressing

GRILLED SALAMI PANZANELLA SALAD

Books and ideas and flavors and dishes all come to me in a fever dream most of the time, but this dish really does make sense. I hope it grabs you by the goat. I feel like I've never seen a grilled salami panzanella salad before, but hey! Could be wrong for sure. This salami is so salty and charred, it rules. This is a salad that Jimmy Kimmel would ask me about on late night. Like, "Hey, my aunt Dottie used to make something like this!" And I'd be like, "Jimmy, come on, I love Aunt Dottie!"

Preheat your oven to 350°F.

Toss the focaccia cubes with the olive oil and season with salt and pepper. Throw them on a baking sheet, then roast until golden brown, 10 to 15 minutes. Sprinkle with salt to taste and set aside.

Peel off all the outside casing of the salami. No one likes to eat the paper. Cut into 3-inch-wide steaks vertically. If you have a propane grill, turn it on full crank and get it nice and hot. If you are cooking inside, get a grill pan super hot.

You don't need any oil. Put each sausage steak flat-side down at a 45-degree angle to get beautiful grill lines and cook until it is really nice and charred, then flip it (still on the flat side) so the char lines make a crosshatch pattern on the flat side. This is going to be quick, so don't walk away and burn your beautiful sausage. Flip over to the round side and repeat. Set aside to cool.

This is kind of like an Italian kitchen sink salad or like a deconstructed Italian sub. It's familiar, but where's it all coming from? My brain. Cut your salami into ½-inch cubes. Make them beautiful oily spicy chunky boys. Set aside.

Set up your sub salad station. Welcome to the deli!! If you are making one big ol' bowl, we are going to pile up everything. Take the red onion, tomatoes, hot pepper, and olives and throw them all in there. I don't use measurements; I just hand bomb everything but here are some guidelines for how to use. Glug the olive oil and vinegar all over everything, then add the oregano and parsley and stir it all up. Season with salt and pepper. Toss it in the air and use the bowl to catch it. Stick your hands in here and there, turn it, turn it, flip it, flip it around like a cement truck, toss it and toss it and toss it until it's glistening and smells like the hairy chest of your nonno. Throw your oven-roasted croutons on top.

There you have it, my friends: the greatest submarine grilled salami salad. Long live the deli.

SERVES 4 TO 6
PREP TIME: 45 MINUTES

1 loaf day-old focaccia, cut into ½-inch cubes

2 tablespoons olive oil

Kosher salt and freshly cracked black pepper

1 pound hot Genoa salami

1 red onion, cut into thin rings and soaked in water for at least 2 minutes

3 hothouse tomatoes, diced

1 cup spicy pickled hot peppers, roughly chopped

1 cup green bar olives, roughly chopped

½ cup extra-virgin olive oil

½ cup red wine vinegar, plus more as needed

1 tablespoon dried oregano

½ cup parsley, roughly chopped

SASHIMI SALAD

This salad is for a fancy night when you want to eat something nice and light, then have fancy time after too. This is the path to continuous fancy play for all-night love. Make sure to get good fish and take your time doing this. No bad fish. Good fish is tough to buy but worth it every time. Please find a good fish shop that will take care of you. Maybe they'll even cut it for you if you're super nice and pay. I love eating like this but never really do it at home. This recipe is a pipe dream. Can we say *pipe* anymore?

Start by making the chile oil. In a small saucepan, heat the grapeseed oil and garlic over medium heat. Stir frequently until the garlic begins to turn golden brown, about 2 minutes, then carefully add the gochugaru, morita powder, Sichuan peppercorns, and salt. Stir constantly for 1 minute. Remove the pot from the heat and allow it to cool completely before straining and discarding the solids. Reserve on the side.

Now, prepare your dressing and vegetables. Place your cabbage and red onion in an ice bath for 15 minutes. This will make them crispy. Drain and pat dry with a paper towel. Set aside.

In a small bowl, mix together your orange juice, lime juice, lemon juice, white shoyu, sesame oil, chile oil, and mirin.

Arrange the hamachi on a large serving plate into a spiral shape and season each piece with Maldon salt. Add your dressing in the negative space on the plate and the olive oil in drops on top to finish.

In a small bowl, mix together your onions, cabbage, and sesame seeds. Make a tall, heaping pile in the middle of your spiral.

Gently rip and tuck the shiso leaves at the base of your cabbage and onion mixture.

SERVES 2
PREP TIME: 30 MINUTES

CHILE OIL
½ cup grapeseed oil
2 garlic cloves, thinly sliced
2 tablespoons gochugaru
1 teaspoon morita chile powder
1 teaspoon Sichuan peppercorns
1 teaspoon kosher salt

¼ head green cabbage, sliced as thin as possible (about 2 cups)
½ red onion, sliced as thin as possible
1 tablespoon orange juice
1 tablespoon lime juice
1 tablespoon lemon juice
2 tablespoons white shoyu soy sauce
2 tablespoons chile oil (from above)
1 teaspoon toasted sesame oil
1 tablespoon mirin
1 hamachi fillet (about 9 ounces), sliced ½ inch thick
Maldon salt
½ teaspoon olive oil
1 tablespoon sesame seeds
4 purple shiso leaves or perilla

FRISÉE AUX LARDONS FAMILY-STYLE

This is one of the most classic salads ever and something I've made a million times working at French bistros in my younger years. This salad eats like a real meal. Maybe it's the poached egg, the bacon, the garlic-rubbed baguette, the bitter frisée with that runny, rich yolk. The tomatoes are just there to be there, a little hit of more acid and sweetness. This is a great salad to make family-style because it's a knife-and-fork salad. As you keep cutting and eating and working the salad, it really becomes a mash, but the frisée holds up.

To clean the endive, cut off any green leaves, keeping only the nice yellow, tender center. Remove this from the stem and soak in ice water for 10 minutes.

Line a plate with paper towels. In a small skillet over medium heat, fry the bacon until lightly browned, 5 to 10 minutes. Transfer to the plate.

Bring a shallow pot of water to a slight simmer. Add the vinegar and poach the eggs, roughly 4 minutes. Make sure the yolk stays nice and runny. Using a slotted spoon, remove the eggs from the water and transfer them to a a small bowl full of cold water.

Lightly salt the frisée and toss with your vinaigrette. Divide the greens among four plates, top each with a gooey egg, the bacon and tomato, and a few toasted baguette slices. Shower with pepper.

SERVES 4 COOL FRANCOPHILES
PREP TIME: 20 MINUTES

4 heads frisée (curly endive)

12 ounces thick-cut bacon, cut into ¼-inch pieces

1 tablespoon white vinegar

7 eggs

Kosher salt and freshly cracked black pepper

Bacon Vinaigrette Dressing (page 335)

2 tomatoes, seeded and diced

16 thin slices French baguette, lightly toasted and rubbed with a garlic clove

WARM POTATO SALAD

This recipe is me working through awakened childhood trauma because I remember when my mom made lame potato salad as a kid. I can still smell it. This is a hero dish and will blow the socks off anyone who eats it. Congratulations to everyone in therapy like I am conquering the traumas of their past.

Place the potatoes in a large pot of cold, salted water. Bring the water to a boil, then reduce the heat and simmer until the potatoes are fork-tender, 15 to 20 minutes. Drain the potatoes and let them cool slightly.

While the potatoes are simmering, let's mix our creamy dip. In a small bowl, combine the cream cheese and 2 tablespoons of the mustard. Set aside.

Place the cooled potatoes on a cutting board and, using the back of a clean pot, gently press them. In a saucepan, melt the butter over medium heat. Add the smashed potatoes and cook until golden brown, 5 to 10 minutes a side. Line a plate with paper towels. Transfer the seared potatoes along with any remaining butter in the pan to a large bowl.

Let's cook our bacon off in a cast-iron skillet set over low heat, until it's cooked to your desired crispiness. Set aside a paper towel-lined plate.

To the same bowl, add the vinegar, mustard, bacon, red onion, scallions, parsley, chives, dill, and kosher salt and pepper to taste. Gently toss everything together until the potatoes are well coated with the dressing; allow any of the larger potatoes to break naturally into smaller pieces. Adjust the seasoning with more salt and pepper. Then add a huge dollop of the creamy dip and make a small indent at the top with the back of your spoon to add the remaining teaspoon of mustard and pickled red onion. Drizzle with olive oil and finish with Maldon salt.

SERVES 6
PREP TIME: 1 HOUR

2 pounds fingerling potatoes

¼ cup unsalted butter

½ cup bacon lardons

¼ cup apple cider vinegar

2 tablespoons whole-grain Dijon mustard

½ cup small-diced red onion

¼ cup thinly sliced scallions

2 tablespoons chopped parsley

2 tablespoons chopped chives

1 tablespoon chopped dill

Kosher salt and freshly cracked black pepper

¼ cup pickled red onion

Olive oil, for drizzling

Maldon salt

CREAMY DIP

¼ cup cream cheese

2 tablespoons whole-grain Dijon mustard, plus 1 teaspoon for garnish

LEFTOVER STEAK SALAD

If you eat this a couple times a week and work out and eat good, you'll be ripped. I make this recipe often because I'm super fit and skinny now. This tastes pretty great and will make you feel good. If you really want to get bulk, don't even make the dressing; just eat it raw dawg with a ton of lemon. Get in the beef barn and work out those demons.

In a skillet over medium heat, warm the butter. Add the onion and sauté until it turns golden brown and caramelized. This may take about 20 minutes. Toss the cubed steak with the onions just until it heats through. Transfer the mixture to a large bowl before the steak begins to cook.

In the same bowl, add the brown rice, arugula, olive oil, lemon zest and juice, vinegar, and salt and pepper to taste. Toss gently until everything is combined. Adjust the seasoning as you see fit. You can either top the salad with the blue cheese dressing or leave it on the side for everyone to dress themselves. Garnish with a couple wedges of lemon.

SERVES 4

PREP TIME: 30 MINUTES

¼ cup unsalted butter

1 large sweet onion, thinly sliced

12 ounces leftover steak, cut into ½-inch cubes

2 cups cooked brown rice, room temperature

2 big handfuls arugula

¼ cup olive oil

Zest and juice of 1 lemon

¼ cup red wine vinegar

Kosher salt and freshly cracked black pepper

Blue Cheese Dressing (page 336)

Lemon wedges, for serving

TACO SALAD

This is another '80s-mom-zone weirdo salad, but it makes me happy, so let's fucking go. Remember when houses had carpets, and you had a TV that was 20 inches wide but weighed 3,832,900 pounds? You'd sit in front of it watching *Astro Boy* at five o'clock on Saturday mornings, or you'd go blow up G.I. Joes with firecrackers or run through the woods until it was dark out. Or ride bikes down some ravine and smoke your first smoke and barf everywhere and get made fun of and get pushed into the creek at the bottom of said ravine. This is the salad of those days. This is the salad of millennials but, like, '80s millennials. Like your dad using superglue instead of getting stitches millennials. This salad rips, and Thousand Island dressing is the king of the village. All together this rules. I love my mom and dad.

In a large skillet over medium-high heat, cook the ground beef until browned. Drain off any excess fat and add one of the taco seasoning packets and the water. Simmer until the water reduces and becomes saucy. Season with salt and black pepper to your liking. Set aside to cool slightly.

In a small bowl, mix your Thousand Island dressing with the remaining packet of taco seasoning.

In a large salad bowl, toss together your ground beef, tomatoes, pickled jalapeños, scallions, corn, beans, and avocados with your dressing. Add your corn chips and toss again. Add your chopped iceberg and toss again. Portion the salad equally on four plates and top with a heaping portion of shredded cheddar.

SERVES 4
PREP TIME: 25 MINUTES

1 pound ground beef

Two 1-ounce packets Old El Paso taco seasoning

⅔ cup water

Kosher salt and freshly cracked black pepper

½ cup your favorite Thousand Island dressing

1 cup cherry tomatoes, halved

¼ cup pickled jalapeños

4 scallions, thinly sliced

1 cup charred corn

½ cup drained and rinsed black beans

2 avocados, diced

2 large handfuls corn chips, crushed (I like a Frito)

1 head iceberg lettuce, chopped

1 heaping cup shredded cheddar cheese

PART III
SANDWICHES

We are going to try our best to understand what a sandwich is. We talk about it so much. The stupidest question I'm always asked is "Is a hot dog a sandwich?" Guess what? SHUT UP.

You know what is a sandwich? A sandwich. Shall we talk about sandwiches? Breads, fillings, meats, vegetables, spreads, sauces, oils. Is it grilled, panfried, baked, melted, or frozen? Is it on bread or in a pita or on a pancake? Is it wrapped in lettuce, in the middle of spinach tortillas, or crunched between portobello mushroom caps? Are these vessels to make sandwiches or just a way to ruin things? Is it just things within other things? Is a sandwich a salad? Is soup a sandwich?

Everyone has their first sandwich love. Is it a bologna sandwich? A grilled cheese? Butter and sugar sandwich? Lettuce and mayo sandwich? I still remember that Raymond Gianfrancesco used to come to school with the most fire Italian sandwiches. I couldn't even understand. He was showing up with prosciutto and mortadella sandwiches. It would blow my mind. And I was there with bologna and white bread, maybe a slice of American cheese, too, if I was lucky.

Still, my first sandwich love is a bologna sandwich. Bologna was a staple where I grew up in the Maritimes. It's an honest meat. I don't understand why bologna gets harped on so much. It's exactly the same as hot dogs, mortadella, or any other emulsified sausage. But for some reason, everyone would make fun of you for eating bologna because they would think you're poor. I love my bologna. I pride myself on eating bologna sandwiches. Also, in my first book, my bologna bowl was the recipe that connected with everyone the most. So suck it, losers. All the kids who made fun of me for eating bologna sandwiches, have you been on Jimmy Kimmel? Do you have an Emmy-nominated TV show? Shut up. I'm fueled by bologna. Bologna is for winners only.

My little brother Grizz's first sandwich love was lettuce and mayo sandwiches. When we were kids, that was the only thing he ate. And still to this day, it makes me wanna fucking barf all over the damn place. Imagine eating a sandwich that is just lettuce, mayo, and bread, Saran wrapped, thrown in a brown paper bag, sweating, with an apple on top smushing it. Grizz would just take it out and eat it, so soft and wet. I love you so much, Grizz, but that is disgusting. You see how mad that still makes me now? I need to work on myself. I love Grizz, and Grizz loves me, and we can't let this disgusting lettuce and mayo sandwich tear us apart, but holy fucking cow shit, a room-temp lettuce and mayo sandwich? COME ON, GRIZZ!

The sandwich has defined the way that we eat. We are excited about sandwiches. Sandwiches are the food of the world. You can throw a sandwich in your breast pocket or your purse. You can take it out at any time. Take a couple bites, put it away for later for a little nibble-nibble treat-treat. How many times have you shared a sandwich, going bite for bite with your best friend, sitting in a tree fort? I LOVE SANDWICHES!

We are going to celebrate a lot of iconic sandwiches. Waiting in line for a desirable Philly cheesesteak is as thrilling as eating one. The people you see coming from all over the world, waiting in line—it's very intimidating. Sometimes you feel like you're gonna mess up when you order, but when you get it right, you get handed that steamy log and open it up and that beef and cheese and the hot steaming bun goes right into your nostrils.

Then you're standing at the stove, frying bacon with your shirt off, making a BLT, willing to risk it all and splatter that hot, greasy bacon fat. Or walking into a Jewish deli and ordering a pastrami sandwich and matzo ball soup to go, eating them on a park bench in the Lower East Side. Getting sand in your jambon beurre on the beaches of Normandy. Eating a late-night shawarma in Copenhagen surrounded by a bunch of weirdo, rave-dancing Euro kids. These are the moments that we live for. These are the days of our lives. These are the people that we are.

In this final section of the book, we will be doing a deep dive into the best sandwiches. We are going all the way in. We are gonna be making iconic sandwiches, dessert sandwiches, breakfast sandwiches, sandwiches you've never thought of, sandwiches I've never thought of until now, some loved, some hated. I like making sandwiches for myself. I love making sandwiches for my friends, something fast and delicious that you can share with somebody in a small amount of time. Sandwiches are truly a beautiful thing. We are allowed to fly as high as we want, soar over the ocean. We can be as brave or as scared as we want, but at the end of the day, we're just making some sandwiches, everybody. And that's beautiful.

TACO SUBMARINE

To this day, my favorite restaurant is Robo Mart, a small gas station under the Peace Bridge on the Niagara River. They used to have a taco sub that was so insane it worked, and it made me happy. Cheesy Mexican pickled jalapeño beef. Texy mexy beefy. Cheesy sexy texy mixy mexy jalapeño beef. After a couple minutes it would relax you, and if you were like me and in high school on a BMX bike eating this in the woods, then you do what you gotta do. Life is not a straight line, but it is not fair if you don't get to have your cake and eat it too. The taco sub is that for me. It's a double-edged sword and double entendre, but it's always worth the fight.

The biggest thing is making this beef. It's so important. Get a large skillet really hot with no oil. Take the ground beef out of the pack and put it into the hot pan. Sear it like one big cheeseburger patty and let it fry up, about 10 minutes. Once it is a little smoky, using a flat wooden spatula, scrape the beef off the pan and chop it all up and break it down. Keep chopping with your spatula while it browns and cooks, about 5 minutes.

When the beef is completely browned, deglaze the pan with the water. Stir that in with the beef. Real quick. Dump in the magic powder (taco seasoning) and pickled jalapeños. Keep stirring until your whole house smells like magic and cook it out for 5 minutes max. Throw in the American cheese and stir until the cheese melts and is incorporated, about 2 minutes. Side note: in Canada we call this cheese processed cheese. It will become stinky cheesy texy mexy beefy. Turn off the beef heat. The residual heat will melt the cheese.

Take the bun. Don't toast it. Slice it open. Take a big spoonful of cheesy beef and throw three clumps of it into the soft sub bun. Throw half the onions, tomatoes, and lettuce on top, then drizzle with the dressing. Squirt some hot sauce all over it. Take your knife and squish it in. Wrap it in parchment paper. Look at the photo. Repeat with the other sub.

Slice the sub down the middle, then peel it all back and take a bite. I told you, the blue cheese dressing works. It's like eating Buffalo chicken. It's a Fort Erie thing. Fort Erie, baby.

SERVES 2
PREP TIME: 30 MINUTES

1 pound ground beef

1 cup water

Two 1-ounce packets spicy taco seasoning

½ cup pickled jalapeños

6 slices American cheese (the correct answer is Kraft singles)

Kosher salt and freshly cracked black pepper

2 submarine buns

1 white onion, thinly sliced

½ tomato, thinly sliced

½ head iceberg lettuce, thinly sliced

1 cup Rizzo's Wedge Salad Dressing (page 125)

Tapatío or Frank's RedHot sauce, for serving

194 SOUPS, SALADS, SANDWICHES

ROASTED SQUASH and MOZZARELLA GRILLED CHEESE with HONEY and BEE POLLEN

Our good friend honey is back. Roasted squash and mozzarella are a match made in heaven, but honey opens the gates and allows both to join in harmony. The roasted squash is sweet but not too sweet. The bee pollen will bring some lovely earthy tones and texture. Grilled cheeses that are cool like this are usually so annoying because what can actually beat a normal grilled cheese, but this one is fair game, I think? What do you think? Leave a comment down below! Subscribe. Turn on that notification bell. Oh wait, this is a book, so just make it and love yourself.

First, we're going to make the persimmon chutney. In a large pot over medium-high heat, combine the apple cider vinegar, rice wine vinegar, water, brown sugar, apples, and persimmons. Simmer until the apples and persimmons are tender, 20 minutes.

Remove the pan from the heat and use a hand blender to blend everything into a chunky sauce. Return the pot to the stove and simmer over medium heat for an additional 20 minutes. Once you see the chutney begin to thicken, with big bubbles floating to the surface, remove it from the heat and allow it to cool slightly. While it is still hot, mix in the ginger, pink pepper, and kosher salt. Let cool completely, then transfer to an airtight container and refrigerate until needed. You can make this a day or two before you make your grilled cheese.

Preheat your oven to 400°F. Line a baking sheet with parchment paper. Cut the acorn squash in half lengthwise and remove the seeds. Place the squash halves on the prepared baking sheet. Drizzle olive oil over the squash halves, making sure to coat them evenly. Sprinkle the kosher salt over the squash and stuff the cavity of each half with the garlic and thyme. Roast the acorn squash until the flesh is tender and easily pierced with a fork, 40 to 45 minutes. Remove the squash from the oven and allow it to cool slightly. Once cool enough to handle, peel the squash and cut the flesh into thin slices.

Heat a large skillet or griddle over medium-low heat. Make sure you have all the ingredients we need to build these sandwiches at hand so we don't burn our bread. Take two slices of sourdough bread and spread butter on one side of each slice. Place buttered-side down on the skillet or griddle. Add a big spoonful of chutney on both inner sides, and then layer a few slices of roasted acorn squash on top of one slice of bread. Tear fresh mozzarella and place it on top of the squash. Drizzle the honey over the cheese. Sprinkle some bee pollen on top. Season with a sprinkle of Maldon salt and black pepper. Place the other slice of bread, buttered-side up, on top and squash to create a sandwich. Grill the sandwich until the bread is golden brown and the cheese has melted, 2 to 3 minutes per side. Remove the sandwich from the skillet or griddle and allow it to cool for a minute. Repeat the instructions to make the three other sandwiches. Cut each sandwich in half and serve with a ramekin of persimmon chutney for dipping.

SERVES 4

PREP TIME: 1½ HOURS

PERSIMMON CHUTNEY

1½ cups apple cider vinegar

1½ cups rice wine vinegar

1 cup water

1 cup packed light brown sugar

2 Granny Smith apples, peeled and diced

2 Fuyu persimmons, peeled and diced

1 teaspoon grated ginger

1 teaspoon ground pink peppercorns

1 teaspoon kosher salt

2 acorn squashes

Olive oil

1 tablespoon kosher salt

2 garlic cloves, thinly sliced

½ bunch thyme

Eight 1-inch-thick slices sourdough country loaf

¼ cup salted butter, room temperature

1 pound ball fresh mozzarella cheese

¼ cup clover honey

1 teaspoon bee pollen

Maldon salt and freshly cracked black pepper

FRIED SPROUTING CAULIFLOWER

This is a way to eat fried cauliflower and make it a real meal. It'll blow your socks and ankles and shins clear off. Please make this. I ate half of this on the shoot and it was so good.

Trim the tough ends of the cauliflower and discard them. In a large bowl, whisk together the buttermilk and salt. Add the cauliflower to the buttermilk mixture and make sure it is fully coated. Cover the bowl with plastic wrap and refrigerate for at least 2 hours to allow the cauliflower to marinate.

Preheat your oven to broil. Place the jalapeños on a baking sheet and broil until the skin is blistered and charred, 4 to 6 minutes. Remove the jalapeños from the oven and let them cool. Once cooled, peel and slice the jalapeños. Set them aside. In a skillet, melt the butter over medium heat. Add the onion to the skillet and cook, stirring occasionally, until the onions are caramelized and golden brown, 10 to 12 minutes. Mix the roasted jalapeños with the caramelized onions and set aside.

Now, make your spicy mayonnaise. Remove the seeds and stems from the pickled peppers and pepperoncini. In a food processor, blend together the pickled peppers, pepperoncini, ketchup, vinegar, paprika, salt, and garlic powder. Transfer to a bowl, add the mayonnaise, and whisk together until thoroughly combined. Place in an airtight container in the fridge and store for up to 1 week.

Now, let's make the cheese sauce. In a medium saucepan, melt your butter over medium heat. Next whisk in the flour and make a little roux, about 10 minutes. After it starts turning a little brown, slowly whisk in your milk. Then turn off the heat and add in your cheese and whisk until it is melted. Put the lid on and save until it's time for the big sandwich show.

Make the cornmeal batter. In a large bowl, whisk together the all-purpose flour, semolina flour, cornmeal, garlic powder, onion powder, smoked paprika, cayenne, and salt. Gradually add the water to the dry ingredients while whisking continuously until a smooth batter is formed. Set the cornmeal batter aside.

To finish, take the marinated cauliflower out of the buttermilk, allowing any excess liquid to drip off. In a large bowl, place the flour and dredge the cauliflower in it, dusting off any excess. Dip the dredged cauliflower in the cornmeal batter, making sure it is evenly coated. Set on a wire rack while heating your oil.

Line a plate with paper towels. In a Dutch oven over medium-high heat, heat the vegetable oil until it's 350°F. Add the cornmeal-battered cauliflower in batches and fry until golden and crispy, turning occasionally, about 30 seconds. Using tongs, remove the fried cauliflower and transfer to the paper towel–lined plate. Season with a sprinkle of salt and the lemon zest.

Preheat a skillet or griddle over medium heat. Butter each slice of brioche and toast both sides. When you're ready to assemble, add your spicy mayo to the base, then the onion mixture, your fried cauliflower, and cheese sauce and top with the other slice of toast. Garnish with a cube of honeycomb on top.

SERVES 4
PREP TIME: 12 HOURS

2 heads sprouting cauliflower
4 cups buttermilk
1 teaspoon kosher salt
2 jalapeños
2 tablespoons unsalted butter, plus more to butter the brioche
1 sweet onion, thinly sliced
2 cups all-purpose flour
4 cups vegetable oil, for frying
Zest of 1 lemon
Eight 1-inch-thick slices brioche
4 cubes honeycomb

SPICY MAYONNAISE

6 pieces pickled cherry pepper
6 pieces pickled pepperoncini
¼ cup ketchup
1 tablespoon white vinegar
1 teaspoon Spanish paprika
½ teaspoon kosher salt
¼ teaspoon garlic powder
2 cups mayonnaise

CHEESE SAUCE

2 tablespoons unsalted butter
2 tablespoons all-purpose flour
1 cup milk
1 cup shredded Monterey Jack cheese

CORNMEAL BATTER

1⅓ cups all-purpose flour
1⅓ cups semolina flour
½ cup cornmeal
½ teaspoon garlic powder
½ teaspoon onion powder
1 teaspoon sweet smoked paprika
¼ teaspoon cayenne
1 teaspoon kosher salt
3 cups water

SUN-WARMED TOMATO

This is the fucking GOAT, period.

When it turns into tomato time in the summer at Blue Goose, I feel so happy and free. Tomatoes warmed by the sun truly do taste different from the stuff you get at the grocery store. This sandwich is all about simplicity. The tomato has to be good because it's just so naked and out there. If you get grocery store rubbery crap, this sandwich will taste like rubbery crap.

Lay your tomato slices out onto a tray and season them well with salt and pepper. Squeeze your lemon over the top of the tomatoes. Let them marinate for 10 minutes.

Spread the mayonnaise on one side of both slices of bread. On one slice of bread, stack the tomatoes at least two layers high, then top your sandwich with the second slice of bread.

Using a bread knife, carefully cut the sandwich in half and eat immediately.

SERVES 1

PREP TIME: 15 MINUTES

2 very ripe heirloom tomatoes, almost bursting, sliced into ½-inch pieces

Kosher salt and freshly cracked black pepper

1 lemon

¼ cup mayonnaise

2 slices artisanal thick-cut white bread

GRILLED CHEESE

How can I even capture the importance of this sandwich? If you came home from school for lunch and your mom was making these bad boys, the whole world was right, no matter how wrong it was before. The smell alone. We all know that smell of butter frying with that shit white bread toasting and the cheese melting. The smell can't be duplicated.

I remember playing *Contra* on Sega, sitting cross-legged on the floor with my brothers, and eating grilled cheeses. It was one of the greatest feelings in the world. Those buttery, crumb-covered fingers all over your controller. Waiting to play. Watching my brothers play or eating with one hand and trying to play with the other, which was impossible.

I would always eat two, obviously. The first one with no ketchup to feel the full flavor and effect. Then the second always dipped in ketchup. No matter how full you are or wherever you are in the world, you have room for one of these. God fucking bless grilled cheese sandwiches.

Preheat your oven to 350°F. The key to a grilled cheese is to also put it in the oven.

Butter one side of each slice of bread.

In a heavy pan like a Matheson cast iron over medium-low heat, put your two slices of bread, buttered-side down. Top each slice with 2 slices of cheese. After it melts a tiny bit, press the cheese ends together. Put the sandwich on a baking sheet and into the oven. Get it nice and golden brown. Flip the sandwich every 2 to 3 minutes. Flip flip flip, it's oozy, it's cheesy, and the bread is nice and crusty. It should only be in there for 6 to 8 minutes total.

Take it out. Cut the grilled cheese in half, right down the middle. No diagonal fancy-pants stuff here.

SERVES 1
PREP TIME: 15 MINUTES

Margarine or butter, room temperature, for buttering your bread

2 slices white bread

4 slices American cheese

CROQUE MADAME

At La Palette during brunch, we made a lot of croque madames. Man oh man, I still love these French bastards. Croque monsieur is OK, but the madame is what everyone needs. Why would you get a cheesy roasted ham sandwich that doesn't have an egg on it? If you can put an egg on it, put an egg on it. It's that simple. Also, the mornay sauce will really tie the whole room together here. Only home runs in this fucking book. This, with a light, bitter salad, is the all-time brunch move.

Make your mornay sauce. Set a heavy-bottomed saucepan over medium heat and add your butter. Once it is melted and bubbling, add your flour and vigorously work it with a wooden spoon to make a roux, 5 minutes. You want to cook the flour and butter mixture but not get any color. Turn down your heat if this happens. Slowly add in your milk, ½ cup at a time, to prevent your sauce from becoming lumpy. Whisk constantly and allow the mixture to simmer before you add your next ½ cup of milk. Once all your milk is added, slowly whisk in the cheese. Season with the mustard, nutmeg, and salt and pepper to taste. Remove from the heat and allow to cool completely. The sauce should coat the back of a spoon when it's done.

Preheat your broiler on high.

Build your sandwiches. Cut the crusts off the bread. Spread a generous layer of your mornay sauce on one side of each slice. Evenly divide your ham among 4 slices of your coated bread. Top each with ¼ cup of the cheese, then add your other piece of bread, and the rest of the cheese. Broil for 7 to 10 minutes on a baking sheet until that cheese begins to really transform but not burn.

While that is going, in a large cast-iron pan over medium-low heat, melt the butter. Add your eggs and cook them low and slow until the egg whites are set—no browning.

Top each sandwich with a sunny-side up egg and 1 teaspoon of the chives.

SERVES 4

PREP TIME: 1 HOUR

MORNAY SAUCE

2 tablespoons salted butter

1 heaping tablespoon all-purpose flour

2 cups whole milk

2 cups shredded Emmental cheese

1 teaspoon Dijon mustard

Pinch of ground nutmeg

Kosher salt and freshly cracked black pepper

8 thick slices challah bread

1 pound freshly sliced French ham

2 cups shredded Emmental cheese

2 teaspoons unsalted butter

4 eggs

4 teaspoons thinly sliced chives

MATTY *and* TRISHY TUNA MELT

This is our love language. There are a lot of days when you're like, "What the fuck are we gonna eat for lunch?" And you know that moment when both parties are so hungry they're furious with each other. No one can make a decision. No one can even think straight and you both turn on each other like a pack of hyenas. But then we lock eyes and say the words "Tuna melts?" And then that beautiful love spark starts glowing. We both run to each other and just say, "I'm sorry." That's the power of a tuna melt.

In a large bowl, add the celery, pickle, red onion, and tuna. Fork it all together to break it up and combine. Add the right amount (50:50 split) of mayonnaise and Miracle Whip. Whip it and smash it around with salt and pepper to taste.

Preheat your broiler on high. Toast your bread, then lather each slice with margarine on one side. Spoon your tuna mix onto each slice of bread. Pat it down and make it nice and flat. The key to a good tuna melt is for the layer of tuna mix to be the same thickness as the toast. Then put on a glorious slice of that godlike Kraft single. Orange god fucked cheese. Put it in the oven on a baking sheet and watch it. Don't walk away, and don't let it burn. Don't ruin this. Let it just get a little warm.

Take it out and eat it with a knife and fork like an adult. I eat mine with Lay's Classic chips on the side and a pickle or a hot pepperoncini. This is me and Trishy's favorite meal. I look at her and say, "Hey, I love making you a tuna melt." Then the oceans part and we start fresh.

SERVES TRISHY AND ME
PREP TIME: 15 MINUTES

½ celery rib, diced

1 dill pickle, diced

¼ red onion, diced

Two 5-ounce cans good canned tuna in water, drained

¼ cup mayonnaise

¼ cup Miracle Whip

Kosher salt and freshly cracked black pepper

4 slices Wonder Bread

2 tablespoons margarine

4 slices American cheese (the correct answer is Kraft singles)

BLT

I always say whatever sandwich I'm eating is the best, but this is my favorite sandwich most of the time. I love it so much. Don't tell the other sandwiches. A shitty diner BLT can be the best and worst sandwich of all time, at the same time. We all know that. But a real BLT with the right amount of salt and pepper and perfect tomatoes and crispy bacon and toasted bread? Holy fuck town, we in the money. I wish people only the best BLTs from here on out, OK?

This is my method for cooking the best bacon with the least amount of splatter. Start by putting your bacon into a large cold pan. Lay the bacon out in a cross-hatching pattern: Place your bacon strips side by side along the base of your pan, and once the bottom is completely covered, start the second layer of bacon on top by placing them in the opposite direction. Use the whole packet!

Set your pan over medium heat. As the pan heats up slowly, the bacon will start steaming and rendering the fat. Keep cooking until your bacon is crispy, 10 to 15 minutes. Set the bacon on a paper towel to soak up the excess fat.

Toast your bread. Spread 1 tablespoon of mayonnaise on each slice of bread. Add salt and pepper to taste. On one slice, add 3 of the lettuce leaves, then add two slices of tomato and season with salt and pepper. Add another slice of tomato, season, and repeat, dividing the tomato between both sandwiches. Place 6 slices of bacon on top of your tomatoes and top with your second slice of toast. Repeat with the other two slices of bread.

Cut in half and enjoy.

SERVES 2
PREP TIME: 20 MINUTES

One 12-ounce package bacon
4 slices thick-cut white bread
4 tablespoons mayonnaise
Kosher salt and freshly cracked black pepper
6 butter lettuce leaves
2 heirloom tomatoes, sliced

STRACCIATELLA DI BUFALA, CAPONATA, SUN-DRIED TOMATOES, CHERRY PEPPERS, *and* BASIL

Stracciatella is the cottage cheese of Italy. It is just cheese curds with some milk added back in. I love cottage cheese. It's pretty underrated and hated, but it's been getting better PR and marketing like stracciatella. What's the deal? These are facts. If you want to believe it or not, that's up to you, but this is a truth machine. Also, now that I'm thinking and writing this, it's like, *Why didn't I just use cottage cheese? I'm such a loser right now; I should have used cottage cheese.* Maybe in the YouTube video I make to promote this book and dish I'll use cottage cheese to pander to the algorithm. Try to make this dish with cottage cheese, but it could end up being horrible because even though cottage cheese is good, stracciatella is probably better, and that's why I did think of using that instead of cottage cheese. Any fucking way, this sandwich is amazing, and the focaccia is lights out. Sun-dried tomatoes are back, by the way. I'm calling it now. Not those rubber band horrible ones but the ones we make. Sun-dried tomatoes are going to have their day in the sun! Again!

Preheat your broiler on high.

Slice the focaccia horizontally and drizzle olive oil on the insides of the focaccia. Toast until golden brown, 3 to 5 minutes.

In a small bowl, mix the cherry bomb peppers and sun-dried tomatoes with a tablespoon of the sun-dried tomato oil. Set aside.

Spread half of the stracciatella di bufala on one side of the focaccia and the rest on the other half. Season the whole thing with a big pinch of Maldon salt and a couple cracks of black pepper. On the bottom layer of each sandwich, add your tomato and pepper mix and basil. Spread your caponata. Then place the top layer of the sandwich, slice into quarters, and serve.

SERVES 4

PREP TIME: 20 MINUTES

One 10 by 13-inch loaf focaccia

Olive oil

4 pickled cherry bomb peppers, seeded and sliced

2 cups chopped sun-dried tomatoes in olive oil

1 pound stracciatella di bufala

Maldon salt and freshly cracked black pepper

1 bunch basil, picked and torn

1 cup caponata (bought from your favorite Italian deli)

CLUBHOUSE

Eating a club sandwich at a diner is a delight. The presentation has a very royal vibe. Even a bad club sandwich is special. I like to add pickle and cheese, so this is kinda a club deluxe. I also like mayo on the side because sometimes I want to spread just a little extra on top of a bite like a bad boy. Every once in a while I'll get it with a side Greek salad, which is a huge flex. A club sandwich with side fries and gravy is all-time one of the greatest meals in the world. I truly think any day where you're sitting down with some friends and eating club sandwiches is a strong-ass day.

First, we're going to make bacon. Line a plate with paper towels. This is the weirdest way to make bacon. It makes my friends uncomfortable. Add the bacon to a cold cast-iron skillet (use that Matheson if you are not a poser) in a cross-hatching pattern. The bacon fat will begin to render. Cook until the bacon is crispy, moving it around so there are no burned bits on the bottom. Set on the paper towel–lined plate to drain.

While the bacon is cooking away, preheat your oven to 400°F.

Coat your chicken breast in a little bit of olive oil, then season it with salt and pepper. Bake on a baking sheet until the internal temperature reaches 160°F, 20 minutes. Let it rest until cool, 30 minutes. Slice your chicken breast against the grain into nice little strips.

Toast the bread until golden brown. Spread a thin layer of mayonnaise on one side of two of the slices of toast. For the third slice, spread a thin layer of mayonnaise on both sides—this is going to be your middle layer. Place half of your lettuce on the first slice of bread. Season your tomatoes with salt and pepper and add them to the sandwich along with all your bacon. Then add your middle piece of bread and top with the rest of your lettuce, the cheddar, and chicken breast. Top with the last slice of bread, mayo side down. Garnish with the pickle.

Throw four long toothpicks in and use a sharp knife to cut the sandwich diagonally into quarters. Serve immediately.

SERVES 1
PREP TIME: 1 HOUR

6 slices bacon

8 ounces cooked chicken breast

Olive oil

Kosher salt and freshly cracked black pepper

3 slices thick-cut white bread

½ cup mayonnaise

3 iceberg lettuce leaves

2 tomatoes, sliced

2 slices cheddar cheese

1 dill pickle

Mayonnaise, for serving

CHICKEN PARM

This is a thick and juicy parmesan. Chicken parmesans are a staple of cities and small towns: good, hot, ooey, and gooey. They're even better cold, hours later, after it all sets into a savory cake. It's the same as eating baked ziti out of the fridge like Tony. You can have roasted sweet peppers, hot peppers, even some fried eggplant as a topper. Maybe add mushrooms or onions. The pepper relish makes for a very even and delicious mouth sensation that will make everyone happy. The bun is very important as well. You need a crusty hard on the outside but soft on the inside roll that holds up. The best chicken parms are from California Sandwiches in Toronto at the OG location on Claremont. These are not anything like those, but anyone reading should definitely get a couple of parms from there because they are absolute fire. I like to get them dry, which means they don't dip the cutlets in the sauce. Then I get marinara on the side and dip, which is a pro move.

First, we're going to make our marinara. In a medium pot over medium heat, add the olive oil and onion and cook until the onion is translucent, about 5 minutes. Add the garlic and cook until slightly golden brown, about 5 minutes. Add the tomatoes, sugar, basil, and salt and pepper to taste. Give it a good stir and cook for 5 more minutes. Remove from the heat and let it rest until ready to use.

Make the hot relish. Preheat your broiler on high. Place a wire rack in a baking sheet. Add the Italian peppers to the rack and broil until the peppers are dark and roasted, then flip and repeat on the other side. This should take 10 to 15 minutes. Add the roasted peppers to a heatproof bowl and cover it with plastic wrap to steam the peppers and wait 20 minutes. Remove from the bowl, peel the skin off the peppers, and cut them into little pieces. Transfer the peppers to a medium bowl and season with the vinegar, olive oil, lemon juice, parsley, salt, and pepper. Stir until combined and set aside.

Set up your breading station. Fill one bowl with the flour and season with salt and black pepper, another with the whisked eggs, and another with the panko. Dip each piece of chicken first in the flour, then the eggs, then the panko. Place on a wire rack set over a baking sheet. In a cast-iron pan over medium-high heat, fill the pot halfway up with olive oil and warm until it hits 350ºF. Add the breaded chicken to the oil and cook in batches until golden brown, 2 to 3 minutes. Flip and repeat on the other side, 2 to 3 minutes. Transfer to a clean wire rack on a baking sheet and season with salt.

Spread the tomato sauce on top of the chicken. Top with a few slices of fresh mozzarella and grated Parmesan. Broil on high until the cheese is melted, 5 to 10 minutes. Add the chicken to the buns and top with hot pepper relish. Enjoy!

SERVES 2
PREP TIME: 1 HOUR

MARINARA SAUCE

¼ cup olive oil

½ yellow onion, chopped

4 garlic cloves, sliced

One 14-ounce can crushed tomatoes

2 tablespoons sugar

6 basil leaves

Kosher salt and freshly cracked black pepper

HOT RELISH

8 long hot Italian peppers

2 tablespoons red wine vinegar

2 tablespoons olive oil

Juice of ½ lemon

10 parsley sprigs, picked and chopped

Kosher salt and freshly cracked black pepper

2 cups all-purpose flour

Kosher salt and freshly cracked black pepper

2 eggs, whisked

2 cups panko bread crumbs

4 boneless, skinless chicken breasts

Olive oil, for frying

8 ounces fresh mozzarella, sliced into 4 pieces

¼ cup grated Parmesan cheese

4 kaiser rolls, halved

BEER-BATTERED HADDOCK

This is a bizarro hot turkey sandwich. When you have your protein ripping hot and then pour some hot thick gravy or chowder on top. That's a unique thing and having been born on the East Coast, I can't help myself; in my blood are hot turkey sandwiches, fried fish, flour-based gravy, and frozen peas. This is just fried fish on toast with a beautiful, creamy pea-filled chowder instead of gravy. Like, chowder is just gravy? Or is that just stew? I'm so confused again. This dish will light you up, and you should eat it while watching *Road to Avonlea* under a knitted blanket that Nan made years ago.

First, we're going to triple-cook the potato wedges. Place the potatoes into a large pot of salted water and bring it to a boil. Cook until the potatoes just begin to feel fork-tender, 8 to 10 minutes. Drain and spread out on a baking sheet lined with a dish towel. Cool completely in the fridge before moving on to the next step.

Heat the vegetable oil in a large, deep pot over medium-high heat until it reaches 325°F. Add the potato wedges and cook until they begin to crisp up but are not yet golden, 6 to 8 minutes. Transfer the partially cooked wedges to a wire rack to cool completely, then transfer the rack to a freezer overnight. Cover and leave the oil on the stove.

The next day, we're going to start by making the beer batter. In a large bowl, combine the flour, cornstarch, baking powder, and salt. Slowly pour in the beer while whisking continuously until the batter is smooth, about 1 minute. Keep this in the fridge until needed, don't push it beyond 36 hours. The colder and fresher the batter is, the better the fry you will get.

Remove the frozen chips from the rack in the freezer. Line a plate with paper towels. Heat the same pot of oil over medium-high heat until it reaches 375°F. Return the cooked chips to the hot oil and fry until they turn golden brown and crispy, 4 to 6 minutes. Remove the wedges from the oil and place them on the paper towel–lined plate to drain. Season with salt while they're still hot.

We're going to use the same pot of oil to fry the haddock fillets. Line a second plate with paper towels. Lightly dust each fillet with flour. Then dip each fillet into the batter, ensuring it is fully coated. Make sure the temperature of the oil is still 375°F. Gently place the coated fillets into the hot oil, one at a time, and fry until they are golden brown and crispy, 3 to 4 minutes per side. Transfer the fried fish fillets to the paper towel–lined plate to drain.

CONTINUED

SERVES 4
PREP TIME: 1 DAY

6 Yukon gold potatoes, cut into wedges

8 cups vegetable oil

Kosher salt

BEER BATTER

1 cup all-purpose flour, plus more for dusting

1 tablespoon cornstarch

1 teaspoon baking powder

1 teaspoon kosher salt

1½ cups lager-style beer

Four 6-ounce haddock fillets

4 cups clam chowder (page 39)

2 cups frozen green peas

Four 1-inch-thick slices milk bread

Coleslaw (page 336), for serving

BEER-BATTERED HADDOCK CONTINUED

Heat the clam chowder in a medium saucepan over medium heat until it begins to simmer. Add the peas and stir well. Allow them to cook for a few minutes until heated through. Turn the heat down to low and keep the chowder warm while you prepare the rest of the dish.

Toast the milk bread slices until they are golden and crispy. Place a slice of toast on each plate. Lay a fried haddock fillet on top of each slice of bread. Spoon a generous amount of the warm clam chowder and peas mixture over the fish fillets, allowing it to cascade over the sides of the bread. Serve with a side of triple-cooked potato wedges and coleslaw.

JERK SHRIMP SALAD

Going to college in Etobicoke and living in Rexdale, you get to eat some really good Jamaican. I lived off beef patties and coco buns my first year of college. That and Taco Bell. I'm very thankful for the diversity in Toronto and being able to eat so much food made by people from all over the world. Toronto has a massive Caribbean and Trinidadian population, as well as Sri Lankan. So much good Indian, it is insane. The food thrives and the flavors pour out into the communities. The idea for this recipe came from a curry shrimp pumpkin roti that I had in Scarborough. I never had anything like that before, and it clicked into an idea to do a broiled jerk shrimp sandwich on a coco bun. It worked out really well.

Let's start by making the jerk marinade. In a food processor, combine the thyme, scotch bonnets, cilantro, parsley, bell pepper, garlic, ginger, tamarind paste, soy sauce, ketchup, citrus zests and juices, allspice, cloves, nutmeg, salt, and black pepper and blend until smooth. Transfer half the mixture to an airtight container and store it until needed in the fridge. Pour the other half of the marinade into a Ziploc bag and add the shrimp, making sure the shrimp are evenly coated. Transfer to the fridge to marinate for 2 hours.

Preheat your broiler to high. Line a baking sheet with parchment paper. Place the marinated shrimp on the prepared baking sheet and broil on both sides until they are slightly charred and cooked through, 6 to 7 minutes total. Allow these to cool for 10 minutes.

In a small bowl, combine the cilantro and scallions.

To assemble, warm your coco buns in a microwave for 15 seconds. Split them open and place a generous amount of the vinegar slaw on the bottom of each bun.

In a medium bowl, toss your cooled shrimp with 4 tablespoons of your remaining jerk marinade (the rest can be frozen for 1 month for another use) and place half on each sandwich. Add the scallions and cilantro salad and top with the other bun.

SERVES 2
PREP TIME: 2½ HOURS

JERK MARINADE
½ bunch thyme, leaves picked
2 scotch bonnets, seeded
1 bunch cilantro
1 bunch parsley
1 green bell pepper
6 garlic cloves
One 1-inch piece ginger
2 tablespoons tamarind paste
¼ cup soy sauce
2 tablespoons ketchup
Zest and juice of 3 limes
Zest and juice of 1 lemon
Zest and juice of 2 navel oranges
1 tablespoon ground allspice
½ teaspoon ground cloves
¼ teaspoon ground nutmeg
1 tablespoon kosher salt
1 tablespoon freshly cracked black pepper

½ pound shrimp, shelled and deveined
½ bunch cilantro, picked
2 scallions, thinly sliced lengthwise
2 coconut bread buns
Vinegar Slaw (page 337)

SALMON KATSU SANDO

Salmon katsu could be a nightmare, but cooking it a little under temperature, like a true medium, is key. No one wants squeaky salmon. No one. That's why everyone uses white fish for frying even though salmon is so fatty. People normally hammer it and it just renders out and becomes squeak town. But this is the perfect salmon; if you cook it right, it will be everything and more. Fuck it up and suffer the consequences.

Let's start by pickling your daikon. In a small saucepan over medium heat, combine your sugar, water, salt, and vinegar. Bring the mixture up to a boil and, once the sugar and salt have dissolved, remove from the heat and put your daikon in. Let it cool, then put it in the fridge for a minimum of 2 hours.

Prepare your salmon katsu. Set up three shallow bowls for your breading station: one with the flour, one with the whisked eggs, and one with the panko. Dip each piece of salmon first in the flour, then the eggs, then the panko. Make sure each salmon piece is completely coated. The best method is to have one wet hand and one dry hand. Alternatively, you can use a fork to pick up the salmon and move it around.

Line a plate with paper towels. Heat 4 inches of oil in a Dutch oven over medium-high heat until it reaches 350°F. Gently place the salmon pieces in the hot oil and fry until golden brown, 1½ minutes per side, then transfer them to the paper-towel lined plate to drain. Season both sides with salt.

Place your salmon on one slice of bread, then add a thin layer of tonkatsu sauce and Kewpie mayo and top with the cabbage, daikon, and another slice of bread. Cut all the crusts off, slice the sandwich in half, and serve cut-side up.

SERVES 2

PREP TIME: 3 HOURS

PICKLED DAIKON

1 cup sugar

1 cup water

1 tablespoon kosher salt

1 cup rice vinegar

¼ daikon, thinly sliced

1 cup all-purpose flour

3 eggs, whisked

1 cup panko

Two 5-ounce salmon fillets

Canola oil, for frying

Kosher salt

Four 1-inch-thick slices milk bread or brioche

2 tablespoons tonkatsu sauce

2 tablespoons Kewpie mayonnaise

¼ head green cabbage, sliced as thinly as possible (about 2 cups)

¼ cup white pickled daikon, sliced as thinly as possible

SHRIMP BURGER

My kids love SpongeBob, but I still have never seen a Krabby Patty. I guess I have Olympic selective hearing or vision, because I can't recall a damn thing my children have watched. It's not that I don't care what they are watching, but Baby Shark or any of that mind-heroin TV doesn't sink in at all. My brain just can't absorb that bullshit. So no Krabby Patty, but this shrimp burger is very easy to make and it's delicious. It's probably not for kids 'cause they would hate it, so make it for you and your buddies. I made a version of this forever ago with Babish and Alvin on *The Burger Show* and I won the competition, lol.

If you are a functioning adult, try to make the wasabi mayonnaise the night before so the wasabi has time to permeate the mayonnaise. In a bowl, combine the Kewpie mayonnaise, Hellmann's mayonnaise, and wasabi paste. Whisk vigorously to ensure there are no lumps of wasabi and set aside. You can store this in an airtight container in the fridge for up to 1 week.

Make the shrimp patties. In a food processor, blend the shrimp, ground pork back fat, fish sauce, Thai chile, white pepper, smoked paprika, and salt until well combined. Shape the mixture into 4 equal-size patties. Cover them and let them rest in the fridge for at least 1 hour and at most overnight to set.

Preheat a large skillet over medium-high heat. Season the shrimp patties with salt and pepper. Add the shrimp patties to the skillet and cook until they are cooked through and have a nice char, 3 to 4 minutes per side. One minute before they are finished cooking, top each piece with a slice of American cheese and allow it to melt.

Meanwhile, in a separate medium pan over medium heat, melt the butter. Place the burger buns cut-side down in the pan and toast them, about 2 minutes

To assemble the burger, spread a generous amount of wasabi mayonnaise on the bottom and top bun. On the bottom bun, add your onion and 3 pickle slices. Then top with a grilled shrimp patty, cilantro, and your top bun. Repeat with the other burgers.

SERVES 4
PREP TIME: 1½ HOURS

WASABI MAYONNAISE

1 cup Kewpie mayonnaise

1 cup Hellmann's mayonnaise

2 tablespoons wasabi paste

SHRIMP PATTIES

1 pound shrimp, peeled and deveined

5 ounces ground pork back fat

1 tablespoon fish sauce

1 Thai green chile, thinly sliced

¼ teaspoon ground white pepper

½ teaspoon smoked paprika

½ teaspoon kosher salt, plus more for seasoning

Freshly cracked black pepper

4 slices American cheese

2 tablespoons unsalted butter

4 sesame seed burger buns

1 white onion, thinly sliced into rounds

3 dill pickles, thinly sliced lengthwise

1 bunch cilantro, picked

BAKE *and* SHARK

I've only eaten these once in my life and it was a mind-blow. I've thought about it a lot. I shot an episode about the incredible Caribana festival celebrating Carribbean culture in Toronto for Vice years and years ago. I was invited into a beautiful home and shown how to make fresh bakes, which is very similar to fry bread or bannock or even a milk bun. This is the perfect fried fish sandwich (even though they use shark and it's obvs named after shark, but we aren't doing shark as we don't live in an area that fishes for shark). I want to eat one of these right now. Also, it's kinda cool, you could make these bakes smaller or bigger if you want. But this is a fried fish killer. This is the full meal-deal version with the pineapple and tomatoes with the slaw. Have at it and share the love.

Let's start by making our buns. In a small pot over medium-low heat, combine the milk and water and heat until it's just above body temperature. Add the yeast and 2 tablespoons of the sugar and let it sit in a warm place until it's foamy and fragrant, about 20 minutes.

Oil a bowl and set aside. In the bowl of a stand mixer fitted with the whisk attachment, whisk the eggs on medium-high speed until fluffy and pale in color. Reduce the speed to medium and slowly pour in the oil until the mixture is thoroughly combined. Reduce the speed to low and slowly add in the yeast mixture and the salt. Turn off the mixer and replace the whisk attachment with the dough hook.

With the mixer on medium speed, slowly add the flour until the dough is completely combined and slightly tacky. Transfer the dough to the oiled bowl, cover it with a kitchen towel, and allow it to proof in a warm area for at least 1 hour.

Next, let's make the green chile marinade. In a food processor, combine the scotch bonnets, jalapeños, bell pepper, cilantro, parsley, garlic, ginger, citrus zests and juices, salt, and black pepper and blend until smooth. Transfer the mixture to an airtight container and add the fish, making sure it's evenly coated. Let it marinate in the fridge for 30 minutes.

Make the fish batter. Sift 1 cup of the flour into a large bowl, then add the salt and sugar. Pour the beer in slowly, stirring continuously, until it's fully incorporated into the batter. It should have a smooth consistency that's thick enough to stick to the fish. Let the batter rest for 10 minutes.

Prepare a plate with the remaining 1 cup flour. Dredge each piece of fish into the flour, then dip it into the batter, ensuring it's fully coated.

CONTINUED

SERVES 4
PREP TIME: 2½ HOURS

BUNS

2 cups whole milk

1 cup water

3 tablespoons instant yeast

1 cup plus 2 tablespoons sugar

4 eggs

1 cup canola oil, plus more to oil the bowl and to fry the buns

2 teaspoons salt

8½ cups all-purpose flour

GREEN CHILE MARINADE

2 scotch bonnets, seeded

2 jalapeños, seeded

1 green bell pepper

1 bunch cilantro

1 bunch parsley

6 garlic cloves

One 1-inch piece ginger

Zest and juice of 3 limes

Zest and juice of 1 lemon

1 tablespoon kosher salt

1 tablespoon freshly cracked black pepper

2 pounds cod, sliced into 1-inch pieces

COD BATTER

2 cups all-purpose flour

½ teaspoon kosher salt

½ teaspoon sugar

1 cup lager

Neutral oil, for frying

228 SOUPS, SALADS, SANDWICHES

BAKE and SHARK CONTINUED

Heat 4 inches of oil in a Dutch oven over medium heat.

Once the dough has risen, make balls about 4 inches in diameter. Use extra flour on your hands to help form them. Using a rolling pin, flatten the balls to about ½-inch thick. Fry each piece of the dough on both sides until golden brown, about 2 minutes per side. Do not overcrowd the pan. Flip them back and forth. Transfer to a wire rack to cool.

Rip that Dutch oven up to medium-high heat until it reaches 350°F. Once the oil is up to temperature, deep-fry the fish until golden brown on both sides, 3 to 4 minutes. Do not overcrowd the Dutch oven, only fry a few pieces at a time. Transfer to the paper towel–lined plate to drain. Season with salt while still hot.

Now it's go time. Slice the bun, add the green chile marinade to both sides, and add mayo to the top bun. Place the vinegar slaw on the bottom bun and add all your little fried cod nuggets. Top with the tomatoes and pineapple. Smack down the top bun and get at it.

¼ cup mayonnaise

Vinegar Slaw (page 337)

½ large beefsteak tomato, cut into thin rounds

¼ pineapple, peeled and sliced into thin half-moons

FRIED SHRIMP PO'BOY

I always crave po'boys when I go to New Orleans. Then I get them, and they are pretty crumbly and fall apart, to be honest. I've never had a po'boy where the bun wasn't two days old and super crusty. I always looked for good ones and have yet to really be fulfilled. I'm not saying this one is better than the ones I've had, but if you follow along here, I promise it will be delicious. The fried shrimp alone are absolute beasts. I don't wanna be negative. I'm just telling my truth.

In a medium bowl, mix together the smoked paprika, white pepper, oregano, garlic powder, 1 teaspoon of the salt, 1 teaspoon of the Old Bay, and the buttermilk. Add the shrimp and marinate for 1 hour. In a separate medium bowl, mix the remaining 1 teaspoon salt with the flour and cornmeal.

Heat 4 inches of canola oil in a large saucepan over high heat until it reaches 350°F, then lower it to medium-high heat to retain the temperature.

Line a plate with paper towels. Working with one shrimp at a time, let the marinade drip off, then coat it completely in the flour mixture. Working in batches, fry the shrimp until golden and crispy, flipping them halfway through, about 2 minutes. Transfer the shrimp to the paper towel–lined plate and season with the remaining teaspoon of Old Bay and salt to taste.

Cut each of your rolls in half and layer the mayonnaise and butter on the inside of both, then layer the sandwiches with the lettuce, tomato, onion, pickle, and the fried shrimp. Serve immediately.

SERVES 2

PREP TIME: 1½ HOURS

Canola oil, for frying

2 tablespoons smoked paprika

1½ teaspoons ground white pepper

1 teaspoon dried oregano

1 teaspoon garlic powder

2 teaspoons kosher salt

2 teaspoons Old Bay Seasoning

1 cup buttermilk

8 ounces tiger shrimp, peeled and deveined

1 cup all-purpose flour

½ cup cornmeal

2 white French rolls

½ cup mayonnaise

2 tablespoons unsalted butter, room temperature

2 cups finely shredded iceberg lettuce

2 vine-ripe tomatoes, thinly sliced

½ cup finely sliced yellow onion

2 dill pickles, sliced into coins

ROASTED CHICKEN THIGH SHAWARMA *with* PICKLED TURNIP *and* HOT PEPPERS

How many times have you gotten hammered, dumb-ass drunk, just falling down all over the place, and then you stumbled into a beautiful shawarma shop? It's delicious, it's filling, it helps the demons stay away. I don't drink anymore. So I go during the daytime. I'm polite now. And the best part, it's still delicious.

Let's set ourselves up for success and make our garlic sauce. In a food processor, blitz the garlic, salt, and lemon juice. After it's well blended into a paste, set the blender on low and slowly drizzle in your grapeseed oil. Give it a taste. It's going to be bold, full of garlicky, salty goodness. Transfer to a container with a lid and let it rest in the fridge while we make the shawarma.

Preheat your oven to 375°F.

It's shawarma time. Trim the excess fat off your chicken thighs and arrange them on a large baking sheet. Let's make this tasty paste. In a small bowl, whisk together the garlic powder, onion powder, paprika, cardamom, cloves, urfa biber pepper, salt, and grapeseed oil. The consistency should be a loose paste. Rub it all over your chicken; really get in there. Throw the chicken into the oven and roast until the internal temperature hits at least 165°F, 35 to 40 minutes.

While the chicken is roasting, let's prep all your toppings and sauces. Roughly chop up your turnips and hot peppers. Set the garlic sauce, turnips, hot peppers, tabouli salad, pickled eggplant, and hummus up in little bowls.

Set a large pot of water over high heat and place a metal strainer on top. When it comes up to a boil, steam your pitas one by one on top of the large pot for 10 seconds each; we are just trying to make them warm. If you want to build your pita, open it up so there is a flap that opens halfway. Smear your hummus and garlic sauce inside, then add your chicken, tabouli, eggplant, all the pickles, and hot sauce. Now tuck your pita flap in and push all the filling to the back pocket of the pita. Roll and secure with a piece of parchment paper. Or for a self-serve option, place a large scoop of delicious chicken inside each pita and hand it to your loved ones so they can pile it with their favorite toppings and sauces.

SERVES 4 TO 6

PREP TIME: 1½ HOURS

GARLIC SAUCE

½ cup peeled garlic cloves

1 tablespoon kosher salt

Juice of 2 lemons

1½ cups grapeseed oil

SHAWARMA

5 pounds boneless, skinless chicken thighs

3 tablespoons garlic powder

2 tablespoons onion powder

2 tablespoons paprika

1 tablespoon ground cardamom

1 tablespoon ground cloves

1 tablespoon urfa biber pepper

2 tablespoons kosher salt

¼ cup grapeseed oil

One 14-ounce jar pickled turnips

One 16-ounce jar pickled hot peppers

Two 7-ounce containers tabouli salad

One 10-ounce container pickled eggplant

One 10-ounce container hummus

4 pitas

One 12-ounce bottle vinegar-based hot sauce

JAMBON BEURRE

Go to the fancy store and buy the most expensive butter. Why is that butter so expensive? Because good butter tastes the best. You deserve it, and so does this iconic sandwich. Don't ask any questions. Also get the good ham. Get it sliced, not thick but not thin. Then get some Dijon and some Maldon salt. Eat this on the beach, on the train, or riding your bike in Paris. Or don't.

Cover your baguette in that butter. Go to town. Next, top with the mustard and Maldon salt. Take that nice French ham, fill that baguette, stuff it in your pocket, and smoke a cigarette. You don't even eat it. Then you ride a bicycle on the cobblestone streets of Nice. Lean up against a wall. Go to the beach and then you eat it with your favorite cornichons.

SERVES 2

PREP TIME: HOWEVER LONG IT TAKES TO SMOKE A CIGARETTE SLOWLY

One 12-inch section fresh baguette, split in half

4 tablespoons unsalted French fancy butter, room temperature

2 tablespoons Dijon mustard

Maldon salt

8 ounces thinly sliced cooked ham, preferably jambon de Paris, room temperature

Jarred cornichons, for serving

BUFFALO CHICKEN FINGER

This is in my top three for last meals. Done perfectly, this is God mode. I've been talking about this sub my whole life. Some people get it, and some people don't. It's OK. But there's something deeper with hot subs. This is a hot sub with cold toppings. That makes it very different from a meatball sub or a baked lasagna sub or a parm with cold tomato. Everything about this is perfection. The blue cheese sauce, the onion, the pickles, and the pickled hots really power together. The steaming-hot Buffalo chicken fingers are just all time. This sub is literally making my mouth water as I write this now. I just almost drowned from saliva. I didn't even realize what was happening. Eat this sub, and don't drown.

Cut each chicken breast into 3 slices lengthwise. Season generously with salt.

Set up your breading station. Place the flour in one dish, beat the eggs in another, and place the bread crumbs in a third dish. Dredge each slice of chicken in flour, then fully immerse in egg, then roll through bread crumbs.

Heat at least 2 inches of oil in a deep skillet over medium-high heat until it reaches 350°F. Fry the breaded chicken strips in batches until golden brown and cooked through, about 3 minutes per side.

In a large bowl, mix the hot sauce, melted butter, 1 teaspoon of salt, and the black pepper. Dip the fried chicken strips in the hot sauce mixture and place on a wire rack.

In a medium bowl, combine 2 tablespoons of the blue cheese, the sour cream, mayonnaise, and lemon juice. Mix until smooth.

Cut the buns in half lengthwise. Remove some of the bread from the inside of the top halves. Spread a generous amount of the blue cheese sauce on the bottom half of the sub buns, then add your lettuce, tomato, onion, pickled peppers, pickles, the remaining 2 tablespoons blue cheese, the chicken fingers, and as much additional blue cheese sauce as your belly can handle. Push the top down to close it up.

SERVES 2
PREP TIME: 30 MINUTES

2 boneless, skinless chicken breasts

Kosher salt

1 cup all-purpose flour

2 eggs

2 cups bread crumbs

Canola oil, for frying

1 cup hot sauce (it better be Frank's RedHot), plus more for serving

½ cup unsalted butter, melted

½ teaspoon freshly cracked black pepper

¼ cup crumbled blue cheese

¼ cup sour cream

½ cup mayonnaise

1 tablespoon lemon juice

Two large submarine buns

½ head iceberg lettuce, thinly sliced, for serving

1 tomato, thinly sliced, for serving

½ cup white onion, thinly sliced, for serving

½ cup hot pickled banana peppers, for serving

¼ cup bread-and-butter pickles, for serving

MEATBALL

A meatball sandwich is best with one meatball. If you're still hungry, you can eat more, but this is the most perfect way to eat a meatball sandwich. I have made a lot of meatballs in my life and a lot of different ones, but these ones are probably the best ones, not gonna lie. Using a whole tray of focaccia is the key. This is obviously perfect for parties or if you are by yourself and you want to slam like twelve meatball sliders. I'm not judging.

In a large bowl, combine the bread crumbs and milk, mixing them thoroughly, and let stand for 10 minutes, until the bread crumbs are hydrated. Add the eggs, onion, garlic, parsley, salt, black pepper, oregano, Parmigiano, Pecorino, and a dash of olive oil and mix everything until combined.

Next, add the beef, pork, and veal. Use your hands to really work the meat until everything comes together into a nice homogeneous mixture. Cover with plastic wrap and let the mixture sit in the fridge for 1 hour. Resting them will help stabilize the mixture and make it easier to handle without overworking.

After the mixture has rested, portion the meat mixture into 2-ounce balls. I always like to use an ice cream scoop to start to get even balls. Afterward I'll wet my hands to prevent them from sticking and shape them into nice balls.

In a medium bowl, add the all-purpose flour. Gently dust each meatball with the flour. This will help with browning.

Preheat your oven to 350°F.

Pour ½ inch of olive oil into a large cast-iron skillet and bring it up over medium heat. Brown your meatballs in batches, about 10 minutes on all sides. Be gentle with them—they're delicate. Transfer the cooked meatballs to a large baking dish and cover them with the marinara.

Bake until they are completely cooked and have reached an internal temperature of 165°F, 30 minutes. Remove the baking dish from the oven and allow them to rest for 10 minutes.

Slice the focaccia down the middle and lightly drizzle it with olive oil. If you have a large grill, you can grill each huge half on its own for about 5 minutes, until golden brown. If you are toasting in your cast-iron pan, cut each half into 16 pieces and toast them individually. After the bread is toasted, rub both sides with a sliced piece of garlic.

CONTINUED

SERVES 8

PREP TIME: 2 HOURS

1 cup dry bread crumbs

2 cups 2% milk

2 eggs

1 small yellow onion, finely diced

6 garlic cloves, minced, plus 1 clove for rubbing the bread

1 cup flat-leaf parsley, chopped

2 tablespoons kosher salt

Freshly cracked black pepper

1 tablespoon chopped oregano leaves

1 cup grated Parmigiano-Reggiano, plus more for serving

1 cup grated Pecorino Romano

Olive oil

1 pound lean ground beef

1 pound lean ground pork

1 pound lean ground veal

4 tablespoons all-purpose flour

4 cups Marinara (recipe follows)

One 13 by 18-inch loaf focaccia

One 8-ounce ball fresh mozzarella, sliced in 16 pieces

MEATBALL CONTINUED

Preheat your broiler on high.

Slice your focaccia horizontally in half. On the bottom half, spread your meatballs 4 by 4. Top with a sprinkle of Parmigiano-Reggiano and one slice of mozzarella per meatball. Place these onto a baking sheet. Broil on high until the cheese is bubbling and lightly browned, 5 minutes. Top each ball with the marinara they cooked in and the remaining slice of bread. Then skewer each ball to cut into 16 sandwiches!

MARINARA

In a medium bowl, use your hands to crush the tomatoes. Remove any seeds and excess liquid. Set aside.

In a heavy-bottomed pot over medium heat, warm the olive oil. Add the onion and garlic and cook until translucent, stirring frequently to prevent any browning, about 5 minutes. Add the crushed tomatoes. Turn the heat down to low, add the basil, and allow the sauce to simmer for 1 hour.

Remove the tomato sauce from the heat. Remove the basil stems and add your salt, sugar, and Parmesan. Using a hand blender on low, gently blend the sauce until the tomatoes break down. You are looking for a sauce that is slightly chunky. Allow the sauce to cool. Store in the fridge for up to 3 days.

MAKES 6 CUPS

Two 28-ounce cans San Marzano tomatoes, drained

1 cup olive oil

1 Spanish onion, finely diced

8 garlic cloves, minced

1 bunch basil

2 tablespoons kosher salt

3 tablespoons sugar

½ cup grated Parmigiano-Reggiano

PORK KATSU SANDO

As classic as it gets, pure and simple. Brine your pork chops; you'll thank me later. Or don't, but still make this sando. It'll still slap if you don't brine, but holy cow, if you brine, you'll win, and winning is what it's all about. For some reason, these eat better than any other sandwich. They seem smaller and more perfect in every way, like most things in Japan. Very thoughtful and no fluff, only 100 percent execution. I love you, sandos. I love you, Japan. Thank you for always leading the way with restraint.

Let's start by making your brine. In a large bowl, dissolve your sugar and salt in the water. Add the pork chops to the bowl, making sure they're completely submerged. Place in the fridge for 2 hours to brine. Then, rinse them off and pat them dry with paper towels.

Next, make your katsu sauce. In a medium bowl, stir together the ketchup, soy sauce, HP Sauce, horseradish, and tonkatsu sauce. Transfer to an airtight container and refrigerate until ready to use.

Prepare your pork katsu. Set up three shallow bowls for your breading station: one with the flour, one with the whisked eggs, and one with the panko. Dip each pork chop first in the flour, then the eggs, then the panko. Make sure each pork chop is completely coated. The best method is to have one wet hand and one dry hand. Alternatively, you can use a fork to pick up the pork and move it around.

Line a plate with paper towels. Heat 4 inches of oil in a Dutch oven over medium-high heat until it reaches 350°F. Gently place the pork chops in the hot oil and fry until golden brown, about 6 minutes total. Then transfer them to the paper towel–lined plate to drain. Season both sides with salt. While the katsu is still hot, brush both sides with your katsu sauce.

Spread your mayo on your bread, place your takuan, then your sauced katsu. Top with a big pile of sliced cabbage and your remaining slice of bread. Repeat with the other sandwich.

SERVES 2
PREP TIME: 3 HOURS

BRINE

1 tablespoon sugar

2 tablespoons kosher salt

4 cups water

Two 6-ounce boneless pork chops, from the shoulder end

1 cup all-purpose flour

3 eggs, whisked

1 cup panko bread crumbs

Canola oil, for frying

Kosher salt

Four 1-inch-thick slices milk bread or brioche

2 tablespoons Kewpie mayonnaise

1 piece of pickled daikon (takuan)

¼ head green cabbage, sliced as thinly as possible (about 2 cups)

KATSU SAUCE

1 cup ketchup

¼ cup soy sauce

¼ cup HP Sauce

1 heaping tablespoon prepared horseradish

1 cup tonkatsu sauce

SCALLION PANCAKE

This is kinda like a Peking duck–pancake situation but a giant scallion pancake sandwich thing. Everyone needs a break from bread loaves, sub buns, and kaiser rolls. These scallion pancakes are the perfect vessel for our supersoft, unctuous pork belly. It's definitely a full-on love letter to the flavors and techniques of Chinatowns all over the world. The crunchy leek and cilantro salad. The bright and intense scallion ginger sauce. The warm heat of the chile oil mayo. Then those bursts of cucumber with the softest pork belly wrapped in the flaky scallion pancake.

Start by making the spicy scallion ginger sauce. In a large metal bowl, add the ginger, garlic, scallions, garlic chives, cilantro, and Thai chiles. In a medium pot over medium-high heat, heat the oil until it begins to smoke. Carefully drizzle the smoking-hot oil over the vegetable mixture. Everything should continue to bubble and sputter after the oil has been added. Allow this to rest on your counter for 30 minutes. Add the sesame oil, sesame seeds, salt, and rice wine vinegar and stir thoroughly. Transfer the sauce to an airtight container and store in the fridge for up to 1 week.

Preheat your oven to 425°F.

In a small bowl, make your hoisin chile mayo by whisking together the hoisin, chile oil, and mayo. Set it aside.

Make your salad mix. In a large bowl, combine the cilantro, cucumbers, leeks, and iceberg lettuce.

To heat up your frozen scallion pancakes, brush each pancake with some of the canola oil. Place your pancakes directly on the oven rack and bake until hot and crispy, 6 to 8 minutes.

Spread your hoisin chile mayo on the base of your pancake, then top with two slices of your pork belly. Top with your scallion ginger sauce, garnish with the salad mix, fold, and eat.

CONTINUED

SERVES 4
PREP TIME: 14 HOURS

SPICY SCALLION GINGER SAUCE

¼ cup minced ginger

4 garlic cloves, minced

1 bunch scallions, thinly sliced

½ bunch garlic chives, thinly sliced

¼ cup cilantro stems, thinly sliced

6 Thai green chiles, sliced

2 cups vegetable oil

1 tablespoon toasted sesame oil

1 tablespoon toasted sesame seeds

2 tablespoons kosher salt

¼ cup rice wine vinegar

HOISIN CHILE MAYO

½ cup hoisin

½ cup chile oil

1 cup mayonnaise

SALAD MIX

¼ cup cilantro

½ cup thinly sliced cucumbers

½ cup thinly sliced leeks

½ cup thinly sliced iceberg lettuce

4 frozen scallion pancakes (buy these from a local Chinese bakery)

2 tablespoons canola oil

1 pound Soy-Braised Pork Belly (recipe follows), cut into ½-inch slices

SCALLION PANCAKE CONTINUED

SOY-BRAISED PORK BELLY

Place the pork belly in a large pot and completely cover it with water. Bring the pot to a boil and immediately remove the pork belly with tongs. Transfer the pork to a colander and run it under cold water until it is completely cooled. Transfer to a baking sheet lined with paper towels and pat it dry.

Return the pork belly to the pot along with the garlic, ginger, scallions, red chile, soy sauce, rice wine vinegar, brown sugar, and chicken stock. Bring the mixture to a simmer over medium heat and cook until the pork belly is tender and the sauce has reduced by half and thickened, 45 minutes to 1 hour. Taste it and adjust the seasoning if necessary. If it's not salty enough, add more soy sauce. If it's not sweet enough, add more sugar.

Remove the pot from the heat and allow everything to cool together for 30 minutes. Transfer the pork belly to a baking sheet lined with parchment paper. Place another layer of parchment on top and press it down with another baking sheet. Place this in the fridge with something heavy on top, like a cast-iron skillet, to help press the pork belly flat. Let this cool in the fridge overnight.

1½ pounds pork belly, skin on

4 garlic cloves, minced

1-inch piece ginger, sliced

2 scallions, cut into 2-inch pieces

1 dried Thai red chile

½ cup soy sauce

¼ cup rice wine vinegar

2 tablespoons brown sugar

2 cups chicken stock

ITALIAN COMBO

In Fort Erie, where I grew up, our subs are very different than normal. A Fort Erie–style combo is more like a cold cut basic sub with sub sauce, not an American Italian–style sub like this. This is more iconic.

If you tried putting mayo on one of these, they would scream at you. I like more red wine vinegar than olive oil to be honest. Also, the iceberg has to be shaved as thin as possible. We've talked about all of this in *Home Style Cookery* already, but it's so important that it's shaved like glass. It creates the best texture to stand up to the fatty meats and the oil and vinegar. Also, the tomatoes need to be as thin as possible and layered with the hot pickled peppers.

In Canada, it fucking sucks how few good-quality Italian preserves, like pickled hot peppers, there are. It's very disheartening. When we first opened Maker Pizza, my goal was to make an American version of a bodega Italian combo. I think we hit the mark. This is my favorite version, and if anyone wants to talk about it, let's go, champ.

This sandwich is all about construction. Anyone can slap together an Italian combo, but we're going to do it together. And we're going to do it right.

Start with the sub heroes. We're looking for a 60:40 ratio of red wine vinegar to olive oil. Or if you like doing splashes like me, it's three splashes of vinegar to two splashes of olive oil directly on the open sub. Give that a little sprinkle of salt and pepper.

Now start stacking. You can make these for TikTok by arranging each layer like shingles. I like starting with the meat. Freak what you feel, do whatever order you would like, but we're going to go mortadella, salami, gabagool—ahem, I mean capicola—and ham, then provolone, tomato, red peppers, and pickled peppers. Dress your iceberg and onions with the olive oil and vinegar mixture and place them on top of the stack. Close them up and get to work.

SERVES 2
PREP TIME: 15 MINUTES

2 sub heroes, split lengthwise but attached on one side

Extra-virgin olive oil

Red wine vinegar

Kosher salt and freshly cracked black pepper

16 slices mortadella

16 slices salami

16 slices capicola

16 slices ham

16 slices provolone

1 tomato, thinly sliced

4 roasted red peppers, torn

6 pickled cherry bomb peppers, finely chopped

1 small head iceberg lettuce, thinly sliced

1 small red onion, thinly sliced and soaked in water for 2 minutes

BEEF ON WECK *with* TOP ROUND ROAST, CREAMED HORSERADISH, *and* BEEF AU JUS

This is a love song to my wife, my life partner, my soul mate, my one and only. Our first kiss was on the Niagara River, sitting on an abandoned dock overlooking the Buffalo city lights. Our love is as strong as the perfect beef on weck served at Bar-Bill. The Kimmelweck bun will be hard to find anywhere else, but you can get them all over western New York and the greater Fort Erie area. It's a salted caraway-seeded crusty roll, perfect for something like shaved top round and creamy horseradish. Most of the time, just prepared horseradish is used, which is perfect, but I made a creamy one to round it out a little more.

This sandwich is served at every birthday party, celebration, graduation, funeral, bachelor party, and stag and doe in Fort Erie that I've been to. It was even served at our prom. Twenty-three years later, Trish still looks stunning in the same dress she wore that night. Obviously, I've had a couple too many beef on wecks over here. I'm wearing a new tuxedo.

It's a huge part of the culinary DNA of Fort Erie. Thank you, Buffalo.

The night before you plan to roast your beef, trim any excess silverskin off your top round and season it with the salt and garlic powder. Store in the fridge, uncovered, to dry it out a bit. We're also going to soak our marrowbone pieces for the au jus to remove impurities. Place them in a container with water to cover, cover with a lid, and refrigerate overnight.

The following day let's start making our au jus. Preheat your oven to 450°F. Drain and dry the bones. Roast them in a roasting pan for 45 minutes, stirring every 15 minutes. They should look golden brown when finished.

Add the beef stock to your roasting pan to deglaze it, then transfer all the juices and the bones to a large pot over medium heat. Add your bay leaf, thyme, soy sauce, and Worcestershire sauce. Simmer, uncovered, for 4 hours to extract the flavor from the bones. Strain through a fine-mesh strainer and reserve the fortified beef stock.

While the stock is simmering, roast the beef. Lower your oven to 400°F. Place your roast on a baking sheet and roast until the center reaches 130°F, about 1 hour. Pull your roast from the oven and crank the oven up as high as it will go, preferably 525°F. Let your roast rest for 30 minutes. Save the accumulated juices for the au jus.

CONTINUED

SERVES 8
PREP TIME: 1 DAY

4 pounds top round roast
2 tablespoons kosher salt
2 tablespoons garlic powder
8 Kimmelweck rolls (caraway seed buns)

BEEF AU JUS

2 (4- to 6-inch) pieces marrowbone, ask your butcher to cut them into 1-inch pieces
6 cups beef stock
1 bay leaf
2 thyme sprigs
½ cup soy sauce
2 tablespoons Worcestershire sauce
¼ cup unsalted butter
⅓ cup all-purpose flour
Kosher salt and freshly cracked black pepper
Reserved roasting juices from your sirloin

HORSERADISH CREAM

1½ cups basic aioli
2 heaping tablespoons prepared horseradish
½ tablespoon kosher salt
1 tablespoon sugar
1½ teaspoons white vinegar

BEEF ON WECK *with* TOP ROUND ROAST, CREAMED HORSERADISH, *and* BEEF AU JUS CONTINUED

While that's roasting, we're going to make the horseradish cream. In a small bowl, whisk together the aioli, horseradish, salt, sugar, and vinegar. Mix vigorously to ensure everything is incorporated evenly. Transfer the cream to a container and refrigerate until ready to use. It will last for 3 days.

After your roast has rested, throw it back into the oven for 10 more minutes to give it a good sear. Remove the roast from the oven and lower the temperature to 350°F. Again, let's save those juices for the au jus. Let your roast rest for an additional 30 minutes.

Let's finish up the au jus. In a medium pot over medium heat, melt the butter. Let's make our roux, add your flour and cook, stirring constantly, until the flour has taken on a blonde color, 4 minutes. Slowly add half of your fortified beef stock, whisking vigorously to prevent lumping. When the gravy comes up to a simmer, add your remaining stock and repeat. Lower the heat if the mixture starts to boil. Once your gravy has thickened enough to coat the back of a spoon, simmer it for an additional 5 minutes.

Strain your gravy using a fine-mesh strainer to remove any lumps of flour that did not get incorporated. Season with salt and pepper, and add any remaining roasting juices from your sirloin.

When the meat is just warmer than room temperature, slice it against the grain as thinly as possible.

Warm your rolls in the oven for 5 minutes directly on the rack. We don't want them toasted, just warm to the touch. Slice them in half and spread a layer of horseradish cream on either side. Top with a generous amount of sliced beef and a small ladle of your au jus. Serve with a large side of au jus. You will have a lot of it, it's pure liquid gold.

FRENCH DIP

Make sure you cook this in the morning and just let it rest all day. That's the best. Using a good baguette is also very important, because you want it to be crusty and crunchy and soft and hold up to the dip. This dish can be trash or so high end. French dip has been ruined for years by chain restaurants with gray-ass, dusty, fake frozen beef. This is our chance to make it right and take it back.

Preheat your oven to 325°F. Season the prime rib generously with salt and pepper, ensuring all sides are coated.

Heat a large Dutch oven over medium-high heat. Add a drizzle of canola oil and sear the prime rib on all sides until browned, about 10 minutes. Transfer the prime rib to a large plate or platter and set aside.

In the same Dutch oven over medium-high heat, add the onion and garlic. Sauté until they become fragrant and begin to caramelize. Add the sliced mushrooms and cook until they release their moisture and start to brown, about 10 minutes. Add the wine and sherry to the pan to deglaze it, scraping up any browned bits from the bottom. Let the mixture simmer for a few minutes to reduce slightly. Add the beef broth, Worcestershire sauce, soy sauce, thyme, rosemary, and bay leaf and bring the mixture to a simmer. Return the seared prime rib with its juices to the Dutch oven, bone-side down.

Transfer the Dutch oven to the oven and roast for about 2 hours, until the internal temperature reaches your desired level of doneness. (I recommend medium-rare, with an internal temperature of around 135°F.)

While the prime rib is cooking, prepare the caramelized onions. In a Dutch oven over medium-low heat, melt the butter. Add the onions and cook slowly, stirring occasionally, until they caramelize and turn golden brown, about 45 minutes. Season with salt and pepper to taste. Set aside.

Once the prime rib is done, remove it from the oven and let it rest for a minimum of 1 hour before slicing. Thinly slice the prime rib. Use a long slicing knife with a rounded tip if you have one. Strain the au jus, the juice that came off the meat after resting, through a fine-mesh strainer, discarding the solids, and transfer the liquid to a serving vessel for dipping.

Preheat your broiler on high. Split the baguettes lengthwise and drizzle them with olive oil. Place them on a baking sheet under the broiler until lightly toasted, about 2 minutes.

To assemble the sandwiches, layer the sliced prime rib on the toasted baguettes. Top with 4 slices of cheese, then put them back under the broiler to let the cheese get melty. Top with caramelized onions. Serve the sandwiches with the au jus on the side for dipping.

SERVES 6
PREP TIME: 4 HOURS

One 2-pound piece bone-in prime rib (6 inches wide)

Kosher salt and freshly cracked black pepper

Canola oil

1 yellow onion, thinly sliced

4 garlic cloves, minced

8 ounces cremini mushrooms, sliced

1 cup red wine

½ cup dry sherry

4 cups beef broth

2 tablespoons Worcestershire sauce

2 tablespoons soy sauce

2 thyme sprigs

2 rosemary sprigs

1 bay leaf

CARAMELIZED ONIONS

¼ cup unsalted butter

2 large yellow onions, thinly sliced

Kosher salt and freshly cracked black pepper

2 crusty French baguettes, each cut into 3 pieces

Olive oil

24 slices provolone

NOT A McRIB SANDWICH

A real American hero. Everyone had one of these as a kid and thought it was the best thing ever. Then it went away and then came back years later. Everyone said *that* was the best and never got it again, and the folklore grew and grew and grew. Now you can make one that doesn't taste like weird, bouncy Styrofoam. The real hero is the ribs. We're using real ribs and not making a farce; getting just a rib sandwich is good enough. We looked into making a "real" McRib, and it was just a pork farce, pretty much, and that's not our vibe. We make the real.

Preheat your oven to 325°F.

Generously season your ribs with salt and pepper. Wrap them in aluminum foil and bake on a baking sheet until tender, about 2 hours. While they are still warm, pull out the bones and cut into patty-size pieces (about 4 bones per piece).

Raise your oven temperature to 350°F. Brush your rib pieces with the BBQ sauce. Bake, uncovered, for 30 minutes, flipping each piece over and basting with BBQ sauce every 10 minutes. We want these to be beautiful and glazed, not burnt.

Dry toast your kaiser rolls in your oven. Place your cooked rib patty on the bottom bun, top with 4 slices of the pickles and a sprinkle of the onion. Put the top bun on and destroy.

SERVES 4

PREP TIME: 2½ HOURS

1 (3-pound) rack pork spare ribs

Kosher salt and freshly cracked black pepper

Two 18-ounce bottles your favorite BBQ sauce (the correct answer is Matheson's)

4 kaiser rolls

2 kosher dill pickles, sliced (we need about 16 slices here)

1 white onion, diced

SABICH *with* CUCUMBER, TOMATO, *and* PICKLED HOT PEPPERS

The first time I ever had sabich was in Montreal, and it was a stand-out for me. Like, why am I always eating falafel? Come on, eggplant as the star with the egg? Everyone, this is some low-key hitter. Maybe people don't want us to know and love the sabich? But we love the sabich and we will tell everyone and we will scream for sabich. We need sabich. It could easily be one of the greats in the world. Thank you, eggplant, you are very kind.

In a medium bowl, mix together the cherry tomatoes and 1 tablespoon of salt. Transfer to a fine-mesh strainer and let it macerate for 1 hour, allowing any excess liquid to drain off.

Line a plate with paper towels. Heat a medium skillet over medium heat and add ¼ cup of the olive oil. Test the oil with a piece of eggplant; if it sizzles right away, your oil is up to temperature. Add all the eggplant and sear on each side until the eggplant is golden brown, 6 to 7 minutes. Transfer to the paper towel–lined plate to drain and cool. Reserve the skillet for toasting the pita.

While the eggplant is cooling, let's make the tahini dressing. In a food processor, combine the garlic and lemon juice. Blend until the garlic is completely broken down, 1 minute. Strain the mixture through a fine-mesh strainer into a medium bowl, discarding the pulp. Combine the garlic and lemon juice mixture with the tahini, cumin, olive oil, and salt. Transfer to an airtight container and refrigerate for up to 1 week.

Once the eggplant is cool, place them in a large bowl. Rinse and pat the tomato dry to remove all moisture and salt. Add the salted tomato, cucumber, hard-boiled eggs, banana peppers, cabbage, parsley, mint, lemon juice, ¼ cup of the tahini dressing, the hot sauce, and 1 tablespoon of salt. Gently toss everything together. Add more tahini dressing, hot sauce, salt, and lemon juice as desired.

In the reserved skillet, drain off the remaining olive oil and toast the pitas until they are warm, 1 minute on each side. Using a bread knife, cut along the side about a quarter of the way around the pita to form a pocket.

Serve the condiments and onions on separate plates for your guests and encourage them to build the sabich of their dreams while asking them about what they dream about.

SERVES 5

PREP TIME: 2 HOURS

2 cups cherry tomatoes, quartered

Kosher salt

¼ cup plus 3 tablespoons olive oil

1 pound Italian eggplant (about 2), cut in ½-inch cubes

2 cups diced cucumber

5 hard-boiled eggs, sliced

¼ cup pickled banana peppers, roughly chopped

3 cups thinly shredded green cabbage

¼ cup parsley, roughly chopped

2 tablespoons roughly chopped mint

Juice of 1 lemon, plus more as needed

2 tablespoons your favorite hot sauce, plus more as needed

5 pitas

½ red onion, thinly sliced

TAHINI DRESSING

8 garlic cloves, peeled

¾ cup lemon juice

1½ cups tahini

1 tablespoon ground cumin

3 tablespoons olive oil

1 tablespoon kosher salt

CANADIAN DONAIR *with* ONION, TOMATO, *and* DONAIR SAUCE

My childhood was spent mostly in Dartmouth, Nova Scotia. We grew up eating donairs, which are the perfect thing. Five great ingredients combine to form the ideal alchemy. The steamed chewy pita. The soft, kinda sweet and spicy beef. The sharp white diced onion. That tomato dice. But we all know the sauce is what will win or destroy people. That's what sets this apart and makes this dish one of a kind. That weird creamy, sweet, vinegary, garlicky sauce that defies science in all its glory. If you've seen my donair episode in the Oscar-winning YouTube show "Just a Dash," you can watch the glory of how to make this. This is one of my death-row meals, easily. You're welcome.

Preheat your oven to 375°F. Line a 9 by 5 by 2½-inch loaf pan with parchment paper.

In a mixer fitted with the paddle attachment, mix the beef, lamb, pork, coriander, garlic powder, oregano, thyme, cayenne, salt, and black pepper on low speed for 30 seconds. Then, begin to increase the speed gradually to medium-high and continue to mix until the meat is even and smooth, about 1 minute. Pack the meat mixture into the prepared loaf pan. Gently bang the pan against the counter to get rid of any air pockets. Really punch it down. Keep punching and banging the pan until you are sure that air couldn't have survived your wrath.

Bake until the internal temperature reaches 150°F, about 1 hour.

While the meat is baking, prepare the donair sauce. In a small bowl, add the condensed milk. While stirring, slowly pour in the vinegar. Stir in the garlic powder. If it's too thick (like it won't move, like a glue), add 1 tablespoon of the water at a time until you get your desired consistency. This is a thick boy. Refrigerate for a minimum of 1 hour. It can last for a few days in the fridge.

Remove the meatloaf from the oven. Carefully remove the meatloaf from the pan and let it rest for a minimum of 30 minutes. Thinly slice the donair meat and place it on a pita. Sprinkle on the onion and tomato, then drizzle with donair sauce. Roll up and enjoy. Repeat with the remaining pitas.

SERVES 4
PREP TIME: 2 HOURS

1 pound ground beef

8 ounces ground lamb

8 ounces ground pork

1 tablespoon ground coriander

2 tablespoons garlic powder

2 teaspoons ground oregano

2 teaspoons ground thyme

1 teaspoon cayenne

1 tablespoon kosher salt

1 tablespoon freshly cracked black pepper

8 pitas

1 white onion, diced

2 tomatoes, diced

DONAIR SAUCE

¾ cup sweetened condensed milk

¼ cup white vinegar

¼ teaspoon garlic powder

½ cup cold water, or less as needed

CUBANO

What a special sandwich we got here, oh boy. The roasted pork, the ham, the mustard, the pickles, and the bread all pressed together. It's all so soft, then you get the pickle crunch in the middle. The sandwich has to be built so that the ratio is perfect. The bread needs to be toasted just right. The filling can't be smushed because it will slide all over the place. The ham can be just OK, but the roasted pork is what you can really judge the sandwich on. That beautiful roasted pork is so crucial. Not too fatty and not dry. We all know that dry roasted pork tastes like cat food.

In a small bowl, mix together the olive oil, orange juice, lime juice, brown sugar, salt, pepper, smoked paprika, cumin, and garlic. This will be your marinade. Score the surface of the pork shoulder with a sharp knife to allow the marinade to penetrate. Place the pork shoulder in a 2.5-gallon jumbo Ziploc bag. Pour the marinade over the pork shoulder, making sure to coat it evenly on all sides. Use your hands to rub the marinade into the meat. Let this marinate in the fridge overnight.

Preheat your oven to 325°F.

Take the pork out of the bag and let any excess marinade drip off. Place it into a large roasting pan. Pour the Coca-Cola into the roasting pan, around the pork shoulder. Cover the pan tightly with aluminum foil, ensuring it is sealed to keep the moisture inside. Roast the pork until the meat is tender and easily pulls apart with a fork, about 2 hours. Every 30 minutes, baste the pork with the pan juices to keep it moist and flavorful. Re-cover it with the foil each time.

Once the meat is tender, remove the foil and increase the oven temperature to 400°F. Roast the pork until the top develops a crispy, golden-brown crust, an additional 15 to 20 minutes. Remove the roasted pork shoulder from the oven and let it rest for at least 30 minutes before slicing or shredding it. Alternatively, you can cool this in the fridge overnight; it will be much easier to slice thinly. You'll need only 8 ounces of the roasted pork to make the sandwiches.

Make the sandwiches. Preheat your oven to 300°F. Preheat your griddle or panini press over medium heat. Slice the bread horizontally and spread a thin layer of mustard on the bottom half of the bread. Spread mayonnaise on the top half. Layer the roasted pork on the bottom half of the bread, followed by the sliced ham. Add the Swiss cheese on top of the ham, and then place the pickles evenly over the cheese. Place the top half of the bread on the filling and spread a thin layer of butter on the outside of the sandwich. Place the sandwich on the preheated griddle with a weight or use a panini press and press it down gently. Cook until the bread is toasted and the cheese has melted, 5 to 10 minutes on each side. Then throw the pan in the oven until the cheese has fully melted, 10 minutes. Take it out, slice it diagonally, and enjoy!

SERVES 4 TO 6

PREP TIME: 2 DAYS

ROASTED PORK

2 tablespoons olive oil

¼ cup orange juice

1 tablespoon lime juice

2 tablespoons light brown sugar

2 teaspoons kosher salt

½ teaspoon freshly cracked black pepper

½ teaspoon smoked paprika

½ teaspoon ground cumin

2 garlic cloves, minced

4 pounds pork butt

One 12-ounce can Coca-Cola

2 loaves Cuban bread (or substitute French or Italian bread)

Yellow mustard

Mayonnaise

8 ounces Roasted Pork (see above)

8 ounces sliced ham (old-ass ham in your fridge preferred)

8 ounces Swiss cheese, thinly sliced

4 large dill pickles, sliced lengthwise

Unsalted butter

MEATLOAF

Meatloaf is another absolute classic, but I feel like not a lot of people are on the meatloaf sandwich kick. It only makes sense in the brain, kinda like how a day-old spaghetti sandwich makes sense. Where you just take out old spaghetti and put it in between two pieces of bread and eat it with a large glass of milk. This is a very soft sandwich and I love it. The only resistance comes from the bread-and-butter pickles, and at the perfect amount. Come join me in this soft party.

Start by preheating your smoker or oven to 325°F.

First, prepare your BBQ sauce. In a small saucepan, heat up enough neutral oil to cover the pan. Add your onion, making sure that the onion caramelizes slowly for 15 minutes. Do not burn. Add the garlic and cook until fragrant, 1 minute. Then, add the smoked paprika, garlic powder, ginger, fennel, allspice, ground mustard, onion powder, cayenne, black pepper, salt, mustard, ketchup, brown sugar, vinegar, and water. Whisk it all together, bring to a boil, and simmer down to a thickened, sticky sauce, about 30 minutes. If you're using a smoker, you can put it in there for 30 minutes, so that the smoky flavor is incorporated throughout.

CONTINUED

SERVES 6
PREP TIME: 2 HOURS

MATTY'S DANK BBQ SAUCE
Neutral oil
1 white onion, grated
3 garlic cloves, grated
1 tablespoon smoked paprika
1 tablespoon garlic powder
1 tablespoon ground ginger
1 teaspoon ground fennel
1 teaspoon ground allspice
1 tablespoon ground mustard
1 tablespoon onion powder
1 teaspoon cayenne
1 tablespoon freshly cracked black pepper
1 teaspoon kosher salt
2 tablespoons yellow mustard
1 cup ketchup
1 cup packed light brown sugar
1 cup apple cider vinegar
1 cup water

MEATLOAF CONTINUED

Make your meatloaf. In a food processor, pulse the Texas toast into small crumbs. In the bowl of a stand mixer fitted with the paddle attachment, add your beef, pork, mustard, fennel, cayenne, smoked paprika, salt, pepper, ketchup, bread crumbs, and eggs. Start your mixer on the lowest speed, and as the ingredients start to incorporate, increase the speed to medium and mix until the consistency starts to look whipped, 5 to 8 minutes.

Scoop your mixture into a nonstick 9 by 5-inch loaf pan and smooth out the top into an even layer. Tap the base of your pan on the table a few times to remove all the air bubbles. Cover the top with a generous layer of BBQ sauce.

In a cast-iron pan, add your onion, generously drizzle with neutral oil, and season with a pinch of salt.

Put your meatloaf and your cast-iron pan with the onion into your smoker (or oven) and close the lid. Allow to smoke (or bake) until the internal temperature of the meatloaf reaches 155°F, about 1 hour, and then pull both the onions and meatloaf out to rest for at least 30 minutes.

Remove your meatloaf from the pan and slice into thick slices. Take two pieces of fresh Texas toast, cover one slice with mayo, and place your meatloaf on top. Add the caramelized onions, more BBQ sauce, and bread-and-butter pickles to finish your sandwich. Make enough soft sandwiches for you and the crew. Enjoy.

MEATLOAF

2 slices Texas toast

2 pounds ground beef

1 pound ground pork

1 tablespoon yellow mustard

1 teaspoon ground fennel

1 teaspoon cayenne

1 teaspoon smoked paprika

1 tablespoon kosher salt, plus more for the onions

1 tablespoon freshly cracked black pepper

3 tablespoons ketchup, plus more for serving

2 eggs

3 white onions, diced

Neutral oil

Twelve ½-inch slices Texas toast

Mayonnaise

Bread-and-butter pickles

MUFFULETTA

Please actually make this. It looks as if you cut the world in half, like one of those pictures of sediment layers or something. I bet you didn't know that muffuletta is named after the bun. Well, it is. Thank you, Louisiana and Sicilian immigrants, for throwing all the good stuff into a muffuletta, 'cause this is the gorgeous and delicious royal flush of sandwiches.

Make the olive salad. In a blender, combine the olives, celery, garlic, Calabrian chili peppers, roasted red peppers, parsley, olive oil, vinegar, oregano, and black pepper and pulse until it's a chunky consistency. Set aside to marinate for at least 10 minutes.

Slice the Italian loaf horizontally. It's up to you if you want to remove some of the soft bread inside. It will help you get more meat and cheese in. On the bottom piece, add a third of the olive salad. Next, start stacking in this order: Italian ham, half of the provolone, the capicola, a third of the olive salad, sweet coppa, mozzarella, soppressata, mortadella, Genoa salami, the remaining half of the provolone, and the remaining third of the olive salad. Press down and let sit for 15 minutes. Serve by slicing into four wedges for you and three of your best friends.

SERVES 4

PREP TIME: 45 MINUTES

OLIVE SALAD

1 cup pitted green olives

¾ cup chopped celery

2 garlic cloves

½ cup peeled roasted Calabrian chili peppers

½ cup peeled roasted red peppers

½ bunch Italian parsley

¼ cup extra-virgin olive oil

2 tablespoons red wine vinegar

½ teaspoon dried oregano

Freshly cracked black pepper

1 loaf crusty Italian bread

6 ounces Italian ham, thinly sliced

4 ounces provolone, thinly sliced

6 ounces capicola, thinly sliced

6 ounces sweet coppa, thinly sliced

4 ounces mozzarella cheese, thinly sliced

6 ounces soppressata, thinly sliced

6 ounces mortadella, thinly sliced

6 ounces Genoa salami, thinly sliced

FRIED SPAM KIMCHI GRILLED CHEESE

There really is something special about Spam. I think it's one of the greatest and most versatile ingredients. It could be fried or grilled or smoked or boiled. Any way you cook it is fire, but here it becomes this perfect storm of flavor with fatty Spam, tangy, crunchy kimchi, buttery fried bread, and the cream town USA American cheese. This is just about as good as it gets.

Slice the Spam into 4 steaks. Drain the kimchi and chop it up so you don't pull kimchi out of your mouth and get slapped with a hot piece of cabbage. Make sure you pull out as much liquid as possible by draining the liquid off and pressing a lot of the juice out.

In a cast-iron skillet over medium-high heat, add the oil and sear the Spam until it's a nice golden brown, about 3 minutes per side. Set that aside and wipe out the pan.

Using margarine or butter, butter one side of each slice of bread. Use margarine if you are a margarine person like I am because I never have room-temp butter.

Preheat your oven to 350°F. The key to a grilled cheese is to also put it in the oven.

In the same pan you used to cook the Spam, put 2 slices of your bread, buttered-side down. Top one bread with 2 slices of the marbled cheddar and the other with 1 slice of the American cheese. Put 2 slices of Spam on the American cheese side, side by side, and kimchi on the marbled cheese side. Flip your Spam side onto the kimchi.

Put the sandwich on a baking sheet and into the oven. Get it nice and hot. Flip every 2 to 3 minutes for about 10 minutes. Flip flip flip, it's oozy, it's cheesy, and the bread is nice and crusty.

Repeat by putting the remaining slices of bread into the pan and building your second sandwich. Do this only if you want to share this sandwich with someone. Or, if you want to crush two sandwiches on your own, this will be our secret. No one will know. This is a good one, though, so I hope you share. Put the second sandwich on the baking sheet and into the oven. Repeat the cook-and-flip process.

Take it out, and in the meantime, let's make a little dipper, shall we? In a small bowl, mix the mayonnaise, sriracha, hoisin, gochugaru, garlic powder, lime juice, and salt and pepper to taste. There's your dip.

Cut each grilled cheese in half, right down the middle. No diagonal fancy-pants stuff here. You want to have a piece of Spam in each half. Get a couple of bites in and then dip it. Or eat half and then eat the other half dipped. Or dip it from the first bite. If I dip, we dip, we dip, dip.

SERVES 2

PREP TIME: 30 MINUTES

One 12-ounce can Spam

1 cup your favorite kimchi

1 tablespoon grapeseed oil

Four ½-inch-thick slices seeded bread

Margarine or butter, room temperature, for buttering your bread

4 slices marbled cheddar cheese

2 slices American cheese

½ cup mayonnaise

¼ cup sriracha

¼ cup hoisin

1 tablespoon gochugaru

1 tablespoon garlic powder

Juice of 1 lime

Kosher salt and freshly cracked black pepper

PHILLY CHEESESTEAK

I love cheesesteaks more than cheeseburgers. I always squeeze and juice the cherry peppers all over my cheesesteaks and stuff the torn shards of the peppers into it. I like eating the first half without ketchup and the second half with ketchup. I don't like to start with ketchup, which is kinda funny. Like maybe I'm treating the second half like dessert, it seems, with my tomato sugar sauce.

Trim the rib eye's fat cap and the connective tissue off the outside, leaving the big piece of meat in the center. Put it in the freezer until it's firm enough to slice thinly, about 30 minutes. Save your trimmings for stewing.

Chop the stems and tops of the mushrooms into ½-inch cubes. In a medium saucepan over medium-high heat, add about 2 tablespoons canola oil, a pinch of salt, a pinch of black pepper, and the mushrooms. Sauté until the mushrooms release their water and get a bit crispy around the edges, about 10 minutes. This should yield about 1 cup. Set aside.

Wipe out the pan and heat another tablespoon of oil. Sauté the peppers with salt and pepper over medium-high heat until the peppers are softened and a little charred, about 3 minutes. Remove the peppers from your pan, add a little more oil, a little bit of salt, and the onion. Lower the heat to medium and cook, stirring often, until your onion is translucent and lightly brown, about 10 minutes. This should yield about 1 cup.

Make your cheese sauce. In a medium saucepan over medium-low heat, combine the milk and Cheez Whiz, stirring until warmed enough to pour easily, about 10 minutes. Set aside for finishing.

By the time you've prepared all your sides, your rib eye should be ready to slice. Remove it from the freezer, and using a very sharp cleaver, slice it into very thin (1⅛-inch to ¼-inch) slices. Don't worry if they aren't perfect slices; they get chopped up in your skillet.

Heat a large cast-iron skillet over high heat with a splash of oil, until it starts to smoke. Add your beef and salt and black pepper to taste. Take two metal spatulas and stir your meat frequently, using the edges of the spatula to chop up the meat as it cooks. When the meat starts to brown after a few minutes, add your mushrooms, peppers, and onions. Continue to chop and stir until completely cooked through, about 2 minutes. Add a drizzle of cheese sauce to the pan to moisten.

Take each of your hoagie rolls and cut them in half lengthwise. Lay the rolls, cut-side down, on top of the meat to slightly steam and warm up the rolls. Let it sit for a few minutes. Flip the rolls over, load the middle with your meat filling, and coat with the cheese sauce. Squeeze the juices of your cherry peppers over your sandwich. Then tear up the cherry peppers and add to your sandwich filling to finish.

SERVES 4
PREP TIME: 50 MINUTES

1 rib-eye roast (2 bones' worth, about 4 pounds)

6 button mushrooms

Canola oil

Kosher salt and freshly cracked black pepper

2 red bell peppers, seeded and diced

1 white onion, diced

¼ cup milk

2 cups Cheez Whiz

4 footlong hoagie rolls

8 pickled cherry bomb peppers

REUBEN

I did an interview once for *Playboy* magazine. It was held at Langer's in Los Angeles. The reporter and I both ordered the #19. It was a perfect day. Reubens are an incredible sandwich and such an icon of Americana. If you are going to make this from scratch, I'll see you in 10 days. If you go get amazing corned beef from your best local deli, I swear I will not tell anyone. It will be our little secret. Here's my ode to the amazing icon that is the #19 at Langer's.

Let's start by making the choucroute. Rinse the sauerkraut under cold water to remove excess brine and squeeze out any excess liquid. Set aside.

In a large pot or Dutch oven, over medium-low heat warm the butter or duck fat. Add the onion, apples, and garlic and sauté until softened and lightly golden. Add the sauerkraut to the pot and stir to combine. Pour in the lager and add the bay leaves, juniper berries, peppercorns, and caraway seeds. Stir well to combine. Bring the mixture to a simmer, then reduce the heat to low. Cover the pot and let the sauerkraut simmer gently for about 1 hour.

While the sauerkraut is simmering, prepare the bacon. In a separate cast-iron pan, cook the bacon over medium heat until browned.

After the sauerkraut has simmered for 1 hour, add the bacon to the pot. Cover and continue to simmer for another 30 minutes to allow the flavors to meld. Season with salt and pepper to taste. The sauerkraut should be tender and flavorful. Remove the peppercorns, bay leaves, and juniper berries. Transfer to an airtight container and store in the fridge.

Now make your Russian dressing. In a medium bowl, combine the ketchup, mayonnaise, pickles, onion, horseradish, Worcestershire sauce, and Tabasco sauce. You can add more or less of each item depending on what you prefer. Season with salt and pepper to taste. Transfer the Russian dressing to a jar or airtight container and store in the fridge.

Now let's make your sandwich. Preheat a large skillet over medium heat and preheat your broiler on high. Butter one side of each slice of bread and toast it in the skillet. To build the sandwich, place each piece of bread on a baking sheet. Spread ½ cup of the Russian dressing on 4 pieces of the rye bread (2 tablespoons per slice), then divide the corned beef into four equal portions on the other 4 pieces of bread. Top the corned beef with a generous amount of choucroute. Layer 3 slices of Swiss cheese on top of the choucroute. Broil for 5 minutes to get it all melty. Top with the coleslaw and remaining dressed four slices of rye bread, dressing side down, to form sandwiches.

Serve with dill pickles.

CONTINUED

SERVES 4
PREP TIME: 12 DAYS

CHOUCROUTE

2 pounds sauerkraut

½ cup butter or duck fat

1 large yellow onion, thinly sliced

3 Granny Smith apples, peeled and thinly sliced

4 garlic cloves, minced

4 cups lager

4 bay leaves

10 juniper berries

10 black peppercorns

1 teaspoon caraway seeds

1 pound smoked bacon, diced

Kosher salt and freshly cracked black pepper

RUSSIAN DRESSING

1 cup ketchup

½ cup mayonnaise

½ cup finely chopped dill pickles

2 tablespoons white onion, finely diced, and chilled

1 tablespoon horseradish

3 squirts Worcestershire sauce

2 squirts Tabasco sauce

Kosher salt and freshly cracked black pepper

8 slices rye bread

¼ cup unsalted butter, softened

2 pounds thinly sliced Corned Beef (recipe follows), or go buy one from your local deli counter

12 slices Swiss cheese

Coleslaw (page 336)

Dill pickles, for serving

REUBEN CONTINUED

CORNED BEEF

In a medium stockpot, add the kosher salt, nitrate salt, garlic, juniper berries, peppercorns, cloves, star anise, cinnamon, bay leaves, mustard seeds, sugar, and water and bring it to a boil. Remove from the heat and add the ice. Stir until the ice is melted, then add the brisket. Cover and refrigerate for 10 days. Check daily to make sure the beef is completely submerged in the brine. You can also give it a stir.

Remove the brisket from the pot. Discard the brine and rinse the stockpot. Return the brisket to the pot and cover it with cold water. Add the onion, celery, garlic, and bay leaves and bring it to a boil. Reduce to a simmer and skim the top to remove any scum. Keep skimming the scum while simmering until the beef is fork-tender, about 3 hours.

BRINE

½ cup kosher salt

1½ teaspoons nitrate salt

2 garlic cloves

6 juniper berries

10 black peppercorns

10 whole cloves

2 star anise pods

1 cinnamon stick

2 bay leaves

1 tablespoon mustard seeds

¼ cup sugar

4¼ cups water

4 cups ice, as needed

One 3½-pound brisket, deckle cut, ½-inch fat cap

1 yellow onion, halved

2 celery ribs, cut into 1-inch pieces

3 garlic cloves

2 bay leaves

SOUPS, SALADS, SANDWICHES

LASAGNA SUBMARINE

I don't wanna be crude, but the number of people who have come up to me and told me they got laid because of the lasagna I made on YouTube all those years ago is wild. So what do you do with the greatest lasagna ever the next day? It's a big question. Obviously, we make this a sub and create an equally significant dish that will rock the world. You're welcome, world. To all my free-loving freaks: I love you and give you another hot take on a classic that has given so much.

In a medium Dutch oven over medium-low heat, combine the olive oil, carrot, onion, and garlic and cook until the onions are translucent but the vegetables do not take on color, about 12 minutes. Add the ground beef and cook for 5 minutes, stirring to work it up but not brown it. Add the tomato paste and cook for another 5 minutes. Add the beef stock and reduce until sludgy and emulsified, about 10 minutes. Add the milk and reduce for 5 minutes. Add the egg yolks and stir immediately until glossy. Add the pepper and season with salt. Set aside.

Preheat your oven to 350°F.

Now it's time to assemble the lasagna. We should be able to do about 4 or 5 layers. Ladle the meat sauce onto the bottom of your casserole dish, then lay down your cheese, then lay down noodles, then another layer of meat sauce, then layer your cheese, then noodles, and so on until your dish is full. Add the parsley in one of the middle layers. Add the Parm on top of the final layer.

Place the casserole dish on a baking sheet so no cheese drips over the sides and burns the bottom of the oven. Cook until golden brown on top, 30 to 35 minutes. Set it on your counter and let it rest for 1 hour, until it's completely cooled. After it has cooled, cut a piece of parchment paper and a piece of cardboard to the size of your lasagna. Put the parchment and then the carboard on top of your lasagna. Get something heavy to put on top, like bricks or tomato cans, to make a lasagna terrine. Keep it in the fridge overnight.

The next day, we're going to assemble this beautiful sub sandwich. About an hour before you want to crush this thing, take the lasagna terrine out of the fridge.

Let's start making the pomodoro dipper. In a medium pot over medium-low heat, heat the olive oil, butter, onion, and a pinch of salt for 4 minutes so the onions get a good sweat. Add the garlic and stir with a wooden spoon to incorporate. Add the crushed red pepper and tomato paste. Stir and cook for another 2 minutes. Add the tomatoes and stir well. Turn the heat down to low and cook for at least 45 minutes, stirring every few minutes to keep it from burning. Season with salt and pepper and set aside.

CONTINUED

SERVES 4

PREP TIME: 2 DAYS

LASAGNA

½ cup olive oil

1 pound carrots, peeled and finely chopped

1 white onion, finely chopped

1 head garlic, cloves sliced

2 pounds ground beef

¼ cup tomato paste

8 cups beef stock

1 cup whole milk

4 egg yolks

1 tablespoon freshly cracked black pepper

Kosher salt

2 pounds mozzarella cheese, shredded

One 16-ounce box oven-ready lasagna noodles

1 bunch flat-leaf parsley, diced

9-ounce wedge Parmesan cheese, grated

POMODORO DIPPER

¼ cup olive oil

6 tablespoons unsalted butter

1 yellow onion, halved

Kosher salt and freshly cracked black pepper

8 garlic cloves, chopped

1 tablespoon red pepper flakes

2 tablespoons tomato paste

One 28-ounce can Bianco DiNapoli Tomatoes, Rustic Crush

LASAGNA SUBMARINE CONTINUED

While the sauce is bubbling away, flip the lasagna out onto a tray. Cut enough of the cold lasagna into 2-inch by 1-inch strips to fit perfectly onto your subs.

Preheat your oven to 350°F.

We're going to make submarine garlic bread. In a bowl, smush the garlic, butter, garlic powder, Parmesan, and salt to taste together with a spatula. Smear the garlic butter inside the submarine buns, and then brush the outside with it. Wrap each in aluminum foil and toast in the oven on a baking sheet for 10 minutes like actual garlic bread.

In a dry, large nonstick pan over medium heat, place the lasagna slices and keep flipping them every minute or so until they are crispy.

Preheat your broiler on low. Pull out the garlic submarines and open each one up, while keeping it on the aluminum foil on the baking sheet. Spread pomodoro on both sides. Carefully place your baby, crunchy lasagna strips in your bun. Smother with the mozzarella cheese and broil for 2 minutes. Do not burn these. You worked too hard to fuck it up now.

Take your subs out of the oven. Receive a round of applause from your hungry audience. Put each sandwich on a plate and serve with a bowl full of the pomodoro dipper on the side. Dip it up, warm it up.

SUBMARINE

12 garlic cloves, grated

1 cup unsalted butter, room temperature

1 tablespoon garlic powder

3 tablespoons finely grated Parmesan cheese

Kosher salt

4 submarine buns, halved

12 ounces mozzarella cheese, shredded

PORCHETTA

Another iconic, powerhouse sandwich. Making a porchetta is an interesting process. Do you score the skin or crosshatch it, or not score it at all? Who knows? Everyone makes it different, but it's still always so good. As long as you get that skin crispy, it should be delicious. It takes a minute to figure out how to perfect it, but it's not that hard. Porchetta is good at room temperature as well. I love sandwiches that are fresh and hot and then hours later are entirely different and equally good just sitting out. Porchetta falls into that category. I almost prefer the hours-later version.

Preheat your oven to 350°F.

Lay your pork belly out flat, underside up. Using a sharp knife, make incisions down the length of the belly, about 2 inches apart, making sure that you don't cut all the way through. Drizzle olive oil all over the pork belly, then add salt and black pepper. Tear the leaves from 3 of the rosemary sprigs and roughly place them along the pork belly.

In a small bowl, mix together the orange zest, 3 of the smashed garlic cloves, the fennel seeds, 2 teaspoons of the pepperoncini oil, and the orange juice. Using your fingers, rub the mix all over the pork belly, making sure that you get some of the mixture into the incisions as well.

Roll your porchetta up super tight and use separate lengths of butchers twine to hold it together. Tie each knot about an inch apart. Generously season the outside of the porchetta with salt and pepper once completely tied and rolled.

Add the oranges you zested earlier, the lemon halves, jalapeños, and onion to a deep baking dish or drip tray. Add the remaining 2 sprigs rosemary and the remaining couple of cloves of garlic. Put your porchetta on top of everything and place it in the oven, you'll use those juices for the salsa verde. Cook until the internal temperature reaches 168°F, 2 hours. Remove the porchetta from the oven and allow it to rest for at least 30 minutes.

While your porchetta is in the oven, bring a medium pot of water to a boil and throw in your rapini. Cover and allow it to blanch, 2 to 3 minutes. Remove, put into an ice bath, then squeeze out excess water. Set aside in the fridge for later!

While the porchetta is resting, in a medium pot, heat the oil to 450°F. Ladle the burning oil over the porchetta to get the skin bubbly and crispy.

Chop your blanched rapini into small bite-size pieces and add to a separate bowl. Add the remaining 2 tablespoons pepperoncini oil, the pickled pepperoncini, and salt and pepper to taste, then combine with your hands.

Spread a little mayonnaise on the bottom half and top half of each bun. Add a small handful of rapini, then your sliced porchetta. Top with salsa verde.

SERVES 6
PREP TIME: 4 HOURS

Half of a pork belly (5 to 6 pounds), skin off

Olive oil

Kosher salt and freshly cracked black pepper

5 rosemary sprigs

2 oranges, zested and halved

5 large garlic cloves, smashed

1 teaspoon fennel seeds

2 tablespoons plus 2 teaspoons pepperoncini oil

Juice of ½ orange

2 lemons, halved

2 jalapeños, halved lengthwise

1 large white onion, roughly chopped

1 bunch rapini

4 cups neutral oil, for frying

¼ cup chopped pickled pepperoncini

4 soft Italian rolls, halved

Mayonnaise

All the Herbs Salsa Verde (page 334)

WAFFLE BREAKFAST SANDWICH *with* MASCARPONE, FREEZER STRAWBERRY JAM, FRIED EGG, *and* BACON

Straight up, this fucking rocks. We are dream-weaving for black hole–diving psychopaths. I used to get everything bagels toasted with herb and garlic cream cheese and sometimes I'd pair strawberry jam with bacon, but I'm healthy now. That's the past, and we don't look back. This is a mega version of that, made with Tricia's help. She's the best waffle maker outside Belgium. The fried egg is just a beautiful cherry on top. Also, just so everyone knows, our kids didn't eat this at all. It's insane to even think they would. And don't forget to make the jam the day before!

Place your baking sheet in your oven and preheat it to 450°F.

Prepare your mascarpone filling. In a large, chilled bowl, whisk your cream with 1 cup of the sugar until you achieve stiff peaks. This can be done with a hand mixer as well if you aren't up for the forearm challenge. Transfer half of this to a second bowl. Add your mascarpone and whisk it together until thoroughly combined. Add the remainder of your whipped cream and gently fold it in with a spatula. Cover and keep in the fridge (about 20 minutes) until ready to use.

Next, we're going to make sheet-pan eggs and bacon. Arrange the bacon on the preheated baking sheet and roast until the fat renders and the bacon curls, about 8 minutes. Take the baking sheet out of the oven and move the bacon to one side of the pan. On the other side, crack your eggs and immediately return it to the oven. Roast until the whites are just set, about 3 minutes. Take it out of the oven and set it aside.

Line a baking sheet with paper towels. In a medium bowl, mix together the remaining 2 cups sugar, the cinnamon, and a pinch of salt. In a large pot, heat your oil to 350°F. Fry your waffles, 4 pieces at a time, until golden brown, 2 minutes per side. Immediately toss them in your sugar mixture and transfer them to the paper towel–lined baking sheet.

Smother 4 waffles with the whipped mascarpone and top with an egg, 2 halves of crispy fried bacon, and ¼ cup of the jam. Top with the remaining fried waffles and eat immediately.

CONTINUED

SERVES 4

PREP TIME: 45 MINUTES

1½ cups heavy cream

3 cups sugar

1 cup mascarpone cheese

4 slices thick-cut bacon, cut in half

4 eggs

1 tablespoon ground cinnamon

Kosher salt

2 cups canola oil

8 frozen waffles

1 cup Strawberry Freezer Jam (recipe follows)

WAFFLE BREAKFAST SANDWICH *with* MASCARPONE, FREEZER STRAWBERRY JAM, FRIED EGG, *and* BACON CONTINUED

STRAWBERRY FREEZER JAM

In a large bowl, combine the strawberries and sugar. Let stand for 15 minutes.

In a small saucepan, bring the pectin powder and water to a boil. Simmer on high for 1 minute, stirring constantly. Add this mixture to the macerated strawberries and stir for another 3 minutes.

Transfer to clean jars and seal tightly. Do not overfill, leave a bit of space in those jars. Let this sit in the fridge overnight to set and transfer to your freezer. This will keep for up to 8 weeks.

MAKES 3 PINTS

2 cups strawberries, hulled and crushed

4 cups granulated sugar

57g (2 ounces) pectin powder

¾ cup water

NYC BACON, EGG, and CHEESE

NEW YORK CITY: Ever heard of it? Food like this is why it's the greatest city in the world. I'd take one of these over a breakfast burrito any day. I'm not trying to pick which coast is the best coast, but man, this warms you up better than anything in the world. It's a global icon.

In a large pan over medium heat, melt the butter. Place both sides of the roll, cut-side down, into the pan and toast until lightly golden brown, 1 to 2 minutes. Set aside and lightly wrap in aluminum foil.

Line a plate with paper towels. In the same pan over low heat, add the bacon and cook until the bacon is crispy. To help it crisp up, press it down with a spatula. Transfer the bacon to the paper towel–lined plate. Don't press the shit out of it, but make sure it's not a grease ball. Open your foil and transfer the bacon to one half of your roll. Wrap it again in the same foil.

Turn your burner a little lower. Pour off all the bacon fat except 2 tablespoons. Pour the eggs in the pan and season with salt and pepper. Using the edge of a spatula, pull the beaten egg toward the center so the uncooked parts get fried. You want the egg to be shiny but not runny. After 2 to 3 minutes, turn off the heat and throw the cheese on top. After a minute, fold the egg around the cheese. Then flip completely over to complete your square omelet with a melty cheese pocket.

Put the egg and cheese pocket on top of your bacon on the roll. I want ketchup on mine, and I don't like hot sauce. Wrap the whole thing in foil and press down. Let it sit for at least 2 minutes. This is important—it's going to all steam together. Eat while avoiding getting kicked in the face by a Timberland.

THIS IS A SOLO EXPERIENCE
PREP TIME: 15 MINUTES

2 tablespoons unsalted butter

1 kaiser roll, halved

4 slices bacon

2 eggs, beaten

Kosher salt and freshly cracked black pepper

1 slice American cheese

Ketchup

PAIN FARCE FRENCH TOAST

Peanut butter and banana sandwiches were a staple in our household, and this is the newest and brightest version for you to make and pass down to your children and their children's children. The challah is clutch for this. It has the perfect buttery, eggy goodness. It's like a crazy Hot Pocket filled with bananas Foster, for freak's sake.

In a large bowl, combine the cream, the eggs, ¼ cup of the sugar, the vanilla, cinnamon, melted butter, and a pinch of salt. Then, soak all of your bread for a minute and really get it covered all over.

In a large pan over medium heat, add the remaining ¼ cup sugar with 2 tablespoons of water. We're going to make a caramel. Allow the mixture to come to boil, after 5 minutes the caramel will start to color at the edges. Gently whisk this for another 5 minutes, until the caramel begins to get darker. Turn off the heat and whisk in your remaining 1 tablespoon butter, bringing the mixture to a simmer. Turn your heat to the lowest setting and gently add the bananas, cut-side down, and cook on low for 2 minutes. Immediately remove from the heat and make sure this doesn't burn.

In a cast-iron pan, throw a little knob of butter. After it melts, start cooking your French toast in batches for 3 minutes on each side. Transfer each piece to a plate and keep that cast-iron buttery.

To assemble, take your French toast and add a swipe of mascarpone, some bananas, and a few tablespoons of the Nutella. Top with another piece of French toast. Cut off the two short sides, slice lengthwise, and cut into thirds to create six small squares, or just cut it in half and eat. Repeat for the other three sandwiches.

SERVES 4
PREP TIME: 1 DAY

1⅓ cups heavy cream

6 eggs

½ cup sugar

1 tablespoon vanilla extract

1 teaspoon ground cinnamon

⅓ cup unsalted butter, melted

Kosher salt

Eight 1-inch-thick slices challah bread

1 tablespoon unsalted butter, plus more for cooking

3 slightly unripe bananas, sliced lengthwise and then in half

1 cup mascarpone

1 cup Nutella

FRIED EGG *and* BOLOGNA BREAKFAST SANDWICH

I love bologna so much. Bologna is just a large hot dog, and if sliced and served on a toasted English muffin, does that make it a sandwich? Then, by God, good idiots, we have our answer. It's the most exciting and boring sandwich at the same time. I have no idea what I'm talking about most of the time, but this sandwich is good. I cook better than I think, I think.

Line a plate with paper towels. In a large skillet over medium-high heat, brown your butter until it begins to foam and throw in your bologna. Fry on both sides until golden brown, 2 minutes. Transfer to the paper towel–lined plate. While the pan is still hot, add your cheese to the skillet to let it melt a bit. Set it aside.

In the same skillet, fry the egg over easy for 2 minutes. We want a soft yolk. Look how much yolk is coming out of this fucking thing. While you are frying your egg, toast your English muffin and generously spread butter on both sides.

To build your sandwich, put your mustard on the base side of the English muffin. Then place your fried bologna on the other half of your English muffin and your egg on top. Stack on your cheese and onion. Pile on the pickle chips and top with the other English muffin half. Squish together so your yolk merges with everything.

SERVES 1

PREP TIME: 10 MINUTES

2 tablespoons salted butter, plus more for your English muffin

One ½-inch-thick slice bologna

1 slice American cheese

1 egg

1 English muffin

Yellow mustard

1 thin slice white onion

8 dill pickle chips

BANANA BREAD FRENCH TOAST *with* FRIED EGG, PEAMEAL BACON, *and* MAPLE SYRUP

As you see, I love weird savory-sweet things. A lot of these sandwiches are just overload, but beautiful. This is your meat boy. If you like meat, make this French toast sandwich. The banana bread French toast is unruly; then the panfried peameal bacon has crispy edges like popcorn and that cured ham center. If you don't know what peameal bacon is, read a Canadian book. The fried egg maxes this out with that runny yolk. Come on! There's nothing like a dessert breakfast sandwich with a fried egg. Also, warm your maple syrup up; you'll thank me.

In a large bowl, whisk together the milk, sugar, 2 of the eggs, the vanilla, and a pinch of salt. Mix vigorously with a whisk.

In a nonstick skillet over medium heat, melt the butter until bubbling.

Quickly dip your banana bread into your batter, knock off the excess batter, and place it in the pan. Fry until golden brown on both sides, about 3 minutes, and transfer to a plate. Repeat with the remaining slices of banana bread.

Line a plate with paper towels. In the same skillet, fry your peameal bacon until golden brown, about 2 minutes a side. Place onto the paper towel–lined plate.

Last, in the same skillet, fry the remaining 4 eggs sunny-side up. Sprinkle them with salt and a few cracks of pepper.

To serve, top each slice of banana French toast with a slice of peameal bacon and one egg. Dust with the powdered sugar and drizzle with the maple syrup.

CONTINUED

SERVES 4

PREP TIME: 1 HOUR AND 15 MINUTES

½ cup milk

½ cup sugar

6 eggs

1 tablespoon vanilla extract

Kosher salt and freshly cracked black pepper

2 tablespoons unsalted butter

4 thick slices Banana Bread (recipe follows)

4 slices peameal bacon

½ cup powdered sugar

½ cup maple syrup

BANANA BREAD FRENCH TOAST *with* FRIED EGG, PEAMEAL BACON, *and* MAPLE SYRUP CONTINUED

BANANA BREAD

Preheat your oven to 350°F. Grease a loaf pan or line it with parchment paper.

In a large bowl, mash the bananas with a fork until smooth (you should have about 1½ cups). Stir the melted butter into the bananas. Add the sugar, eggs, and vanilla and mix well until combined.

In a separate bowl, whisk together the flour, baking soda, and salt. Gradually add the dry ingredients to the banana mixture, stirring until just combined. Be careful not to overmix, as it can result in a denser bread. Pour the batter into the prepared loaf pan and smooth the top with a spatula.

Bake until a toothpick inserted into the center comes out clean, 50 to 60 minutes. The baking time may vary depending on your oven, so start checking around the 50-minute mark. Baking is science and I'm not a scientist. Let the banana bread cool in the pan for about 10 minutes, then transfer it to a wire rack to cool completely before slicing.

MAKES 1 LOAF

2 to 3 ripe bananas
½ cup unsalted butter, melted
1 cup sugar
2 eggs
1 teaspoon vanilla extract
1½ cups all-purpose flour
1 teaspoon baking soda
½ teaspoon kosher salt

PEANUT BUTTER COOKIE *with* NUTELLA *and* SALTED CARAMEL ICE CREAM SANDWICH

You gotta dip this. But you can only dip like half in caramel because your hot little fingers will make a mess. And we don't like messes, do we? No! We don't. We like clean hands and lots of napkins and people eating delicious peanut butter cookies sandwiched with Nutella-swirled salted caramel ice cream. This is a true legend happening right now. You want to put all the yummy stuff together? You can do it, we're all adults. We can live free and love free and eat as many of these as possible.

Let's start by making the cookies. Preheat your oven to 350°F. Line a baking sheet with parchment paper.

In a medium bowl, whisk together the flour, baking powder, baking soda, and kosher salt.

In the bowl of a stand mixer fitted with the paddle attachment, cream the butter, granulated sugar, and brown sugar on medium-high speed until light and fluffy, about 1 minute. Add the peanut butter, egg, and vanilla and mix on medium speed until well combined. Gradually add the dry ingredients to the wet ingredients and mix on medium speed until a dough forms, 2 to 3 minutes.

Using a 2-ounce ice cream scoop, portion the cookie dough onto the prepared baking sheet, leaving 2 inches between each cookie. Place a 4-inch ring mold around a cookie, then press and flatten the cookie slightly with the back of a fork, creating a crisscross pattern on top. Repeat with the remaining cookies.

Bake the cookies until they are lightly golden around the edges, 10 to 12 minutes. Remove from the oven and let the cookies cool for a few minutes on the baking sheet, then transfer them to a wire rack to cool completely.

CONTINUED

SERVES 6

PREP TIME: 6 HOURS

PEANUT BUTTER COOKIES

1¼ cups all-purpose flour

½ teaspoon baking powder

½ teaspoon baking soda

¼ teaspoon kosher salt

½ cup unsalted butter, softened

½ cup granulated sugar

½ cup packed light brown sugar

½ cup smooth peanut butter

1 egg

1 teaspoon vanilla extract

PEANUT BUTTER COOKIE *with* NUTELLA *and* SALTED CARAMEL ICE CREAM SANDWICH CONTINUED

Let's make our salted caramel. In a small pot over medium heat, melt the granulated sugar until it fully melts and reaches a deep amber color, 10 minutes. Don't touch it or else you risk crystallizing your caramel. ALSO, be careful not to let it burn—it can go from golden to burned quickly.

Immediately add the cubed butter and gently whisk until the butter is completely melted and incorporated, about 1 minute. Remove the saucepan from the heat and carefully add the cream while whisking constantly. The mixture will bubble up vigorously. Whisk until the cream is fully incorporated and the caramel sauce is smooth. Add the sea salt and mix until incorporated.

Allow the salted caramel sauce to cool for at least 15 minutes in the saucepan, then transfer it to a heatproof, airtight container and store in the fridge for up to 3 days.

Now that you have your cookies and caramel ready, let's make the ice cream filling. In a large bowl, combine the ice cream, peanut butter, and Nutella and mix them together until well combined. You should have a smooth and creamy ice cream mixture with swirls of peanut butter and Nutella.

Line a baking dish with parchment paper. Make sure you are using a dish that fits in your freezer. Scoop the ice cream mixture into the prepared dish and spread it evenly. Cover the container with a lid or more parchment paper and place it in the freezer to firm up until it's solid, at least 2 to 3 hours.

Place a scoop of the ice cream on the flat side of a peanut butter cookie. Make sure to softly flatten it with the back of the scoop, then top the ice cream with another cookie, flat-side down, to create a sandwich. Repeat the process with the remaining cookies and ice cream. You'll have enough for 6 ice cream sandwiches. If you have extra of either, eat them in the kitchen while hiding from your family and friends.

If serving the ice cream sandwiches immediately, dip the cookie halfway into the caramel sauce and serve. Maybe have a little extra on the side for extra dips. If you're not serving them right away, wrap each sandwich individually in parchment paper and store them in the freezer. Eat within 4 days.

SALTED CARAMEL

1 cup granulated sugar

¼ cup unsalted butter, cubed

½ cup heavy cream, room temperature

1 teaspoon sea salt

2 cups salted caramel ice cream

⅓ cup chunky peanut butter

¼ cup Nutella

APPLE PIE TOASTER STRUDEL *with* CHEDDAR CHEESE

It all comes down to Nannie's apple pie with cheddar cheese. This is an East Coast thing or a small-town thing. Maybe it's a growing-up-in-the-1940s thing, but it's a good thing that I love. My kids don't really like pie, but they crushed these. So I thought, why not make a couple of apple pie–filled toaster strudels with some grated cheese? The mouthfeel is perfection with the cold, shredded cheddar, the hot filling, and the warm, flaky pastry full of icing. Baking in the afternoon with your family is the best. Music playing, sun shining, cold or hot out, windows open, or even a fire going in the fireplace.

In a large pot over medium heat, combine the apples, brown sugar, butter, cinnamon, vanilla, cornstarch, flour, and pinch of salt and cook for 20 minutes, stirring frequently to prevent the mixture from burning. This part is crucial: cook the filling just enough for the liquid to leach out and activate the starch. The apples should be just tender. Think of this more as a glazed caramel apple and less as an apple compote. The more you reduce, the less gooey filling you have in the end, and you want that gooey filling!

Place the filling in a bowl, cover, and allow it to cool completely in the fridge. It should be cool within 2 hours. You can also make this the day before.

Line a baking sheet with parchment paper. Cut each sheet of puff pastry into 6 equal rectangles. Place 2 heaping tablespoons of pie filling into the center of 6 of the rectangles. In a small bowl, combine the egg yolks and cream to make an egg wash. Brush the edges of the puff pastry with it and top with the remaining 6 rectangles. If you're looking to get beautiful dark golden brown strudels, brush a thin layer of egg wash onto their tops before baking. You can apply up to three coats of the egg wash, allowing it to dry between coats, to achieve a beautiful lacquered finish. Crimp the edges of the strudel with a fork and cut two diagonal slashes across the top of each to act as vents so the pies do not burst in the oven. Place this on the prepared baking sheet in the fridge to cool completely before baking, about 15 minutes.

While the pies are cooling, preheat your oven to 350°F.

Bake the pies until golden brown, about 25 minutes.

Meanwhile, make your strudel glaze. In a small bowl, whisk together the powdered sugar and milk. Immediately after the strudels are baked, drizzle the glaze onto each pie. To serve, grate a heaping pile of cheddar on top of each pie.

SERVES 6

PREP TIME: 4½ HOURS

4 Granny Smith apples, peeled and diced

3 heaping tablespoons light brown sugar

1 tablespoon unsalted butter

1 teaspoon cinnamon

¼ teaspoon vanilla extract

2 teaspoons cornstarch

1 teaspoon all-purpose flour

Kosher salt

Two 16-ounce packages puff pastry, thawed

2 egg yolks

1 tablespoon heavy cream

1 cup powdered sugar

2 tablespoons 2% milk

1 pound aged orange cheddar cheese

TEMPURA BANANA SPLIT SANDWICH *with* ALL THE FIXINGS

Is there anything better than a banana split? Well, maybe a tempura banana split! This gives carnival fried-dough vibes and is everything that's great about the carnival while leaving the creeps at home. I'd never even had a fried banana until I thought of this while we were doing the shoot. I was like, *We aren't even cooking anything. Is this even a sandwich?* I was losing hope in myself and, boom, tempura, the bananas—that's something, right? A little powdered sugar, heck yeah. This is idiotic, and maybe someone has done this, but I haven't seen it. Suck an egg.

Make the tempura batter. In a medium bowl, mix the club soda with the egg. Gently fold in the flour. Don't overmix this shit; it's all fine to have some lumps.

Line a plate with paper towels. Heat 3 inches of oil in a large Dutch oven over medium-high heat until it reaches 350°F. Peel the banana and split it down the middle. Dip both banana slices in the batter, making sure they're fully coated. Carefully drop each banana piece into the hot oil and fry each side for 3 minutes. Take the bananas out with a slotted spoon and let them rest on the paper towel–lined plate.

On a long oval dish, place each banana half on opposite ends. Dust the tempura banana with the powdered sugar. Put one scoop of each ice cream between the bananas. Spoon the pineapple on top of the three ice creams. Dollop each scoop with whipped cream. Pour the chocolate fudge all over and pour that strawberry syrup all over. Then top that baby with the nice little cherries and blast it with some sprinkles.

SERVES 1

PREP TIME: 30 MINUTES

TEMPURA BATTER

½ (12-ounce) can club soda, ice-cold

1 egg

½ cup all-purpose flour

Canola oil, for frying

1 ripe banana

2 tablespoons powdered sugar

1 scoop vanilla ice cream

1 scoop strawberry ice cream

1 scoop chocolate ice cream

½ cup minced canned pineapple in syrup

One 6.5-ounce can whipped cream

½ cup chocolate fudge

½ cup strawberry syrup

3 maraschino cherries

¼ cup round mixed colored sprinkles

NOT A JOS LOUIS

We are rocking only the classics, making only the highest, most adorned GOATs. You thought we were just over here making grilled cheeses? Please! The Jos Louis is one of the greatest cake sandwiches of all time. It is two chocolate cake rounds with cream in the middle and then covered in a chocolate shell. Get out of here with that crumbly wagon-wheel fake cookie biscuit stuff. Naw, dudes, this cake sandwich is as good as it gets. When I was in elementary school and saw kids with these in their lunches, I just thought how rich they must be. Imagine getting premade packaged cake sandwiches! I would be maybe getting a sugarless Rice Krispies square, *maybe*. Lol, now we can make these at home and even the playing field.

Let's start by making the cream cheese filling. In the bowl of a stand mixer fitted with the paddle attachment, cream the cream cheese and powdered sugar on medium speed until smooth. With the mixer running, slowly pour the butter into the cream cheese and sugar mixture until fully incorporated. Be sure to scrape down the bowl halfway through with a spatula. Chill in the fridge while you make the cake.

Next up is the cake. Using a 9 by 13-inch pan that's at least 2 inches deep, bake the chocolate cake according to the package instructions, then let it cool to room temperature. Remove your cake from the pan and take a 4-inch ring mold and begin to cut out your circles. After your circles are cut, then slice each one and make sure they are ½ inch thick.

For the chocolate glaze, boil a small pot of water. In a glass bowl that is larger than your pot, place the dark chocolate, cocoa butter, and chocolate chips. Place the glass bowl over the pot of water. Stir until the mixture is melted and fully incorporated, about 5 minutes. Remove it from the heat and leave it at room temperature so it's not ripping hot but still warm for pouring over.

Put your cream cheese filling into a Ziploc bag. Then cut about ½ inch off the tip at one corner, so you can pipe the filling between the two chocolate cake halves. Once they're all filled, place your sandwiches on a wire rack set over a baking sheet and begin to pour your chocolate glaze over your "Jos Louis." Let the chocolate set completely and go to town.

SERVES 4

PREP TIME: 45 MINUTES

CREAM CHEESE FILLING

1 pound cream cheese, room temperature

2 cups powdered sugar

½ cup unsalted butter, melted

One 15.25-ounce box chocolate cake mix

CHOCOLATE GLAZE

1 pound dark chocolate

½ cup cocoa butter

1 cup semisweet chocolate chips

NOT A PASSION FLAKIE

I love Passion Flakies. It's a delicious flaky pastry that's full of a fruit filling and a whipped topping. This reminds me of sitting behind a convenience store on my BMX, high as shit, eating one of these and drinking a Becker's chocolate milk. We never had stuff like this in our house growing up. So, taking your weekly lawn-cutting money and using it to secure a couple Flakies never hurt. Now you can make them at home so your kids don't hate you later.

Let's start by making the cream cheese frosting. In the bowl of a stand mixer fitted with the paddle attachment, beat the butter, cream cheese, and vanilla on medium-high speed until smooth and creamy, about 2 minutes. Gradually add the powdered sugar in three batches, beating well after each addition, until the frosting is smooth and fluffy, about 2 minutes.

In a large bowl, whip the cream until stiff peaks form using your stand mixer or, if you have diesel forearms, take out all your aggression.

Working in two batches, gently fold the whipped cream into the cream cheese mixture until well combined. Store in the fridge in an airtight container until ready to use. It will keep for about 3 days.

Next up is the peach compote. Bring a large pot of water to a boil. Using a large serving spoon, gently place the peaches in the water and boil for 1 minute. Transfer the peaches to a large bowl filled with ice water. Once the peaches are cooled, use a paring knife to peel the peaches, then dice them.

In a large saucepan over medium heat, combine the diced peaches, granulated sugar, and lemon juice and cook, stirring occasionally, until the peaches break down and the mixture thickens to a compote consistency, 30 to 45 minutes.

Remove from the heat and let the compote cool completely. Transfer to an airtight container and store in the fridge until ready to use. It will keep for about 3 days.

Preheat your oven to 350°F. Line a baking sheet with parchment paper.

In a small bowl, whisk together the egg yolks and cream. Place the puff pastry squares on the prepared baking sheet. Brush the tops of the squares with the beaten egg mixture and sprinkle with the turbinado sugar. Bake the puff pastry squares until they are golden and puffed up, 20 to 25 minutes. Remove them from the oven and transfer them to a wire rack to cool completely.

Cut the cooled puff pastries horizontally with a bread knife to create a top and a bottom layer for each flakie. Using a piping bag, pipe the cream cheese frosting onto the bottom layer of each puff pastry square. Spoon a generous amount of the peach compote over the cream cheese frosting. Place the top puff pastry layer over the compote to create a sandwich.

SERVES 8
PREP TIME: 3 HOURS

CREAM CHEESE FROSTING

1 cup unsalted butter, room temperature

1 pound cream cheese, room temperature

1 tablespoon vanilla extract

2 cups powdered sugar, sifted

1 cup heavy cream

PEACH COMPOTE

6 ripe peaches

½ cup granulated sugar

1 tablespoon lemon juice

2 egg yolks

1 tablespoon heavy cream

Two 16-ounce packages puff pastry, thawed, cut into 4-inch squares

¼ cup turbinado sugar

STRAWBERRIES *and* WHIPPED CREAM *on* MILK BREAD

Thank you, Japan. Fruit sandwiches with cream are an incredible creation. These little cuties make you want to eat so softly, like a little happy chipmunk. You want to make sure you're all alone. Just gently nibble away at this and taste it and feel it all. The softest bread, the pillowy whipped cream, and the perfectly ripe strawberries. Not like these ones from somewhere in the world. We couldn't get good ones for the shoot because, guess what? They are seasonal, and they were not in season, so these were the best we could get. Not like those ninety-dollar ones you can find in Japan. Those taste like actual angels. This is a low-risk, high-reward sandwich—enjoy.

In the bowl of a stand mixer fitted with the whisk attachment, combine the cream, sugar, and vanilla and mix on high speed until you achieve stiff peaks, about 8 minutes. Transfer the mixture into a separate bowl and place in the fridge for 20 minutes.

Wipe the bowl of the stand mixer clean. Once again, using the stand mixer fitted with the whisk attachment, whip the cream cheese and Miracle Whip on high until the mixture is soft, light, and fluffy, about 2 minutes.

Working in batches, fold the whipped cream mixture into the cream cheese mixture.

Get out your bread. Working from the edges inward, carefully spread the cream cheese mixture evenly across all slices. Place the strawberries diagonally on top of four slices of bread. Top each of those with another slice so the cream is covered with strawberries. Carefully cut off the crusts. Wrap the sandwich nicely in plastic wrap and finish by cutting it in half diagonally, slicing through the strawberries.

SERVES 4
PREP TIME: 30 MINUTES

1 cup whipped cream, very cold

¼ cup sugar

¼ teaspoon vanilla extract

½ cup cream cheese, room temperature

½ cup Miracle Whip

8 slices Wonder Bread

1 pack (16-ounce) ripe strawberries, stemmed and cut in half

FLUFFERNUTTER *on* WONDER BREAD *with* PEANUT BUTTER *and* CHOCOLATE CHIPS MICROWAVED *for* 10-SECOND SANDWICH

This is my childhood. This is my secret. This is my safe place. Don't make fun of me, you fucks. I'm ready to fight over this. I grew up not being allowed to have sugar, so it truly was a righteous quest when I could make these and eat them. Not often, but like once or twice a year. It was that feeling of doing something bad and getting away with it, like when I used to steal chocolate bars at our local corner store. It felt crazy at the time, stealing a Mars bar and ripping down the street like a cowboy who just robbed a train. I haven't had that feeling in a long, long-ass time. Maybe it's time to make this.

On one slice of bread, spread the Marshmallow Fluff edge to edge. On the other slice, spread the peanut butter. On the peanut butter side, evenly sprinkle the choccy chips. I like to pat mine down so they're flat like the earth.

Place the marshmallow side on top of the peanut butter side. Put it on a plate and microwave on high for 10 seconds. The microwave is crucial—10 seconds is where it gets warm. Some of the chocolate chips melt, but some don't. The joy of the contrasting texture of semimelted chocolate chips is something to die for. Don't even bother grabbing the plate out of the microwave; just yank the sandwich right off and eat it right away.

I used to eat these every once in a while as a small child. I would eat at least two before I got caught. It's a time-sensitive situation.

I would get sent to my room for one month if I got caught eating this. If you are a god-fearing individual, don't eat this. You will go to hell.

SERVES 1, THIS IS PERSONAL

PREP TIME: 15 SECONDS, FASTEST RECIPE EVER

2 slices Wonder Bread

2 tablespoons Marshmallow Fluff (another marshmallow crème is OK, but not ideal)

2 tablespoons smooth peanut butter

3 tablespoons semisweet chocolate chips

CLASSIC ICE CREAM SANDWICH

I'm just a plain-old sucker for chocolate chip mint. Or is it mint chocolate chip? However you freaks say it, it's OK. But what is not OK is eating white ice cream. That shit needs to be nuclear green. I don't know why, but I kinda do, 'cause it fucks with my brain. If it's white, it hurts my head. Green is GO, THAT'S IT. Making homemade ice cream sandwiches is the best. If you have kids, you get to see their excitement. It's tenfold stoke, the stoked championships of stoke. Make these for your kids or your friends and see what makes you happier. Nuclear green or bust.

When the cookies are completely cooled, take a scoop of mint chocolate chip ice cream and place it onto the flat side of one cookie. Take another cookie and gently press it down on top of the ice cream, creating a sandwich. Repeat this process with the remaining cookies and ice cream. Place the ice cream sandwiches in the freezer until the ice cream is firm, at least 1 to 2 hours.

CONTINUED

SERVES 6

PREP TIME: 2 DAYS

12 York Peppermint Chocolate Chip Cookies (recipe follows)

4 cups Mint Chocolate Chip Ice Cream (recipe follows)

CLASSIC ICE CREAM SANDWICH CONTINUED

YORK PEPPERMINT CHOCOLATE CHIP COOKIES

Preheat your oven to 400°F. Line a baking sheet with parchment paper or a silicone baking mat.

In a medium bowl, whisk together the flour, baking powder, and baking soda.

In a stand mixer fitted with the paddle attachment, cream the butter, granulated sugar, and brown sugar over medium speed until light and fluffy, about 1 minute. Add the salt, egg, egg yolk, and vanilla and mix on medium speed until combined, 2 to 3 minutes. Gradually add the dry ingredients to the wet ingredients, mixing until just combined. Be careful not to overmix the dough. Fold in the chunks of dark chocolate.

Scoop the cookie dough using a 2-ounce ice cream scoop. One at a time, take a portion of cookie dough and flatten it slightly in your hand. Place a York Peppermint Patty in the center of the flattened dough. Fold the dough around the mint patty, ensuring it is completely enclosed. Repeat this process for each cookie. Place them onto the prepared baking sheet, leaving about 2 inches between each cookie. Bake until the edges are golden brown, 10 to 12 minutes.

Remove from the oven. Sprinkle a pinch of Maldon salt on top of each cookie. Let the cookies cool on the baking sheet for a few minutes before transferring them to a wire rack to cool completely.

MAKES 12 LARGE COOKIES

2 cups all-purpose flour

1 teaspoon baking powder

½ teaspoon baking soda

½ cup unsalted butter, softened

¾ cup granulated sugar

¾ cup packed light brown sugar

½ teaspoon kosher salt

1 egg

1 egg yolk

1 tablespoon vanilla extract

One 3.5-ounce dark chocolate bar (78% cacao), cut into chunks

12 York Peppermint Patties (one for each cookie)

Maldon salt, for sprinkling

CLASSIC ICE CREAM SANDWICH CONTINUED

MINT CHOCOLATE CHIP ICE CREAM

In a medium saucepan over medium heat, warm the milk, stirring occasionally until it reaches a gentle simmer.

In a large separate bowl, whisk together the egg yolks and sugar until smooth. Gradually pour the hot milk into the egg yolk mixture, whisking constantly, to temper the eggs and prevent them from curdling.

Pour the tempered egg mixture back into the saucepan and set it over low heat. Cook the mixture, stirring constantly with a spatula, until it thickens slightly and coats the back of the spoon.

Remove the saucepan from the heat. Strain the mixture through a fine-mesh strainer into a large bowl. Stir in the cream, peppermint and vanilla extracts, and green food coloring. Add more or less food coloring to get your desired color. Mix well to combine. Let the mixture cool to room temperature, then cover and refrigerate for at least 4 hours or overnight to chill completely.

Pour the chilled mint ice cream base into an ice cream maker and churn according to the manufacturer's instructions until it reaches a soft-serve consistency. During the last few minutes of churning, add the dark chocolate curls, allowing them to mix evenly. Transfer the ice cream to a container with a lid and let this set in the freezer overnight. It can keep for up to 1 week in an airtight container.

MAKES 4 CUPS

1 cup whole milk

4 egg yolks

¾ cup sugar

2 cups heavy cream

1½ tablespoons peppermint extract

1 teaspoon vanilla extract

Green food coloring

1 cup dark chocolate curls or chopped dark chocolate

DRESSINGS *and* MORE

CREAMY HONEY DRESSING

In a small bowl, whisk together the mustard, garlic, vinegar, honey, and salt and pepper to taste until combined. Keep whisking and slowly add the olive oil until the mixture is emulsified.

MAKES 1 CUP

2 tablespoons Dijon mustard

1 garlic clove, minced

¼ cup champagne vinegar

3 tablespoons honey

Kosher salt and freshly cracked black pepper

½ cup extra-virgin olive oil

ALL THE HERBS SALSA VERDE

In a blender, combine the almonds, cashews, shallot, garlic, tarragon, parsley, jalapeño, and canola oil. Blend on medium speed, adding your water little by little until you have a loose salsa. Pour the salsa verde into a bowl and fold in the lime zest and juice. Season with salt and set aside until serving.

MAKES 4 CUPS

½ cup almonds, toasted and chopped

½ cup cashews, toasted and chopped

¼ cup small-diced shallot

1 tablespoon minced garlic

1 cup tarragon leaves

1 cup parsley leaves

2 to 3 jalapeños, halved and seeded (about ⅓ cup)

⅓ cup canola oil

¼ cup water

Zest and juice of 2 limes

Kosher salt

SCOTCH BONNET SALSA

In a blender, add your parsley, cilantro, ginger, garlic, scotch bonnet, jalapeño, scallions, salt, sugar, and oil. Pulse everything together until it begins to break down and form a paste. At this point, you can blend on high until everything comes together into a smooth sauce. Try to be as quick as possible so you don't heat up the mixture and accidentally turn the herbs brown.

Quickly transfer to a bowl, cover, and cool in the fridge until needed. Try to make this as close to when you will be serving it as possible.

MAKES 1½ CUPS

½ bunch parsley, stemmed

½ bunch cilantro, stemmed

1 knob ginger, peeled

4 garlic cloves, peeled

1 scotch bonnet, seeded

1 jalapeño, seeded

2 scallions

1 tablespoon kosher salt

1 tablespoon sugar

1 cup grapeseed oil

BACON VINAIGRETTE DRESSING

Dice the bacon into nice, thick cubes. Add them to a small, cold pan. Turn the heat to medium and slowly cook the bacon until it is golden brown but still tender, with ample bacon fat in the pan, about 10 minutes. Save the fat in your favorite bacon fat jar.

Transfer the bacon to a small bowl along with the mustard, maple syrup, garlic, and vinegar and stir to combine thoroughly. Add a good amount of pepper, nice big chunks. Adjust with salt and vinegar as desired.

MAKES 1 CUP

6 ounces double-smoked bacon

3 tablespoons grainy mustard

2 tablespoons maple syrup

2 garlic cloves, grated

¼ cup apple cider vinegar, plus more as needed

Kosher salt and freshly cracked black pepper

BLUE CHEESE DRESSING

In a medium bowl, whisk together the mayonnaise, sour cream, and buttermilk until smooth and well combined. Add the blue cheese, garlic, chives, and lemon juice and stir until everything is well mixed. Taste the dressing and adjust the seasoning with salt and pepper as needed.

Transfer the dressing to a jar or bottle with a tight-fitting lid and store in the fridge until ready to use.

MAKES 4 CUPS

1 cup mayonnaise

1 cup sour cream

½ cup buttermilk

1 cup crumbled blue cheese

2 garlic cloves, grated

¼ cup chives, finely diced

2 tablespoons lemon juice

Kosher salt

1½ teaspoons freshly cracked black pepper

COLESLAW

In a large bowl, combine the cabbage, carrot, and onion with the sugar and salt and let macerate until wilted. Mix in the mayonnaise and vinegar. Adjust the sugar, salt, and pepper to taste. Cover with plastic wrap and store in the fridge. This is best when it is made the night before serving.

MAKES 3 CUPS

½ green cabbage, cored and shredded

1 carrot, peeled and grated

½ white onion, chopped

1 big pinch of sugar

Kosher salt

1 cup mayonnaise

¼ cup white wine vinegar

VINEGAR SLAW

In a large bowl, combine the cabbage, scotch bonnet, and carrot. Gently toss the slaw with the vinegar, lime juice, sugar, and salt. You want to make the slaw at least 20 minutes before serving to allow the cabbage to wilt slightly and become tender.

MAKES 2 CUPS

¼ head green cabbage, thinly sliced (about 2 cups)

1 scotch bonnet, thinly sliced

½ carrot, peeled and thinly julienned

¼ cup white vinegar

Juice of 2 limes

2 tablespoons sugar

1 tablespoon kosher salt

THANK-YOUS

Patricia, Macarthur, Rizzo, Ozzy
Mom Zone and Steve Savage, Grizz
Sister Sarah, Cameron, Cail
Steve Jr., Dooms Jr. Jr., Ellie Pearl, Nat
Carol and Bill
Our loving sister we love you so much and will forever miss you, Rebecca
Jeff, Evan, and Rhys
Jude the Obscure and David
The brother, Sandy, Alyssa, Nate and Theo
Deanna, Rob, their dog Donut
Lisa, Jacqueline, Danielle, Marika
Coulson, Connor, Ryan the sous chef, Justin, Katherine
Ellie, Adam, Ever, Myer
Sam and Raj crew
Garrett, Quentin Bacon and his nephew
Blue Goose Farm forever: Keenan, Ashley, Miles
Shlomo Buchler, his beautiful family, Maker Pizza
Matheson Cookware forever: Brian, Kei, Nathan, Adam, Adam
Gary, David, Keegan, Michelle, Caroline
The entire Our House H.C. teams: Love to Rizzo's House of Parm, Cà Phê Rang,
Matty's Patty's Burger Club, Prime Seafood Palace
Matheson Food Company

INDEX

Note: Page numbers in *italics* indicate photos separate from recipe.

A
aioli, garlic, 78
All the Herbs Salsa Verde, 334
anchovies, salads with, 145, 152
Apple Pie Toaster Strudel with Cheddar Cheese, 306–9
Avgolemono (soup), 54–55

B
bacon
 Bacon Vinaigrette Dressing, 335
 Banana Bread French Toast with Fried Egg, Peameal Bacon, and Maple Syrup, 300–302
 BLT, 210–*11*
 Brussels sprouts salad with, 146–47
 Clubhouse sandwich, 214–15
 Frisée aux Lardons Family-Style, 174–75
 NYC Bacon, Egg, and Cheese, 294–95
 soups with, *18–19, 38–39*, 48–51, *52–53*, 66–67
 Waffle Breakfast Sandwich with Mascarpone, Freezer Strawberry Jam, Fried Egg, and Bacon, 288–*93*
Bake and Shark, 228–*31*
Baked Potato Buffet Vichyssoise, 48–*51*
bananas
 Banana Bread French Toast with Fried Egg, Peameal Bacon, and Maple Syrup, 300–302
 Pain Farce French Toast, 296–97
 Tempura Banana Split Sandwich with All the Fixings, *310*–11
Bánh Mì Salad with Roasted Pork Belly, 164–*65*
barley
 Cock-a-Leekie Soup, 60–*61*
 Oxtail Barley Yam Soup, 88–89
 Turkey Drumstick and Barley Soup, 68–69

basil, salads with, 152–*55*, 160–*61*
basil, stracciatella sandwich with, 212–13
BBQ sauce, Matty's, 271
beans
 Black Beans with Cotija, Cilantro, Red Onion, Crumbled Pork Rinds, Oregano, and Salsa Macha, 150–51
 Butter Beans with Lemon, Confit Garlic, Canned Sardines, and Baby Gem Lettuce, 148–49
 Cannellini Bean and Kale Soup with Lots of Shallots, 32–33
 Cannellinis with Roasted Red Peppers, Raisins, Capers, Anchovies, and Parsley, 144–45
 Chickpea Casserole, 134–36
 Cranberry Beans with Comté, Tarragon, Mint, and Sherry Vinegar, 142–43
 Lupinis with Stracciatella di Bufala, Basil, and Anchovies, 152–55
 Soupe au Pistou, 16–17
bee pollen, sandwich with, 196–97
beef
 Beef Noodle Soup, 96–99
 Beef on Weck with Top Round Roast, Creamed Horseradish, and Beef Au Jus, 254–59
 Bollito Misto (with ox tongue), 74–75
 Canadian Donair with Onion, Tomato, and Donair Sauce, 266–67
 Corned Beef, 282
 French Dip, 260–61
 Giant Meatball Soup in Beefy Tomato Broth, 84–85
 Lasagna Submarine, 283–85
 Leftover Steak Salad, 178–79
 Meatball (sandwich), 84–85
 Meatloaf (sandwich), 270–73
 Oxtail Barley Yam Soup, 88–89
 Philly Cheesesteak, 278–79
 Reuben, 280–82
 Taco Salad, 180–*81*
 Taco Submarine, *192*–95

Beer-Battered Haddock, 218–21
beets, in Dumplings, Roasted Baby Beets, Pork Belly, and Pork Broth, 20–22
BLT, 210–*11*
Blue Cheese Dressing, 336
Bollito Misto, 74–75
bone marrow
 other dishes with, 70–71, 74–75, 254–55
 Roasted Bone Marrow in Light Bone Broth with Fresh Peas, 72–73
bread and such. *See also* sandwiches; sandwiches, breakfast/sweet
 about: making croutons, 24, 129
 Frisée aux Lardons Family-Style, 174–75
 Grilled Salami Panzanella Salad, 168–*71*
 Roasted Shallot Salad with Sherry Vinegar and Rye Bread Crumbs, 126–27
 Stuffed Acorn Squash Soup with Emmental and Bread Crumbs, 62–65
breakfast sandwiches. *See* sandwiches, breakfast/sweet
broccoli
 Broccoli Salad with Bacon Vinaigrette Dressing, Fried Egg, and Gorgonzola, 116–17
 Broiled Broccoli and Cheddar Soup, 30–31
broccoli rabe. *See* rapini
Broiled and Burnt Roasted Tomato Soup with Grilled Cheese Crostini Thing, 28–29
Broiled Broccoli and Cheddar Soup, 30–31
Brussels Sprouts with Bacon, Mint, Pistachio, Fish Sauce, Pickled Pepper Caramel, and Lime, 146–47
Buffalo Chicken Finger, 240–*41*
Butter Beans with Lemon, Confit Garlic, Canned Sardines, and Baby Gem Lettuce, 148–49

C

cabbage
- Bánh Mì Salad with Roasted Pork Belly, *164–65*
- Cabbage Soup with Crème Fraîche, Smoked Trout Roe, and Chives, *18–19*
- Coleslaw, 336
- Nuoc Mam Gung, 164
- Vinegar Slaw, 337

Caldo de Pollo, *58–59*

Canadian Donair with Onion, Tomato, and Donair Sauce, *266–67*

cannellini beans. *See* beans

caramel (salted), ice cream sandwich with, *303–5*

Caramelized Maple Parsnip Soup with Sunchoke Chips and Ricotta, *26–27*

Caramelized Onions, 261

cauliflower, fried sprouting, *198–99*

Celery Salad with Creamy Honey Dressing, *114–15*

Charred Corn Esquites-Style with Fried Oaxacan Cheese Curds, *130–31*

cheese
- about: dumplings with, *20–22*
- Apple Pie Toaster Strudel with Cheddar Cheese, *306–9*
- Blue Cheese Dressing, 125, 336
- Broiled and Burnt Roasted Tomato Soup with Grilled Cheese Crostini Thing, *28–29*
- Broiled Broccoli and Cheddar Soup, *30–31*
- Caramelized Maple Parsnip Soup with Sunchoke Chips and Ricotta, *26–27*
- Cheese Sauce, 198
- Corn Maple Parmesan Soup, *34–37*
- Creamy Dip, 176
- Fried Spam Kimchi Grilled Cheese, *276–77*
- Goat Cheese and Mascarpone Spread, 16
- Grilled Cheese, *202–3*
- Muffuletta, 274
- Not a Jos Louis, *312–13*
- Not a Passion Flakie, *314–15*
- NYC Bacon, Egg, and Cheese, *294–95*
- other sandwiches with (*See* sandwiches)
- Philly Cheesesteak, *278–79*
- Pumpernickel, Beer, Cheese Curds Soup, *24–25*
- Roasted Squash and Mozzarella Grilled Cheese with Honey and Bee Pollen, *196–97*
- salads with (*See* salads)
- Stracciatella di Bufala, Caponata, Sun-Dried Tomatoes, Cherry Peppers, and Basil, *212–13*
- Stuffed Acorn Squash Soup with Emmental and Bread Crumbs, *62–65*
- Waffle Breakfast Sandwich with Mascarpone, Freezer Strawberry Jam, Fried Egg, and Bacon, *288–93*

chicken
- Avgolemono (soup), *54–55*
- Bollito Misto, *74–75*
- Buffalo Chicken Finger, *240–41*
- Caldo de Pollo, *58–59*
- Chicken Consommé, 8
- Chicken Finger Crouton Salad, a Tribute to the Breakfast Beacon, *166–67*
- Chicken Parm, *216–17*
- Clam, Sausage, Orecchiette, Kale, and Chicken Brodo, *44–45*
- Clubhouse sandwich, *214–15*
- Cock-a-Leekie Soup, *60–61*
- Cubed Mortadella, Macaroni, and Chicken Broth, *90–93*
- Gumbo, *80–81*
- Roasted Chicken Leg Pastina Soup, *56–57*
- Roasted Chicken Thigh Shawarma with Pickled Turnip and Hot Peppers, *234 35*

Chickpea Casserole, *134–36*

chiles. *See* peppers/chiles

chocolate
- Chocolate Glaze, 312
- Classic Ice Cream Sandwich, *320–25*
- Fluffernutter on Wonder Bread with Peanut Butter and Chocolate Chips Microwaved for 10-Second, *318–19*
- Mint Chocolate Chip Ice Cream, *324–25*
- Not a Jos Louis, *312–13*
- Tempura Banana Split Sandwich with All the Fixings, *310–11*
- York Peppermint Chocolate Chip Cookies, 323

Cioppino, *40–41*

clams. *See* seafood

Clubhouse sandwich, *214–15*

Cock-a-Leekie Soup, *60–61*

Coleslaw, 336

cookies, peanut butter, *303–5*

cookies, peppermint, 323

corn
- Caldo de Pollo, *58–59*
- Charred Corn Esquites-Style with Fried Oaxacan Cheese Curds, *130–31*
- Corn Maple Parmesan Soup, *34–37*
- Cornmeal Batter, 198

Court Bouillon with Fresh Garlic and Ginger Oil, *12–13*

crab. *See* seafood

Cranberry Beans with Comté, Tarragon, Mint, and Sherry Vinegar, *142–43*

Cranberry Vinaigrette, 143

Creamy Honey Dressing, 334

Creamy Sausage Soup with Rapini and Tortellini, *82–83*

crème fraîche, cabbage soup with smoked trout roe and, *18–19*

Crispy Lamb Pho, *70–71*

Croque Madame, *204–5*

croutons
- about: making, 24, 129
- Chicken Finger Crouton Salad, a Tribute to the Breakfast Beacon, *166–67*

Cubano, *268–69*

Cubed Mortadella, Macaroni, and Chicken Broth, *90–93*

cucumber
- Sabich with Cucumber, Tomato, and Pickled Hot Peppers, *264–65*
- Sichuan Chili Oil Smashed Cucumber Salad and Soy-Cured Egg, *120–23*

Cullen Skink, *52–53*

D

daikon, in Rutabaga and Daikon Broth with Tofu, *14–15*

daikon, pickled, 164, 224

dessert sandwiches. *See* sandwiches, breakfast/sweet

INDEX 345

Donair Sauce, 267
dressings, sauces, and more
   about: dressing a salad, 109
   All the Herbs Salsa Verde, 334
   Bacon Vinaigrette Dressing, 335
   Black Vinegar Chili Crisp Dressing, 121–22
   Blue Cheese Dressing, 125, 336
   Cheese Sauce, 198
   Coleslaw, 336
   Congee Sauce, 47
   Cranberry Vinaigrette, 143
   Creamy Dip, 176
   Creamy Honey Dressing, 334
   Donair Sauce, 267
   Fresh Garlic and Ginger Oil, 13
   Garlic Aioli, 78
   Garlic Sauce, 235
   Goat Cheese and Mascarpone Spread, 16
   Green Chile Marinade, 228
   Hoisin Chile Mayo, 248
   Horseradish Cream, 254
   Hot Relish, 216
   Jerk Marinade, 223
   Katsu Sauce, 247
   Larb Sauce, 163
   Mango Marmalade, 136
   Marinara Sauce, 216, 244
   Matty's Dank BBQ Sauce, 271
   Mornay Sauce, 204
   Nuoc Mam Gung, 164
   Persimmon Chutney, 197
   Pomodoro Dipper, 283
   Russian Dressing, 280
   Salsa Macha, 151
   Salsa Verde, 75
   Scotch Bonnet Salsa, 335
   Spicy Mayonnaise, 198
   Spicy Scallion Ginger Sauce, 248
   Tahini Dressing, 264
   Vinegar Slaw, 337
   Wasabi Mayonnaise, 226
   Yellow Curry Dressing, 136
Dumplings, Roasted Baby Beets, Pork Belly, and Pork Broth, 20–22

E
eggplant, sabich with, 264–65
eggs
   Broccoli Salad with Bacon Vinaigrette Dressing, Fried Egg, and Gorgonzola, 116–17
   Crab Congee (with omelet), 46–47
   Croque Madame, 204–5
   Fried Egg and Bologna Breakfast Sandwich, 298–99
   NYC Bacon, Egg, and Cheese, 294–95
   Sichuan Chili Oil Smashed Cucumber Salad and Soy-Cured Egg, 120–23
   Waffle Breakfast Sandwich with Mascarpone, Freezer Strawberry Jam, Fried Egg, and Bacon, 288–93
Everyone's Mom's Macaroni and Tuna Salad, 137–39

F
farro, salad with, 156–57
fish. *See* seafood
flowers, in Lightest Broth of Garden Herbs with One Chile, 8–11
Fluffernutter on Wonder Bread with Peanut Butter and Chocolate Chips Microwaved for 10-Second, 318–19
French Dip, 260–61
French toast. *See* sandwiches, breakfast/sweet
Fried Egg and Bologna Breakfast Sandwich, 298–99
Fried Shrimp Po'boy, 232–33
Fried Spam Kimchi Grilled Cheese, 276–77
Frisée aux Lardons Family-Style, 174–75
fruit salad, 140–41

G
garlic
   Confit Garlic, 148
   Fresh Garlic and Ginger Oil, 13
   Garlic Aioli, 78
   Garlic Sauce, 235
   Roasted Garlic Schmaltz, 56
Giant Meatball Soup in Beefy Tomato Broth, 84–85
ginger
   Fresh Garlic and Ginger Oil, 13
   Spicy Scallion Ginger Sauce, 248

Green Chile Marinade, 228
Grilled Salami Panzanella Salad, 168–71
Grilled Cheese, 202–3
Gumbo, 80–81

H
ham
   Croque Madame, 204–5
   Cubano, 268–69
   Italian Combo, 252–53
   Jambon Beurre, 236–39
   Muffuletta, 274–75
   Smoked Ham Hock with Haddock Soup, 94–95
herbs
   All the Herbs Salsa Verde, 334
   Lightest Broth of Garden Herbs with One Chile, 8–11
Hoisin Chile Mayo, 248
honey
   Creamy Honey Dressing, 334
   Peaches with Goat Cheese, Mint, Honeycomb, and Olive Oil, 112–13
   Roasted Squash and Mozzarella Grilled Cheese with Honey and Bee Pollen, 196–97
Horseradish Cream, 254

I
ice cream sandwiches, 310–11, 318–19, 320–25
Irish Lamb Stew, 66–67
Italian Combo, 252–53

J
Jambon Beurre, 236–39
Jerk Shrimp Salad (sandwich), 222–23
Jos Louis, not, 312–13

K
kale
   Cannellini Bean and Kale Soup with Lots of Shallots, 32–33
   Clam, Sausage, Orecchiette, Kale, and Chicken Brodo, 44–45
Katsu Sauce, 247
kimchi, in Fried Spam Kimchi Grilled Cheese, 276–77
Kimchi Stew, 86–87

L

lamb
- Canadian Donair with Onion, Tomato, and Donair Sauce, 266–67
- Crispy Lamb Pho, 70–71
- Irish Lamb Stew, 66–67

larb, cold ground pork, 162–63

Large Crab Cake with Clam Chowder and Aioli, 76–79

Leftover Steak Salad, 178–79

lemon, butter beans with, 148–49

Lightest Broth of Garden Herbs with One Chile, 8–11

lobster soup, red curry, 42–43

M

mangoes
- Mango Marmalade, 136
- Vasos de Fruta, 140–41

maple
- Banana Bread French Toast with Fried Egg, Peameal Bacon, and Maple Syrup, 300–302
- Caramelized Maple Parsnip Soup with Sunchoke Chips and Ricotta, 26–27
- Corn Maple Parmesan Soup, 34–37
- Maple Walnuts, in Peaches with Goat Cheese salad, 112–13

Marinara Sauce, 216, 244

marshmallow. *See* Fluffernutter on Wonder Bread...

Matty and Trishy Tuna Melt, 206–9

Matty's Dank BBQ Sauce, 271

mayonnaise, spicy/wasabi/hoisin chile, 198, 226, 248

meatball
- Giant Meatball Soup in Beefy Tomato Broth, 84–85
- Meatball (sandwich), 242–45

Meatloaf (sandwich), 270–73

Mini Shells with Crab and Basil, 160–61

mint
- Classic Ice Cream Sandwich, 320–25
- Cranberry Beans with Comté, Tarragon, Mint, and Sherry Vinegar, 142–43
- Mint Chocolate Chip Ice Cream, 324–25
- Peaches with Goat Cheese, Mint, Honeycomb, and Olive Oil, 112–13
- Spaghetti with Mint, Ricotta, and Olive Oil–Baked Bread Crumbs, 128–29

Mornay Sauce, 204

Muffuletta, 274

N

Not a Jos Louis, 312–13

Not a McRib Sandwich, 262–63

Nuoc Mam Gung, 164

nuts and seeds
- All the Herbs Salsa Verde, 334
- Brussels Sprouts with Bacon, Mint, Pistachio, Fish Sauce, Pickled Pepper Caramel, and Lime, 146–47
- Fluffernutter on Wonder Bread with Peanut Butter and Chocolate Chips Microwaved for 10-Second, 318–19
- Maple Walnuts, in Peaches with Goat Cheese salad, 112–13
- other salads with nuts, 115, 126, 143, 151, 164
- other salads with seeds, 121, 151, 172
- Pain Farce French Toast, 296–97
- Peanut Butter Cookie with Nutella and Salted Caramel Ice Cream Sandwich, 303–5
- Tahini Dressing, 264
- Zucchini Salad with Manchego, Salsa Verde, and Pepper and Pine Nut Relish, 118–19

NYC Bacon, Egg, and Cheese, 294–95

O

okra, in Gumbo, 80–81

olive oil
- Peaches with Goat Cheese, Mint, Honeycomb, and Olive Oil, 112–13
- Spaghetti with Mint, Ricotta, and Olive Oil–Baked Bread Crumbs, 128–29

Olive Salad, 274

onions, leeks, and shallots
- Black Beans with Cotija, Cilantro, Red Onion, Crumbled Pork Rinds, Oregano, and Salsa Macha, 150–51
- Cannellini Bean and Kale Soup with Lots of Shallots, 32–33
- Caramelized Onions, 261
- Cock-a-Leekie Soup, 60–61
- Pickled Red Pearl Onions, 136
- Roasted Shallot Salad with Sherry Vinegar and Rye Bread Crumbs, 126–27
- Spicy Scallion Ginger Sauce, 248

orecchiette and orzo. *See* pasta

Oxtail Barley Yam Soup, 88–89

P

panzanella salad, 168–71

parsnips, in Caramelized Maple Parsnip Soup with Sunchoke Chips and Ricotta, 26–27

pasta
- Avgolemono (soup), 54–55
- Beef Noodle Soup, 96–99
- Clam, Sausage, Orecchiette, Kale, and Chicken Brodo, 44–45
- Creamy Sausage Soup with Rapini and Tortellini, 82–83
- Cubed Mortadella, Macaroni, and Chicken Broth, 90–93
- Everyone's Mom's Macaroni and Tuna Salad, 137–39
- Lasagna Submarine, 283–85
- Mini Shells with Crab and Basil, 160–61
- Orecchiette with Smoked Mussels and Bottarga, 158–59
- Orzo and Goat Cheese Salad, 132–33
- Spaghetti with Mint, Ricotta, and Olive Oil–Baked Bread Crumbs, 128–29

peaches
- Not a Passion Flakie (with Peach Compote), 314–15
- Peaches with Goat Cheese, Mint, Honeycomb, and Olive Oil, 112–13

peanut butter. *See* nuts and seeds

peas, roasted bone marrow in light bone broth with fresh, 72–73. *See also* Beer-Battered Haddock

peppers/chiles
- Black Vinegar Chili Crisp Dressing, 121–22
- Cannellinis with Roasted Red Peppers, Raisins, Capers, Anchovies, and Parsley, 144–45
- Green Chile Marinade, 228
- Hoisin Chile Mayo, 248
- Hot Relish, 216
- Lightest Broth of Garden Herbs with One Chile, 8–11

Pepper and Pine Nut Relish, 118

Roasted Chicken Thigh Shawarma with Pickled Turnip and Hot Peppers, *234–35*

Sabich with Cucumber, Tomato, and Pickled Hot Peppers, *264–65*

Stracciatella di Bufala, Caponata, Sun-Dried Tomatoes, Cherry Peppers, and Basil, *212–13*

Persimmon Chutney, 197

Philly Cheesesteak, *278–79*

pho, crispy lamb, *70–71*

Pickled Carrots and Daikon, 164

Pickled Daikon, 224

Pickled Red Pearl Onions, 136

pineapple, recipes with, *140–41, 228–31*

pistou soup, *16–17*

Po'boy, fried shrimp, *232–33*

Porchetta, *286–87*

pork. *See also* bacon; ham; sausage and salami

    Bánh Mì Salad with Roasted Pork Belly, *164–65*

    Canadian Donair with Onion, Tomato, and Donair Sauce, *266–67*

    Cold Ground Pork Larb, *162–63*

    Cubano, *268–69*

    Dumplings, Roasted Baby Beets, Pork Belly, and Pork Broth, *20–22*

    Giant Meatball Soup in Beefy Tomato Broth, *84–85*

    Kimchi Stew, *86–87*

    Meatball (sandwich), *84–85*

    Meatloaf (sandwich), *270–73*

    Not a McRib Sandwich, *262–63*

    Porchetta, *286–87*

    pork belly (sandwich), *248–51*

    Pork Katsu Sando, *246–47*

potatoes

    Baked Potato Buffet Vichyssoise, *48–51*

    Caldo de Pollo, *58–59*

    Cullen Skink, *52–53*

    Warm Potato Salad, *176–77*

Prime Seafood Palace, radicchio salad from, *110–11*

Pumpernickel, Beer, Cheese Curds Soup, *24–25*

R

Radicchio Salad from Prime Seafood Palace, *110–11*

raisins, bean salad with, *144–45*

Rang, Chef, 6, 164

rapini

    Creamy Sausage Soup with Rapini and Tortellini, *82–83*

    Porchetta, *286–87*

Red Curry Lobster Soup, *42–43*

Reuben, 280–82

Rhode Island Clam Chowder, *38–39*

rice

    Crab Congee, *46–47*

    Kimchi Stew, *86–87*

    Leftover Steak Salad, *178–79*

    Roasted Chicken Thigh Shawarma with Pickled Turnip and Hot Peppers, *234–35*

Roasted Garlic Schmaltz, 56

Roasted Squash and Mozzarella Grilled Cheese with Honey and Bee Pollen, *196–97*

Russian Dressing, 280

Rutabaga and Daikon Broth with Tofu, *14–15*

S

Sabich with Cucumber, Tomato, and Pickled Hot Peppers, *264–65*

salads

    about: appreciating, and expanded view of, 108–9; dressing, 109

    Bánh Mì Salad with Roasted Pork Belly, *164–65*

    Black Beans with Cotija, Cilantro, Red Onion, Crumbled Pork Rinds, Oregano, and Salsa Macha, *150–51*

    Broccoli Salad with Bacon Vinaigrette Dressing, Fried Egg, and Gorgonzola, *116–17*

    Brussels Sprouts with Bacon, Mint, Pistachio, Fish Sauce, Pickled Pepper Caramel, and Lime, *146–47*

    Butter Beans with Lemon, Confit Garlic, Canned Sardines, and Baby Gem Lettuce, *148–49*

    Cannellinis with Roasted Red Peppers, Raisins, Capers, Anchovies, and Parsley, *144–45*

    Celery Salad with Creamy Honey Dressing, *114–15*

    Charred Corn Esquites-Style with Fried Oaxacan Cheese Curds, *130–31*

    Chicken Finger Crouton Salad, a Tribute to the Breakfast Beacon, *166–67*

    Chickpea Casserole, *134–36*

    Cold Ground Pork Larb, *162–63*

    Coleslaw, 336

    Cranberry Beans with Comté, Tarragon, Mint, and Sherry Vinegar, *142–43*

    Everyone's Mom's Macaroni and Tuna Salad, *137–39*

    Frisée aux Lardons Family-Style, *174–75*

    Grilled Salami Panzanella Salad, *168–71*

    Jerk Shrimp Salad (sandwich), *222–23*

    Leftover Steak Salad, *178–79*

    Lupinis with Stracciatella di Bufala, Basil, and Anchovies, *152–55*

    Mini Shells with Crab and Basil, *160–61*

    Olive Salad, 274

    Orecchiette with Smoked Mussels and Bottarga, *158–59*

    Orzo and Goat Cheese Salad, *132–33*

    Peaches with Goat Cheese, Mint, Honeycomb, and Olive Oil, *112–13*

    A Radicchio Salad from Prime Seafood Palace, *110–11*

    Rizzo's Wedge Salad, *124–25*

    Roasted Shallot Salad with Sherry Vinegar and Rye Bread Crumbs, *126–27*

    Roasted Sunchokes, Fresh Ricotta, and Farro, *156–57*

    Sashimi Salad, *172–73*

    Sichuan Chili Oil Smashed Cucumber Salad and Soy-Cured Egg, *120–23*

    Spaghetti with Mint, Ricotta, and Olive Oil–Baked Bread Crumbs, *128–29*

    Taco Salad, *180–81*

    Vasos de Fruta, *140–41*

    Vinegar Slaw, 337

    Warm Potato Salad, *176–77*

    Zucchini Salad with Manchego, Salsa Verde, and Pepper and Pine Nut Relish, *118–19*

salmon. *See* seafood
Salsa Verde, 75, 334
sandwiches
  about: definition, virtues, and first loves, 190; overview of recipes, 191
  Bake and Shark, 228–31
  Beef on Weck with Top Round Roast, Creamed Horseradish, and Beef Au Jus, 254–59
  Beer-Battered Haddock, *218*–21
  BLT, 210–*11*
  Buffalo Chicken Finger, *240–41*
  Canadian Donair with Onion, Tomato, and Donair Sauce, *266*–67
  Chicken Parm, 216–*17*
  Clubhouse, *214*–15
  Croque Madame, 204–*5*
  Cubano, 268–*69*
  French Dip, *260*–61
  Fried Shrimp Po'boy, *232–33*
  Fried Spam Kimchi Grilled Cheese, 276–*77*
  Fried Sprouting Cauliflower, 198–*99*
  Grilled Cheese, *202*–3
  Grilled Cheese Crostini Thing, *28–29*
  Italian Combo, *252*–53
  Jambon Beurre, 236–*39*
  Jerk Shrimp Salad, *222*–23
  Lasagna Submarine, 283–85
  Matty and Trishy Tuna Melt, *206*–9
  Meatball, 242–*45*
  Meatloaf, *270*–73
  Muffuletta, 274–*75*
  Not a McRib Sandwich, 262–*63*
  Philly Cheesesteak, *278*–79
  Porchetta, 286–*87*
  Pork Katsu Sando, *246*–47
  Reuben, 280–82
  Roasted Chicken Thigh Shawarma with Pickled Turnip and Hot Peppers, *234*–35
  Roasted Squash and Mozzarella Grilled Cheese with Honey and Bee Pollen, *196*–97
  Sabich with Cucumber, Tomato, and Pickled Hot Peppers, 264–*65*
  Salmon Katsu Sando, 224–*25*
  Scallion Pancake, 248–*51*
  Shrimp Burger, 226–*27*
  Stracciatella di Bufala, Caponata, Sun-Dried Tomatoes, Cherry Peppers, and Basil, *212*–13
  Sun-Warmed Tomato, 200–*201*
  Taco Submarine, *192–95*
sandwiches, breakfast/sweet
  Apple Pie Toaster Strudel with Cheddar Cheese, 306–9
  Banana Bread French Toast with Fried Egg, Peameal Bacon, and Maple Syrup, 300–302
  Classic Ice Cream Sandwich, *320–25*
  Fluffernutter on Wonder Bread with Peanut Butter and Chocolate Chips Microwaved for 10-Second, *318–19*
  Fried Egg and Bologna Breakfast Sandwich, *298*–99
  Not a Jos Louis, *312–13*
  Not a Passion Flakie, *314*–15
  NYC Bacon, Egg, and Cheese, *294*–95
  Pain Farce French Toast, *296*–97
  Peanut Butter Cookie with Nutella and Salted Caramel Ice Cream Sandwich, 303–5
  Strawberries and Whipped Cream on Milk Bread, 316–*17*
  Tempura Banana Split Sandwich with All the Fixings, 310–11
  Waffle Breakfast Sandwich with Mascarpone, Freezer Strawberry Jam, Fried Egg, and Bacon, 288–*93*
Sashimi Salad, *172–73*
sauces. *See* dressings, sauces, and more
sauerkraut, in Reuben, 280–82
sausage and salami
  Bollito Misto, 74–75
  Clam, Sausage, Orecchiette, Kale, and Chicken Brodo, *44*–45
  Creamy Sausage Soup with Rapini and Tortellini, 82–83
  Cubed Mortadella, Macaroni, and Chicken Broth, *90*–93
  Grilled Salami Panzanella Salad, *168*–71
  Gumbo, *80*–81
  Italian Combo, *252*–53
Scallion Pancake, 248
Scotch Bonnet Salsa, 335

seafood
  Bake and Shark, 228–*31*
  Beer-Battered Haddock, *218*–21
  Cabbage Soup with Crème Fraîche, Smoked Trout Roe, and Chives, *18–19*
  Cioppino, 40–*41*
  Clam, Sausage, Orecchiette, Kale, and Chicken Brodo, *44–45*
  Crab Congee, *46–47*
  Cullen Skink, *52–53*
  Everyone's Mom's Macaroni and Tuna Salad, 137–*39*
  Fried Shrimp Po'boy, *232–33*
  Gumbo, *80*–81
  Jerk Shrimp Salad (sandwich), *222*–23
  Matty and Trishy Tuna Melt, *206*–9
  Mini Shells with Crab and Basil, *160–61*
  Orecchiette with Smoked Mussels and Bottarga, *158*–59
  Red Curry Lobster Soup, *42–43*
  Rhode Island Clam Chowder, *38–39*
  Salmon Katsu Sando, 224–*25*
  Sashimi Salad, *172–73*
  Shrimp Burger, 226–*27*
  Smoked Ham Hock with Haddock Soup, *94–95*
shallots. *See* onions, leeks, and shallots
shrimp. *See* seafood
Sichuan Chili Oil Smashed Cucumber Salad and Soy-Cured Egg, *120–23*
slaw, vinegar, 337
Smoked Ham Hock with Haddock Soup, *94–95*
soups
  about: benefits, appeal, and history of, 6–7
  Avgolemono, *54–55*
  Baked Potato Buffet Vichyssoise, *48–51*
  Beef Noodle Soup, *96–99*
  Bollito Misto, 74–75
  Broiled and Burnt Roasted Tomato Soup with Grilled Cheese Crostini Thing, *28–29*
  Broiled Broccoli and Cheddar Soup, *30–31*
  Cabbage Soup with Crème Fraîche, Smoked Trout Roe, and Chives, *18–19*

INDEX 349

Caldo de Pollo, 58–59
Cannellini Bean and Kale Soup with Lots of Shallots, 32–33
Caramelized Maple Parsnip Soup with Sunchoke Chips and Ricotta, 26–27
Cioppino, 40–41
Clam, Sausage, Orecchiette, Kale, and Chicken Brodo, 44–45
Cock-a-Leekie Soup, 60–61
Corn Maple Parmesan Soup, 34–37
Court Bouillon with Fresh Garlic and Ginger Oil, 12–13
Crab Congee, 46–47
Creamy Sausage Soup with Rapini and Tortellini, 82–83
Crispy Lamb Pho, 70–71
Cubed Mortadella, Macaroni, and Chicken Broth, 90–93
Cullen Skink, 52–53
Dumplings, Roasted Baby Beets, Pork Belly, and Pork Broth, 20–22
Giant Meatball Soup in Beefy Tomato Broth, 84–85
Gumbo, 80–81
Irish Lamb Stew, 66–67
Kimchi Stew, 86–87
Large Crab Cake with Clam Chowder and Aioli, 76–79
Lightest Broth of Garden Herbs with One Chile, 8–11
Oxtail Barley Yam Soup, 88–89
Pumpernickel, Beer, Cheese Curds Soup, 24–25
Red Curry Lobster Soup, 42–43
Rhode Island Clam Chowder, 38–39
Roasted Bone Marrow in Light Bone Broth with Fresh Peas, 72–73
Roasted Chicken Leg Pastina Soup, 56–57
Rutabaga and Daikon Broth with Tofu, 14–15
Smoked Ham Hock with Haddock Soup, 94–95
Soupe au Pistou, 16–17
Stuffed Acorn Squash Soup with Emmental and Bread Crumbs, 62–65
Turkey Drumstick and Barley Soup, 68–69

spaghetti. *See* pasta
Spam, in Fried Spam Kimchi Grilled Cheese, 276–77
Spicy Scallion Ginger Sauce, 248
squash
    Roasted Squash and Mozzarella Grilled Cheese with Honey and Bee Pollen, 196–97
    Stuffed Acorn Squash Soup with Emmental and Bread Crumbs, 62–65
    Zucchini Salad with Manchego, Salsa Verde, and Pepper and Pine Nut Relish, 118–19
Strawberries and Whipped Cream on Milk Bread, 316–17
strawberry jam, waffle breakfast sandwich with, 288–93
Stuffed Acorn Squash Soup with Emmental and Bread Crumbs, 62–65
sunchokes
    Caramelized Maple Parsnip Soup with Sunchoke Chips and Ricotta, 26–27
    Roasted Sunchokes, Fresh Ricotta, and Farro, 156–57
Sun-Warmed Tomato, 200–201
sweet sandwiches. *See* sandwiches, breakfast/sweet

T
Taco Salad, 180–81
Taco Submarine, 192–95
Tahini Dressing, 264
Tempura Banana Split Sandwich with All the Fixings, 310–11
tofu
    Kimchi Stew, 86–87
    Rutabaga and Daikon Broth with Tofu, 14–15
tomatoes
    Broiled and Burnt Roasted Tomato Soup with Grilled Cheese Crostini Thing, 28–29
    Giant Meatball Soup in Beefy Tomato Broth, 84–85
    Marinara Sauce, 216, 244
    Pomodoro Dipper, 283
    sandwiches with (*See* sandwiches)
    Sun-Warmed Tomato, 200–201
    Turkey Drumstick and Barley Soup, 68–69

V
Vasos de Fruta, 140–41
veal
    Giant Meatball Soup in Beefy Tomato Broth, 84–85
    Meatball (sandwich), 84–85
vichyssoise, baked potato, 48–51
vinaigrette (bacon) dressing, 335
Vinegar Slaw, 337

W
Waffle Breakfast Sandwich with Mascarpone, Freezer Strawberry Jam, Fried Egg, and Bacon, 288–93
walnuts. *See* nuts and seeds
Warm Potato Salad, 176–77
Wasabi Mayonnaise, 226

Y
yams, in Oxtail Barley Yam Soup, 88–89
Yellow Curry Dressing, 136

Z
Zucchini Salad with Manchego, Salsa Verde, and Pepper and Pine Nut Relish, 118–19

CONVERSIONS GUIDE

Notes for this edition

The tablespoon measurements in this book refer to 15 ml tablespoons, not the 20 ml tablespoons commonly found in Australia and New Zealand. You can use 3 teaspoons (5 ml each) to achieve the same measure.

The cup measurements in this book refer to US (237 ml) cups, so if you have metric (250 ml) cups at home, we recommend using roughly 2 teaspoons less than a full cup to give the closest results.

Included here are weight, liquid, length and temperature conversions, which you may find useful.

WEIGHT MEASURES

General

US (OUNCES / POUNDS)	METRIC (GRAMS)
1 OUNCE	30
2 OUNCES	55
3 OUNCES	85
4 OUNCES (¼ POUND)	115
5 OUNCES	140
6 OUNCES	170
7 OUNCES	200
8 OUNCES (½ POUND)	225
9 OUNCES	255
10 OUNCES	285
11 OUNCES	310
12 OUNCES (¾ POUND)	340
13 OUNCES	370
14 OUNCES	395
15 OUNCES	425
16 OUNCES (1 POUND)	455
24 OUNCES (1½ POUNDS)	680
32 OUNCES (2 POUNDS)	910

Butter

STICKS	METRIC (GRAMS)
¼	30
½	55
1	115

LIQUID MEASURES

US (QUARTS)	METRIC (ML)	IMPERIAL (FL OZ)
1	950	32½
2	1890	65
3	2840	100
6	5680	200

OVEN TEMPERATURES

FAHRENHEIT (°F)	CELSIUS (°C)	GAS MARK
150	70	¼
200	100	½
225	110	½
235	120	½
250	130	1
275	140	1
300	150	2
315	160	2–3
325	170	3
350	180	4
375	190	5
400	200	6
410	210	6–7
425	220	7
450	230	8
475	240	8
480	250	9
500	260	10

LENGTH MEASURES

IMPERIAL (IN)	METRIC (CM)
1/16	0.2
⅛	0.3
3/16	0.4
¼	0.6
⅜	0.8
½	1
⅝	1.5
¾	2
1	2.5
1¼	3
1½	4
1¾	4.5
2	5
2¼	5.5
2½	6
2¾	7
3	7.5
3¼	8
3½	9
3¾	9.5
4	10

Published in 2024 by Murdoch Books, an imprint of Allen & Unwin.
First published in 2024 by Ten Speed Press, an imprint of Random House,
a division of Penguin Random House LLC, New York.

Murdoch Books Australia
Cammeraygal Country
83 Alexander Street
Crows Nest NSW 2065
Phone: +61 (0)2 8425 0100
murdochbooks.com.au
info@murdochbooks.com.au

Murdoch Books UK
Ormond House
26–27 Boswell Street
London WC1N 3JZ
Phone: +44 (0) 20 8785 5995
murdochbooks.co.uk
info@murdochbooks.co.uk

For corporate orders and custom publishing, contact our business development team at salesenquiries@murdochbooks.com.au

Acquiring editor: Kelly Snowden | Co-Project editor: Claire Yee
    Production editor: Serena Wang | Editorial assistant: Gabby Ureña Matos
Designer: Isabelle Gioffredi | Art director: Emma Campion
    Production designers: Mari Gill and Faith Hague
Prepress color manager: Jane Chinn
Cowriter and recipe developer: Garrett McGrath
Digitech: Dominic Matos and Josh Bacon | Photo retoucher: Allison Hunter
Copyeditor: Heather Rodino | Proofreader: Erica Rose | Indexer: Jay Kreider
Production director: Lou Playfair

Text © Matty Matheson 2024
The moral right of the author has been asserted.
Design © Ten Speed Press 2024
Photography © Quentin Bacon 2024
Use of the "Steal Your Face" logo courtesy of Grateful Dead Productions.

Murdoch Books acknowledges the Traditional Owners of the Country on which we live and work. We pay our respects to all Aboriginal and Torres Strait Islander Elders, past and present.

Product safety EU representative: EU Authorised Representative: Easy Access System Europe, Mustamäe tee 50, 10621 Tallinn, Estonia, gpsr.requests@easproject.com

All rights reserved. No part of this publication may be reproduced, stored in a retrieval system or transmitted in any form or by any means, electronic, mechanical, photocopying, recording or otherwise, without the prior written permission of the publisher.

ISBN 978 1 76150 058 9

 A catalogue record for this book is available from the National Library of Australia

A catalogue record for this book is available from the British Library

Printed in Slovenia, by DZS Grafik

OVEN GUIDE: You may find cooking times vary depending on the oven you are using. For fan-forced ovens, as a general rule, set the oven temperature to 20°C (35°F) lower than indicated in the recipe.

10 9 8 7 6 5 4